DATE DUE

DEVELOPING YOUNG MINDS

DEVELOPING YOUNG MINDS

From Conception to Kindergarten

Rebecca Shore

ROWMAN & LITTLEFIELD
Lanham • Boulder • New York • London

Published by Rowman & Littlefield
A wholly owned subsidiary of The Rowman & Littlefield Publishing Group, Inc.
4501 Forbes Boulevard, Suite 200, Lanham, Maryland 20706
www.rowman.com

Unit A, Whitacre Mews, 26-34 Stannary Street, London SE11 4AB

British Library Cataloguing in Publication Information Available

Library of Congress Cataloging-in-Publication Data Available

Shore, Rebecca.
Developing young minds : from conception to kindergarten / by Rebecca Shore.
p. cm.
Includes bibliographical references and index.
ISBN 978-1-60709-352-7 (cloth : alk. paper) -- ISBN 978-1-60709-354-1 (electronic)

∞ ™ The paper used in this publication meets the minimum requirements of American National Standard for Information Sciences Permanence of Paper for Printed Library Materials, ANSI/NISO Z39.48-1992.

Printed in the United States of America

This book is dedicated to my first teachers,
Bruce and Wynona, my parents; and

My most profound teachers,
Lily and Bobby, my children; and

My husband Marcus,
Who continually shows me alternative ways of learning.

With deepest gratitude to all the wonderful
Teachers of the world including my students; and

Miss Bobby Germany, my mentor teacher,
Melissa and Jenny, my sisters
And finally and especially the carpenter's son and
The Old Wig.

CONTENTS

LIST OF FIGURES

ACKNOWLEDGMENTS

It definitely takes a village and I want to start out by thanking mine. First, to the medical doctors: Dr. Kathi Kemper, Dr. Robyn Humphries, Dr. Whitney Lane, Dr. Kerry Brionnes, Dr. Shanon Moran, Dr. Matthew Samarel, Dr. Holly Smith. You all offered varying assortments of advice, support, and in some cases, love and friendship over the years, and I cherish each of you.

Also, special thanks to Dr. Richard Lambert, Dr. Paula Goolkasian, Dr. Pamela Shue, Dr. Corey Lock, Drs. Bob and Kate Algozzine, Dr. Dawson Hancock, Dr. Mary Lynne Calhoun, Dr. Ellen McIntyre, Dr. Jim Bird, Dr. Alan Mabe, Dr. Debra Morris,and all of my wonderful colleagues in the College of Education at the University of North Carolina at Charlotte. To the Department of Educational Leadership and all professional educators transforming lives as we try to do each and every day. Thank you for opening your minds (and in some cases course content) to early childhood education and brain science and for your incredible patience helping guide a practitioner toward becoming a scholar.

To my personal extended village represented here mostly by acronyms— you know who you are! CMS, AKHS, JMR, PRES, FCDS, CCRI, and UNCC. Also, thanks to each and every one of my students in the CUSU, MSA, and EdD programs at UNCC for always sharing diverse perspectives through enriching dialogue and creative insights; thank you for teaching me! A special shout out to Ching Yi, my devoted graduate assistant, who brought joy and excellence to the toughest aspect of the book for me. Also to Amazing Amy and to Jazzy Kathy and all of the amazing exercise teachers from Jazzercise at the Fountains, who brought my brain back from the brink through body movement. Thank you all!

My sincere thanks are still extended to those dear friends and family members who read early versions of my first book, *Baby Teacher*, and gave me their invaluable feedback on concepts that are further expanded in *Developing Young Minds*: Bonnie Bruce, Dr. Fenwick English, Dr. Beverly Jones III, the late Dr. Gordon Shaw, Dr. Daniel Sher, Dr. Bruce Brasher and his wonderful wife, Cindy, Bruce and Wynona Martin, Melissa Dowd, Joel Whitten, Ellen Wenner, and especially Dr. Kathi Kemper and Dr. Robert Greenberg. Thank you, Kathryn Bornac and Melissa Dowd, for their creative illustrations and their assistance with dreaded technological and computer-assisted design aspects, and to Bobbie Collins at Wake Forest University for her research assistance. Thanks go to Dr. Lorraine Cooke, of the National Association for the Education of Young Children, for her contribution to the New Jersey story. And to Janet Singerman, Jennifer Johnson, Lisa Shporer, and the many amazing North Carolina ECE experts from who I learned so much! Also, I still hold dear my Mom's Night Out group, and especially Janet, for their support of a mom writer in progress.

An important member of my village deserves her own paragraph. Laura Pace, a brilliant early childhood expert who, by fate's good fortune, became my next-door neighbor in North Carolina, a fellow USC Trojan no less, who gave invaluable and insightful feedback on almost every page from an authentic practitioner's point of view; I thank you!

A tremendous debt of gratitude to Carlie Wall, Elaine McGarraugh, and the wonderful team at Rowman & Littlefield, and especially to Tom Koerner, for believing in this project (and all of my projects) right from the start. Thank you to Marcus, an amazing provider and the father of my children, and to my phenomenal mother, not only for her unceasing love and support throughout the decades, but her incredible insights and sensational editing abilities! Thanks also to Suzanne from Learner's Edge, and May and Kit Armstrong, for their brilliance and invaluable contributions.

Finally, deepest thanks to my children, Lily and Bobby, from the bottom of Mommy's heart, for being such amazing teachers and igniting the initial spark of inspiration for this literary child. You are the ultimate reason for my passion to improve learning environments for all children, and I love you!

INTRODUCTION

Eye-Opening Discoveries

Thinking can never be unreasonable.
—Wolfgang Amadeus Mozart (25 years old), in a letter to his father
December 15, 1781

Have you ever traveled in a country that doesn't speak your language? Perhaps you found yourself in a shop needing an answer to an important question. You ask a salesperson, "Where is the restroom?" The salesperson looks at you, but you soon discover that she does not understand a word of what you asked. Do you then repeat your question more slowly and perhaps more loudly? "Where is your restroom?" Perhaps you speak English and your potential information source speaks only Japanese or Farsi. Perhaps the salesperson's language doesn't even use the same alphabet as yours.

If this particular scenario has never happened to you, you have probably seen it happen to others or portrayed in movies, plays, or television programs. Step back from it now and analyze some faulty assumptions that you have intuitively relied upon.

In this scenario, does the salesperson have a hearing impairment? You have no data to support this assumption as she did look at you when you spoke. Yet you automatically raised the volume of your voice in an attempt to communicate better. Did the salesperson misunderstand your pronunciation? Perhaps. However, you could speak at a speed that would make a southerner sound like a New Yorker and it would never be slow enough for your potential information source to understand if the only spoken language she understands is different from yours. This effort to communicate by speaking louder and slower was based on faulty assumptions, and decision making based on faulty assumptions is not uncommon.

There was a time when the planet Earth was believed to be flat and left-handedness was considered a human defect, and even a time when only Euro-Americans were considered to be human, at least to other Euro-Americans. Fortunately, as more and more seemingly correct (yet incorrect) assumptions have been disproved, some societies have become more inclined to consider alternative viewpoints. Different doesn't mean defective; in fact, it provides new learning opportunities that could increase dendritic branching between neurons in the brain and ultimately increase brain function. And increased dendritic branching, as this book will show, is a very good thing!

This book is about potentially faulty assumptions—assumptions that can actually stifle the development of your most valued contribution to life, your child. If you are a parent, teacher, or caregiver, you could at best be missing magical moments in the child's life that can never be returned to, and at worst could be harming a child's development.

This book proposes that infants and young children can take in and process far more complex data from their environment than was previously thought possible. In fact, the complex data taken in from an enriched early environment actually stimulates and then increases neural networking in the infant brain. The wonderful world we live in doesn't have to be completely watered down for babies, but simply presented to them in a conscientious and purposeful manner, one that works for them developmentally.

Contrary to some traditional thinking on child rearing, most babies come into the world hardwired for receiving complex data and, in most cases, the sky's the limit so to speak on building neural networking. In many cases this natural, high-level data processing should not be stifled by, say, the comforts of a constant car seat or carrier, which may provide convenience but serves as an obstacle to the child's developing motor functions. Or the sippy-cup lid that reduces or eliminates messy spills but denies the child an important physics lesson regarding liquid and gravity.

This book is inspired by a true story: the story of what happened to me when research coincided with real life throughout motherhood. And as is so often the case, real life became the greater of the learning experiences and fortunately has now informed the research; research describes and gives order to what is. Ask Jean Piaget. Ask John Dewey.

IN THE BEGINNING: A TRUE LIFE STORY

In 1994, I got a big surprise. I found out that I was pregnant. I was thirty-seven years old and had never slowed down long enough even to think about the possibility of bearing children. I had just defended my doctoral dissertation at the University of Southern California and was ready to finish my research study on new professional opportunities for teachers in charter schools. I was working full time as an assistant principal at a large comprehensive high school in Southern California and teaching at a local university, all the while desperately seeking ways to fix our country's education system.

As fate would have it, becoming a mother was going to be added to my resume of life's experiences. It was also to become the most wonderful (and challenging) experience—greater than any job I ever held, any degree I ever earned, anything I ever accomplished. And perhaps, most importantly, it would become my greatest learning experience, leading me to what I am now confident is the answer to our education system's primary problem—bridging the learning gap that is present on the first day of kindergarten. *This gap, which research has proven that no amounts of money or other interventions infused into the system can fill, appears to be unable to be bridged for students between kindergarten and twelfth grade.*

When confronted with the unknown, I turn immediately to research and science. So when I found out that I was pregnant, I began voraciously devouring everything in print about early childhood. After almost two decades of working in secondary schools, I knew a lot about adolescents but very little about babies. Fortunately, my quest to fix schools had already led to an interest in how and why learning occurs in the brain the way that it does.

Simultaneously with my new quest, scientists discovered that magnetic resonance imaging (MRI) could become functional (fMRI) by measuring the oxygen levels of blood. This revolution in imaging occurred in 1990 and began to transform our understanding of the goings on inside our heads. Rather than simply viewing brain structure as a still photo-graph—for example, the location of a tumor—this new approach to look-ing into the brain revealed countless new insights into the actual *function-ing* of the brain—which areas are more active when and why.

SEEING IS BELIEVING

In an attempt to become a self-made early childhood expert in the mid-1990s, I had read much of the latest research about infant development, sometimes even resorting to tackling the medical journal articles when translations for educators were not yet available. Of particular interest to me was the research on infant sight. I found this interesting because it showed me how little we had looked through the eyes of babies through-out history and how we had designed infant environments around what adults saw rather than what babies saw.

I read the research reporting that babies were not born with the ability to distinguish pinks and blues and all of those other light pastel colors that parents had traditionally used to decorate babies' cribs and bedrooms.[1] Therefore, their primary visual environment was virtually invisible to them! The sophistication of seeing lighter colors would develop a little later. The research said that initially the vision of babies operated best when viewing sharp contrasts; namely, objects in black and white.[2] Al-ways looking for opportunities to apply research, I was one of those progressive moms who bought a black-and-white crib mobile when they first hit the market, instead of one of the pretty pink ones.

I read several new books that recommended using black-and-white flash cards with babies to stimulate their visual neural networks. I had also seen the baby flash cards when they first arrived in stores: white 3x5 cards with a black circle, triangle, parallel lines, or other such imprint on them. While I'm no artist, I was confident that I could recreate those simple flash cards for less than $7.95! So yes, I admit it. I went to the local office supply store and bought white cardboard and black markers and made my own.

My daughter, Lily, loved working with flash cards. She would smile and giggle and obviously enjoyed the gist of the activity. However, she rarely actually looked at the cards for more than a second or two. She spent considerably more time looking at (laughing at) Mommy. (She did, however, love to chew on the cards and bend them into interesting shapes.)

When Lily was about four months old, I noticed something that initiated much thinking and questioning on my part and ultimately led to the writing of this book. I was holding Lily on my hip while looking through a stack of mail on the kitchen counter, when she clearly became mesmerized by a particular picture hanging on our kitchen wall about a foot or two away from her direct line of vision. It was a large black-and-white print of an Ansel Adams photograph of Yosemite National Park.

What surprised me about Lily's attention to this particular photo was not just the intensity of her long gaze, but also the incredible complexity of what she was viewing. Her body language, the evidence that baby researchers rely upon so heavily, made it clear to me that she was highly focused and taking in much data from gazing at this picture. She was also enjoying the view and did not want to stop. I was quickly reminded of one of my favorite quotes by Renate Caine, who at a conference of school administrators remarked that "the mind is virtually inexhaustible when it is engaged in something it perceives as meaningful."[3]

Yosemite National Park, by Ansel Adams.

The lower portion of the Ansel Adams picture, the area at which Lily was directly staring, depicted hundreds of pine trees covered with light snow. There were patterns, yes, but not simple, predictable, man-made patterns. Each tree had a trunk with protruding branches. The number of lines created by all of the tree branches must have reached into the hundreds of thousands, and just like the mind of every child, every tree and every branch was slightly different. However, the combinations of the vast number of irregular branches into groups protruding from the hundreds of trunks did depict an overall pattern of trees in winter, whether they are irregular or complex. This was indeed a far cry from the simple lines and shapes on the flash cards for babies in the baby departments of the stores.

Babies may not be able to see light pastel colors, but it seemed to me that in the colors they could see—blacks, whites, and other sharply contrasting hues—they were able to, and in fact enjoyed, working hard to distinguish highly complex images and to decipher enormously complex patterns. *Different did not necessarily mean simpler.* It just meant different or not-the-same-as, and therefore the brain's natural ability to determine differences must *already* be at work at birth.

It occurred to me that perhaps my husband and I should drive up to Yosemite and show Lily the reality of its magnificence in person, but research abounds that infant vision doesn't extend much beyond a foot in the first few months, just about the distance from mom's breast to her face, and that the scope of their sight increases gradually over time.[4] Obviously, distance vision isn't necessary in the womb, so vision in a newborn is not yet well developed at birth.

In fact, a newborn baby's eyesight is roughly 20/500.[5] In addition, they cannot see objects moving well at all until after two months of age.[6] Early researchers assumed that babies were not interested in objects more than a foot or so away from them. We know now that this was a faulty assumption. They just couldn't see them clearly!

Some promoters of the simple flash cards claimed that the lovely, simple, black-and-white pictures for babies helped them learn to focus more quickly. However, more recent research suggests that the cards may only help babies focus in the first ten to twelve days of life, if even then. By week three, babies are focusing just fine on those simple black-and-white symbols and are ready for more. More what? More complexity.

One additional ancillary benefit of those early flash cards might have been to bring Mom or the caregiver's focus (and consequently her face) closer to the infant more frequently. I had read the research that claimed that babies seem to enjoy studying human faces.[7] And whose face do they seem to like best? Mom's, of course.[8] Again I saw the flash cards arrive in the baby stores, and I took one look at those simple smiley faces drawn on card stock and recreated them myself. Once again, Lily clearly preferred gazing at my expectant face to the drawings on the cards.

What is it about a human face that seems to so engage babies? Early researchers suggested that it might help babies distinguish different people and perhaps even distinguish friend from foe.[9] However, a baby's sense of smell is so highly sensitive at birth that it would surely help to accomplish that task easily in infancy.

On the other hand, ask any anatomy professor which area of the human body is the most complex to view, and he or she will say it is the human face. The face has many muscles and movable parts, and it is expressive beyond quantification. The data transmitted by the combination of the facial muscles, eyes, lips, teeth, tongue, eyebrows, forehead, and even nostrils are exponentially more complex than those conveyed by any other part of the body. The subtle and quick changes from expression to expression add a depth to the complexity of the vision that photographs or flash cards cannot capture. Scientists began working on computer-assisted facial-recognition programs in the mid-1960s, and this technology has only been made fully operational at the national level through the Federal Bureau of Investigation (FBI) in the fall of 2014. The human face is extraordinarily complex.

At last count, the face transmits over seven thousand different expressions.[10] Furthermore, have you ever seen a more expressive face than that of a mother gazing at her newborn? No pleasure is more joyful and no concern more fearful. The human face is a tremendously complex data transmitter, and babies love it, but Mom's face is even more dynamic, and babies love it even more.[11]

A week or two after the Ansel Adams picture incident with Lily, I heard the remark, "You have to crawl before you walk and walk before you run." The underlying assumption, so common in our culture, was that we have to move from the simple to the more complex. It's a concept that is certainly deeply embedded in our education system. In some cases, it may be true.

However, after interviewing several prominent doctors, I found that in terms of the brain and body working together, moving from a sedentary position to mobility—crawling—is a much more complex task for a baby than moving from walking to running is for a child. It reminded me of times in schools when children were failed or held back for an inability to memorize multiplication facts. Some of these children were capable of much more complex higher-order mathematical thinking, but they just had a memory deficiency for those facts—facts that are so easily retrievable on calculators or computers.

The point is that perhaps we still carry some misperceptions on what is simple and what is complex from a baby's perspective. Perhaps we have underestimated the level of the functioning of the infant mind and its real capacity for making sense of its world. And perhaps the simple truth is that developmentally appropriate complexity can build better and more high-functioning brains.

In trying to decide and define what is best for babies rather than merely determining what care is needed for basic survival, just where is the line between abuse or neglect and cognitive enrichment? Is feeding, clothing, and not shaking our babies really enough? Should it be all that we expect from parents or infant caregivers? Are we only interested in the survival of our youngest citizens? Or, do we truly care about the development of the whole child?

Cognitive development in very young children has been either overlooked or misunderstood for centuries and overshadowed by attention to their physical, social, and emotional growth and development. Those aspects of a child's development are all important components, but they are intricately linked to the child's brain development. Overall, consider how important it is that we mandate healthy cognitive developmental environments in addition to physical environments.

The history of our attention to the cognitive development of newborns appears to be a classic case of what is now called the *positivistic fallacy*.[12] This is a fallacy that arises when we infer that absence of evidence is evidence of absence. When it comes to the intentional development of the brains in babies, this faulty assumption has certainly clouded our view.

Consider how a newborn acquires language. What evidence can babies show behavioral psychologists that would suggest they are learning language? Psychologists measure and record such behaviors as breathing, heartbeat, and sucking motions and try to conclude whether a baby shows more or less interest in a particular activity. Unfortunately, none of these behaviors appears to provide the evidence needed to determine what complex mental representations are forming in their purposeful little brains.

Should we wait to speak to a child until the child can speak? Of course we shouldn't, even though it is largely through anecdotal evidence that we conclude that infants learn language long before they can provide evidence of that learning. It is through hearing language, and more importantly, being spoken to that babies learn language themselves, long before the first "mama" emerges.

Newborn babies think and know much more than we previously realized. More important, however, is how much they could think and know given a developmentally appropriate enriching environment. What is the potential learning capacity of a newborn? Unfortunately, babies don't initially appear to know much of anything, or if they do, they can't readily communicate it to us. Therefore, historically, on the great continuum of knowing, babies have been viewed as existing on the opposite end from the great philosophers.[13]

Babies arrive in this world nearly helpless. Their physical development, indeed their very survival, depends almost entirely upon the behaviors of the caregivers in their early environment. So traditionally it has been the health and safety of babies that has concerned parents and other care providers. But what about cognitive development? When do they become educable? When do they learn to think, and when can their thinking capacity be enhanced or broadened? Correspondingly, if an infant is not exposed to a developmentally stimulating environment, could they suffer potentially lifelong delays as a result?

They may not upon first blush appear to be doing much complex thinking at all. We know now, however, that they are in fact incredibly high-powered thinking machines right from birth. Human beings in fact have more brain cells at birth than at any other time in their lives. Later, the brain cells prune themselves, surely a case of "use them or lose them," as the saying goes.

Babies who have been neglected physically show outward signs of the neglect rather early on. Battering leaves bruises. Insufficient nutrition can often be detected through the size of the baby or other physical cues. The effects of cognitive neglect, however, may not show up until the child reaches kindergarten—which, tragically, may be too late to overcome them.

Deprived of stimulation, connections in the brain that could become neural networks of high-level thinking and understanding do not connect later on, and in many cases, these brain cells lose the capacity to connect at all. Babies simply have not been able to communicate this to us in a language that we can easily understand. Fortunately, modern technology is helping us to decode their understanding at breathtaking speed. The critical implications of this new outpouring of data need rapid dissemination and are thus the impetus of this book.

Failure to nurture complex neural networks and thus lay a strong, broad foundation in the infant brain upon which higher-level thought may later transpire has significantly more tragic consequences than our prior historical misunderstandings because in many cases the neglect of the infant brain cannot be overcome or corrected later in life.[14] The cumulative unfulfilled potential that has resulted from this neglect is mind-boggling.

At this point, the past possibilities of greatly increased brainpower are spilled milk. We cannot go backward. However, with the incredible advances in brain research brought about by modern technology, we no longer have excuses for any "sparrows" arriving at the kindergarten door; all children can and should be provided with the opportunity to be "bluebirds" by age five. This is not a how-to book for "tigermoms" trying to create "superbabies." It is a book that is dedicated to helping every single child develop their full, innate potential right from birth. It is also a challenge to society to rethink and reframe a child's first day of "school."

NOTES

1. G. W. Bronson, "Infant Differences in Rate of Visual Encoding," *Child Development* 62, no. 1 (1991): 44–54.

2. Penelope Leach, *Your Baby and Child: From Birth through Age Five*, rev. ed. (New York: Alfred A. Knopf, 2000), 13.

3. Renate Nummela Caine and Geoffrey Caine, "Understanding a Brain-Based Approach to Learning and Teaching," *Educational Leadership* 48, no. 2 (October 1990): 66–70.

4. M. L. Courage, and R. J. Adams, "Visual Acuity Assessment from Birth to Three Years Using the Acuity Card Procedure: Cross-Sectional and Longitu-

dinal Samples," *Optometry and Vision Science: Official Publication of the American Academy of Optometry* 67, no. 9 (1990): 713–18.

5. Thomas Verny with John Kelly, *The Secret Life on the Unborn Child* (New York: Dell, 1981), 40.

6. O. J. Braddick, and J. Atkinson, "Infants' Sensitivity to Motion and Temporal Change," *Optometry and Vision Science* 86, no. 6 (2009): 577–82.

7. John Cleese, "The Human Face," *Newsweek*, August 27, 2001, 5.

8. W. R. Bushnell. "Mother's Face Recognition in Newborn Infants: Learning and Memory," *Infant and Child Development 10* (2001): 67–74.

9. O. Pascalis, S. DeSchonen, J. Morton, C. Deruelle, and M. Fabre-Grenet, "Mother's Face Recognition by Neonates: A Replication and an Extension," *Infant Behavior and Development* 18 (1995): 79.

10. Cleese, "The Human Face," 5.

11. Charles A. Nelson, "The Development and Neural Bases of Face Recognition," *Infant and Child Development* 10, no. 1–2 (March–June 2001): 3–18.

12. David Huron, "Music and Mind: Foundations of Cognitive Musicology," Lecture 1 of the 1999 Ernest Bloch Lecture Series at the University of California at Berkeley, September–December 1999, http://www.musiccog.ohio-state.edu/ Music220/Bloch.lectures/Bloch.lectures.html.

13. Alison Gopnik, Andrew N. Meltzoff, and Patricia K. Kuhl, *The Scientist in the Crib* (New York: Morrow, 1999), 12.

14. Sarah D. Sparks, "Scientists Trace Adversity's Toll," *Education Week*, November 7, 2012.

I

FINDING FAULTY ASSUMPTIONS

Error flies from mouth to mouth, from pen to pen, and to destroy it
takes ages.

—Voltaire

"What if the world really isn't flat?" Early astronomers contemplated
this notion, although they usually did so quietly because of the political
and religious ramifications if it were found to be true. In 1492, Christopher Columbus helped prove those early astronomers correct: Earth
wasn't flat after all! Then in the early 1530s just before his death, Nico-
laus Copernicus released his great work, *De Revolutionibus Orbium Co-
elestium (On the Revolution of the Celestial Spheres)*, in which he suggested that Earth rotates around the sun and not vice versa. This new
knowledge could not initially penetrate the long-standing belief that Earth
was the center of God's universe. Two well-known Italian scientists,
Bruno and Galileo, believed Copernicus. Bruno was burned at the stake.
In 1633, Galileo was tortured into renouncing this belief. His life was
spared, although he spent the rest of his days in prison.[1] Truth can have
tragic consequences.

"All men are created equal" is the now infamous statement of the
famous American founding father, Thomas Jefferson. All men, that is,
except for Indians, Africans, Aborigines, Jews, women—the list could go
on and on. Manifest Destiny, slavery, and the Holocaust represent just a
few of the more tragic by-products of our misconceptions regarding definitions. In this case, one major misconception was of the definition of the
word *men*.

Throughout history, our realization of greater truths, our cumulative societal evolution as a species on this planet, has often resulted from recognition that our prior thinking was based on faulty assumptions, assumptions that may have once appeared true or real to some of us but became obviously erroneous with the addition of new data over time—often embarrassingly so and sometimes with tragic consequences. As we learned, our thinking changed, and we saw prior beliefs through new lenses.

A slightly more recent, and perhaps less-than-tragic, case is that of left-handedness. There was a time when left-handedness was considered to be the result of a defect of some kind. Children in school who exhibited left-handed tendencies were forced to try to learn to write with their right hands. This view of left-handedness resulted in some less-than-flattering expressions still found in our language today, such as "left-handed compliment." The words *sinister* and *gauche* are derived from the Latin and French words for *left*.

Earth was initially considered flat because that's the way it appeared to the unaided human eye. Since a straight horizon was all man could see at the time, how could Earth possibly be round? And if it looked flat to them at the time, with their limited vision capabilities (including their limited vision of what could come along in the future to enhance and expand our "vision"), the assumption was made that the world was, in fact, flat. Indeed, at the far border cartographers would sometimes inscribe on maps, "Beyond here there be dragons!"

Initially, Indians, Africans, Aborigines, and others were considered nonhuman by Europeans because these people could not communicate with the dominant society. Their language was unintelligible, and they shared a different culture from the dominant culture of their geographic location at the time. Consequently, they were not believed to be human or to have souls and, therefore, mistreating or killing them was considered no more immoral than mistreating or killing any other beast.

A hundred years ago, women in the United States were not permitted to vote, own their own homes, or sign contracts. They used the events surrounding the Emancipation Proclamation to gain rights for their gender. Today we continue to strive for universal recognition of, and respect for, all people, regardless of language, culture, gender, or other differences.

Regarding hand dominance, lefties were considered faulty because they wrote, threw, or used knives, forks, and chopsticks differently from the majority. Thanks to modern technological developments in brain research, we now know that the corpus callosum, the brain part that helps the left and right hemispheres in the brain communicate, is actually 11 percent larger in lefties. And while lefties make up only about 10 percent of the population, left-handedness is much more common among mathematicians, musicians, architects, artists, and professional baseball players—not a motley crew to be among! Who would object to possessing the talents of a Marie Curie, Michelangelo, Albert Einstein, Benjamin Franklin, Bill Gates, or Sandy Koufax, left-handed or not?

In each of these samples, the truth was "different," yes, but "faulty," no.

The commonality among these scenarios is that they come from the sometimes ugly list of the unfortunate results of thinking and acting upon faulty assumptions. Throughout history, these faulty assumptions have resulted in the loss or ruin of countless lives, leaving an embarrassing blemish on our evolutionary history.

The subject of this book is another tragedy based on a faulty assumption. It is a tragedy, a destruction that is easily overlooked but may exceed others in history because it has been and continues to be so pervasive and far-reaching. There is no way to calculate its cumulative loss over the generations of civilized humanity. The misunderstanding addressed here is that of the development of the infant brain and its remarkable capabilities when properly nurtured during the first years of life.

So, is this another nature versus nurture debate? No. Genetics matter, but intelligence is not fixed at birth. Environment matters so very much that it can, by conservative estimates, alter IQ by twenty to forty points in either direction, depending upon the environmental circumstances of a newborn baby.[2] The environment of the first few years of life can truly make or break our intellectual futures. Simply put, we are our brains. And since so much of what is considered "success" in life rides upon the facility of the brain, failure to do everything possible to maximize the potential of every child not only falls short of preserving the common good, it can also contribute to the common bad.

A century of educational and social reform all points to one plausible solution to the learning problem that has haunted schools, educators, and parents of schoolchildren for eons. It is only through increased complexity in the data received by the brain in early childhood that more complex neural networks can form, creating a foundation for increased brain capacity in later life. Nurturing neural networks in the developing brains of infants is as important as providing food for tummies and clean diapers on bottoms, and a failure to do so is a form of child abuse. This book will lay out the case for a high-quality, free, and appropriate education to begin at birth, or better yet, on our maternity wards, and *high quality* means, in a word, *complex*.

COMPLEXITY DEFINED

Webster's Eleventh New Collegiate Dictionary says that something that is *complex* is "a whole made up of complicated or interrelated parts; a group of obviously related units of which the degree and nature of the relationship is imperfectly known; hard to separate, analyze, or solve."[3] A usage note says, "Complex suggests the unavoidable result of a necessary combining or folding and does not imply a fault or failure; complicated applies to what offers great difficulty in understanding, solving, or explaining." Some of Webster's definitions of the term *simple* include "not complex," "innocent," "uneducated," "easy, straightforward, causing little difficulty." Which of these words or phrases have you heard most frequently with reference to babies?

There is abundant research indicating that parents who speak more words to their infants will usually hear their children speak words back sooner and in more abundance. Parents who use more complex sentence structures when talking to their babies, using phrases that include word such as *which* and *because*, generally hear seven- and eight-word sentences back from their children long before parents with simpler speech patterns.

While babies cannot talk to us in their infancy, they clearly absorb and process as much data as they are exposed to; the more complex the data input, the more complex and sophisticated the output. This was documented in Betty Hart and Todd Risley's 1995 book, *Meaningful Differences in the Everyday Experiences of Young American Children*, which describes their longitudinal study of the effects of the language of parents on the cognitive development of their offspring.

The researchers used forty-two families with newborns in their homes for the study. They visited the families monthly for an hour, collecting and transcribing over 1,300 hours of conversations within the families in the presence of the babies. The amount of data they gathered over the three years that the study encompassed would fill fifteen books (twenty-three megabytes of computer storage).[4]

To summarize their initial findings in a few sentences: they found that the more educated the mother, the more she spoke to her child. Less-educated moms of low socioeconomic status spoke the least. By the age of three, children of educated, professional parents had heard appropriately thirty million words. Children of working-class parents had heard about twenty million, and children of moms with lower socioeconomic standing around ten million. Varied races and genders were represented in each of the three parent groups and had no bearing on the results. However, the vocabularies and IQs of the professional parents dwarfed those of the welfare parents regardless of race and gender differences.

There was also a notable difference in the quality of the words spoken to the children. Professional parents used multisyllabic words in long, complex sentences and provided extensive explanations to their young children almost constantly. Poor children heard much less, as well as less complex language in their environments. Professional parents were also quick and generous with positive feedback to their children, while poor parents were much more critical. Poor children were much more likely to hear words such as, "NO," "BE QUIET," "BE STILL!"

To follow up, Hart and Risley investigated their initial subjects through ages nine or ten, until the children reached the third grade. The early parental behaviors continued, and researchers predicted correctly that performance on language and IQ tests continued to be higher for the children of professional parents. The researchers found that 86 percent to 98 percent of the words in the children's vocabularies were also in the parent vocabularies.[5] Beginning and participating in "school" from kindergarten to third grade did not change the vocabulary acquisition trajectory set in the first three years of life.

So clear is the importance of the research on speaking to babies that it can be expected that, unless brain abnormalities of some kind are present, a child's speaking ability could be more a result of the stimulation that he receives early in life rather than genetic or socioeconomic factors. By contrast, a child who is not exposed to complex speech patterns early in life usually does not develop them.

In Noam Chomsky's 1988 compilation of lectures, *Language and Problems of Knowledge*, he writes, "It is something that happens to the child placed in an appropriate environment."[6] There appear to be no limits to the level of complexity of speech that the infant brain can process given an enriched, complex environment, and assuming a developmentally appropriate stimulating environment. Yet as the brain ages, so does its capacity for learning new things, including language.

Research has shown that it is far simpler to learn second and third languages as a young child than as a teenager. In fact, research by Dr. Patricia Kuhl at the University of Washington suggests that not only can babies learn languages faster and better than teens or adults, they can simultaneously learn two languages just as fast as one.[7] (For more in-depth study of how infants crack the speech code, Dr. Kuhl's work is a great starting point.)

This notion alone has implications with respect to processing complexity and the capacity of the infant brain. More recent research shows us that a newborn baby comes into the world able to distinguish all of the possible human sounds produced by every language in the world. Yet after only a year of life, babies no longer have the capacity to hear such subtleties and complexity. They can only hear those sounds they have repeatedly heard during their first year of life. This is almost always the language spoken in their home environment.[8]

Clearly, establishing an environment of rich, complex language is a critical concept with regard to the acquisition of speech. When the sound waves from outside the ear journey inward to stimulate the neurons in babies' brains, those neurons do what they were designed to do—connect with one another. Complex sound creates a complex neural network that is more broad and dense and far-reaching than a neural network created by exposure to less-complex stimuli. This will be further explained in our next chapter. For now, it is important to understand that complex stimulus in general leads to a more complex result; in this case, more complex language skills and/or multiple language acquisition.

THE NATURE (OR NURTURE) OF INTELLIGENCE

One fundamental faulty assumption that managed to blind researchers in the first half of the twentieth century, and continues to prevail in the thinking of many educators and parents today, is this: intelligence is fixed. It is determined genetically at birth and remains the same until death. This was believed for generation after generation, and many are still misinformed today.

The roots of this misconception may lie in a simple oversight. In the mid-1800s before any IQ tests existed, Charles Darwin was investigating the origin of the species. While interested in his cousin's work, Francis Galton became curious about the heritability of human intelligence. While Darwin was studying the differences in species, Galton was studying the differences between individual human beings.

Ironically, while Galton's vast travels contributed to his fascination with people on many continents and inspired his thinking on the heritability of intelligence, he somehow overlooked the possible influence of environmental factors on intelligence. He published a book, *Hereditary Genius* (1869), and in it he included a lengthy narrative of data supporting his theory that mental abilities in humans were essentially inherited and did not change over time. Could it be that children raised in families surrounded by highly intelligent caregivers had a more enriched learning environment and consequently developed greater mental abilities through nurture rather than entirely by nature? The oversight of an environmental factor combined with the widespread publication of this work probably contributed to the persistence of the concept of fixed intelligence over time. Many intelligence tests, even many used today, were developed according to this faulty assumption.

The social consequence of this assumption reinforced the social and cultural norms of the time. In eighteenth-century Europe, babies were born and grew into children basically on their own based on privilege or lack thereof. At some point, their intelligence was somehow assessed, and they took their place in what was considered to be the natural hierarchy of society: the haves, the have-nots, and a few in between. The American dream of all people being created equal with equal opportunity was not yet a twinkle in the founding fathers' eyes.

When the U.S. Constitution was crafted and adopted, the principle of all people being created equal was one that, in practice, did not actually include all people. Who could have imagined the lives that would be lost over time through war and the changes that would have to be undertaken to achieve a society that today more closely resembles the concept of equality?

In 1905, the French government commissioned Alfred Binet to develop a test that would separate the slow learners from the "more intelligent" in schools. The prevailing assumption was that slow learners could not ever become more intelligent and therefore should not be allowed to hold the faster learners back. They should be sorted out. Binet's writings of the time reveal that he did not believe that intelligence was fixed; he suggested that intelligence was "educable." Yet somehow this aspect of his views and research was not circulated for nearly six decades.

The Stanford-Binet Intelligence Scale test was a combined effort of Binet and Lewis Terman of Stanford University. The original test, created in 1921, was used to sort students in schools for curricular programs, to sort people in the military for rank or placement, and to help determine future vocational matches. Despite Binet's view, the way IQ (intelligence quotient) numbers were used reflected a belief that intelligence was fixed. Surprisingly, even today, revised versions of the test reflect a somewhat fixed-intelligence assumption.

Throughout the 1930s and 1940s, testing became particularly popular in and outside school. In addition to scholastic aptitude testing, tests were used for everything from assisting with career planning to choosing the best personality in a future wife or husband. In schools, the IQ of children was initially kept secret from parents. Educators believed that since this magic number, determined usually around the age of six, predicted mental capacity, it could not be entrusted to the general public.

A logical outgrowth of this notion of fixed intelligence was that of predetermination. If children were programmed from birth to develop in a particular way regardless of environmental factors, why should their growth be guided at all? Some educators recommended that parents simply watch their children "bloom like a flower" and not interfere.

Fortunately, over time, some dissonant data began to appear. Evidence emerged that suggested that IQ is not fixed. The early work of Maria Montessori, who developed a system of early childhood care, is an example of this and is discussed further in chapter 3. She, like Binet, believed that a person's intelligence was educable, and she set out to prove it. And while her work was tremendously successful, it was extremely slow to be recognized and accepted.

It took many more years of replication research to begin to turn the tide of belief in a fixed IQ. Many educators and psychologists in the 1940s and 1950s risked their reputations by producing evidence that intelligence may not be fixed. Among them were many female professors, who also may have faced credibility questions at the time because of their gender. Regardless of the reasoning, it was slow to be considered seriously.

Finally, in the 1960s, studies with orphan children in model nursery schools became too dramatic to ignore. Following up on the work begun by Beth Wellman at Iowa University in 1938, Harold Skeels and Harold Dye found that children removed from the original orphanage and placed in a significantly more stimulating environment gained more than twenty IQ points when retested.[9] Even more remarkable, those children who were left in the orphanage had lost thirteen to forty-five IQ points when retested.

Follow-up studies published in 1957 by Wayne Dennis and Pergrouhi Najarian investigating orphans in Beirut, Lebanon, found that even the maturation and developmental stages of the children could be altered by environment. These researchers presented evidence to support their theory in year-old babies who could not sit up and four-year-olds who could not yet walk. This was so developmentally contrary to every other normal child studied that the only plausible answer was that nurture could influence development more than nature in some cases.

If intelligence were fixed, these children would have automatically figured out these basic developmental activities regardless of their environment. However, robbed of an appropriate environment for learning even these essential skills, the children reported on in this study had floundered.[10]

Other theories came to light and were tested. For example, the work of the Russian researcher Lev Vygotsky, which was long suppressed, eventually was translated into English and disseminated. Vygotsky believed that learning actually leads development and that intelligence, as well as development, changes constantly as a result of that learning. (Vygotsky's work will be further explored in chapter 3.)

Combining the data primarily from Europe and the United States, scholars considered a new hypothesis. Perhaps IQ changes over time.

Perhaps the brain can be altered by experience. Perhaps the Earth isn't flat.

By 1970, the concept of fixed intelligence was considered disproved among researchers. More longitudinal studies that followed children from birth into adulthood, with data gathered all along the way, revealed unquestionable changes in IQ scores over time. In 1964, Jerome Bruner made an important observation: "The significance about the growth of the mind in the child is not to what degree it depends upon capacity but upon the unlocking of capacity."[11] This process, he reported, could only be accomplished through interaction with the child's environment.

At the same time, two psychologists studying human intelligence helped change the concept of a single and sometimes fixed model to new paradigms for looking at intelligence altogether that included differing types or patterns with multifaceted aptitudes within one individual. In 1983, Howard Gardner proposed the Multiple Intelligences concept, a new definition that included, among other areas, problem-solving ability, creativity, divergent thinking, and interpersonal expertise.

Gardner suggested that individuals could display intelligence in any of eight areas (additional areas have since been added), including bodily-kinesthetic, logical-mathematical, linguistic, interpersonal, intrapersonal, musical, spatial, and naturalist.[12] He also suggested that each intelligence area was semiautonomous and that a person's combined intellectual capacity was a combination of that which is contributed by genes as well as that developed as a result of environmental influences. (Shockingly, today in many public schools children are still tested as early as the end of first grade for "gifted" or "talent development" designation and sometimes never tested again.)

Two years following the release of Gardner's book on Multiple Intelligences, Robert Sternberg of Yale University presented a different theory that distinguished between three different patterns of intelligence depicted by behavior. One person may have stronger abilities in analyzing and evaluating; others may be better at discovering or inventing; and still others may be excellent at applying or implementing different concepts or skills. In his model of intelligence, the ability to perform skills in one of these three overarching areas presented differing intelligences or "strengths." Consequently, Sternberg's theory led to the approach that students should be taught in the ways that best matched their pattern of intelligence, suggesting that a one-size-fits-all approach to teaching may be discriminatory based on one's learning preference.

Also in the 1980s, researchers such as Stephen Buell, Paul Coleman, and Marian Diamond followed up with studies that proved that if we didn't use our brains, we would actually lose brain capacity. Diamond further reported that remaining curious and active and maintaining a love of life were all-important ingredients for neural tissue in the brain to remain stimulated and healthy. Love of life, self, and others was basic, she said. [13]

A TURNING POINT THROUGH TECHNOLOGY

As briefly referenced in the introduction, a critical new finding in imaging began to inform our understanding of how our brains operate beginning in 1990; this was the discovery that oxygen-rich blood is repelled by magnetic fields, but oxygen-depleted blood is attracted to magnetic fields. In essence, prior to this time, MRI (magnetic resonance imaging) could primarily be used for locating a tumor or structural problem in the brain. However, this finding gave birth to the notion that "function" could be observed in the brain. In other words, regional neural activity of the brain could be measured by blood oxygenation level–dependent (BOLD) contrast that followed blood oxygen changes. [14] The fMRI, or functional MRI, was born.

Being able to look into living brains catapulted the neurosciences to the forefront of study on how brains function (and therefore learn). Profound findings that could inform teaching and learning had been published in scientific journals, and authors such as David Sousa and Eric Jensen (and this author) are working to help translate this research into jargon that educators can understand and readily apply in their classrooms in an attempt to improve learning environments. Through action research collaboration, we can work to further inform which findings may bear fruit in our present school learning structures and, conversely, which may not.

Harvard University and Johns Hopkins University developed master's degrees and certificate programs for educators specializing in these new areas in an effort to bring more science into the field of education. Other university Colleges of Education are reaching out to the sciences in efforts to collaborate and improve the present system. Today the message is clear that not only do teaching methods need to change but also the boundaries within which we have traditionally thought of as "schooling" need change. This need becomes more critical each year as new studies are released showing that the first three years of life set the stage in a nearly unalterable way for the K–12 years of schooling to come.

Today, we see tremendous gaps between high-achieving kindergartners and children of the same age who struggle to identity colors and shapes. Educators report, and research backs up the claim, that if children are experiencing failure in their schoolwork by the end of the third grade, that they rarely catch up with their more successful peers. Over time, this lack of success in school can translate into a lack of interest in continuing one's education or, more seriously, discourage learning altogether, particularly school learning. It has also been determined that the majority of these failing students appear to come from low socioeconomic and minority backgrounds.

Huge sums of federal and foundation funds have been injected into the education system over the last half century in an attempt to bridge this learning gap. Unfortunately, research abounds indicating that we have not been able to bridge that gap through compensatory programs. From the Annenberg Foundation millions to the Title I billions, from whole school restructuring efforts to reducing class sizes, from the four decades of Effective Schools reform efforts (leaving no child behind), no silver bullet has surfaced. How can so much hard work, so much money, and the best of intentions fail to produce some kind of "best practices" that work for educating all of our children?

Perhaps the critical question is not *"How* do children learn best?" but *"When* do children learn best?" Do we believe that children of poverty or children from particular races are genetically incapable of developing performance levels equal to those of their higher-socioeconomic peers? To believe this could be viewed as racist and may simply be based on a faulty assumption. Clearly, babies learn, and teaching them in developmentally appropriately manners changes their brains and ultimately their lives.

The most startling research to be shared in the last decade may be the recently established finding that we cannot go back and "remediate" that which is lost in the first few years of child development in a K–12 setting. It appears now that a severely stressful or dysfunctional home life cannot only poison a child's brain development in early childhood but that it can also derail a child's learning capacity altogether, sometimes before the child even enters kindergarten.

A research summary appeared in the November 7, 2012, issue of *Education Week*, written by Sarah D. Sparks and titled "Scientists Trace Adversity's Toll."[15] In it, Dr. Jack P. Shonkoff, the director of Harvard's Center on the Developing Child, is quoted as pointing out that over time, we cannot go back and rewire a brain that has suffered an impoverished or overly stressful early childhood. Scientists and educators alike hoped that we could. Many billions of dollars of failed reform efforts over the decades are clear indicators of this sincere hope.

Today, however, we have every evidence that funneling more millions (or even billions, as in the case of the generous Bill & Melinda Gates Foundation effort) into our schools, particularly our high schools, is not money well spent if increasing student learning is the goal. In short, perhaps when a free and appropriate education begins in our maternity wards will we begin to see the learning gap bridged. In the meantime, parents, caregivers, or other early childhood educators need the information to do what they can to increase neural networking in infant brains. This book is intended to serve as a part of the curriculum for the crib and beyond.

We have established that the development of our brain is critical to the development of our intelligence(s) and ultimately to our personality. It is a major factor in determining our future options and ultimate life experiences as adults. To fully understand how to develop our brain capacity and the brain capacity of the babies in our care, we must first understand at least some of the complex structures and functions of our brains. Let's begin that journey in the next chapter.

SALIENT POINTS

- Intelligence is influenced by the environment and can change over time.
- More complex language in the early childhood environment usually results in more sophisticated language skills throughout life.

- More complex stimuli in the early childhood environment can result in increased dendritic branching and a more complex neural network formation in the brain.
- The potential for some aspects of brain development can be permanently lost if not nurtured through language and developmentally appropriate practice (DAP) in infancy.

NOTES

1. "The Scientists: Nicolas Copernicus," Blupete.com, http://www.Blupete.com/Literature/Biographies/Copernicus.htm.

2. Barbara Clark, *Growing up Gifted* (Columbus, OH: Merrill, 2012), 11.

3. *Merriam-Webster's Collegiate Dictionary*, 11th ed. (Springfield, MA: Merriam-Webster, 2005).

4. Betty Hart and Todd R. Risley, "The Early Catastrophe: The 30 Million Word Gap by Age 3," *American Federation of Teachers* (Spring 2003): 4–9.

5. Hart and Risley, "The Early Catastrophe."

6. Noam Chomsky, *Language and Problems of Knowledge: The Managua Lectures* (Cambridge: MIT Press, 1988).

7. Patricia K. Kuhl, "Cracking the Speech Code: How Infants Learn Language," *Acoustical Science and Technology* 28, no. 2 (2007): 71–83.

8. Joan Raymond, "The World of the Senses," *Newsweek* (special issue), Fall/Winter 2000, 18.

9. Harold M. Skeels and H. B. Dye, "A Study of the Effects of Different Stimulation on Mentally Retarded Children," *Proceedings of the American Association on Mental Deficiency* 44 (1939): 114–36.

10. Wayne Dennis and Pergrouhi Najarian, "Infant Development under Environmental Handicap," *Psychological Monographs* 71, no 7 (1957): 1–13.

11. Jerome Bruner, "The Course of Cognitive Growth," *American Psychology* 19 (1964): 1–15.

12. Howard Gardner, *Frames of Mind: The Theory of Multiple Intelligences* (New York: Basic Books, 1983).

13. Marian Diamond, "Brain Research and Its Implications for Education," paper presented at the Twenty-Fifth Annual Conference of the California Association for the Gifted, Los Angeles, February 1986.

14. Seiji Ogawa, T. M. Lee, A. R. Kay, and D. W. Tank, "Brain Magnetic Resonance Imaging with Contrast Dependent on Blood Oxygenation," *Proceedings of the National Academy of Sciences of the United States of America* 84, no. 24 (December 1990): 9868–72.

15. Sarah D. Sparks, "Scientists Trace Adversity's Toll," *Education Week*, November 7, 2012.

2

BRAIN SCIENCE FOR NON-NEUROLOGISTS

With our new knowledge of the brain, we are just dimly beginning to realize that we can now understand humans, including ourselves, as never before, and that this is the greatest advance of the century, and quite possibly the most significant in all human history.
—Leslie A. Hart, *Human Brain and Human Learning*

"The Decade of the Brain." This was the title given to the decade of the 1990s by the U.S. Congress because of the explosion of research on the brain brought on by new technological advances. The pace at which scientists began discovering the interplay between biology, behavior, and the brain as the century turned has been nothing short of exhilarating, and many scientists consider the human brain to be the most complex object in the known universe today.

Almost every day, a new study enlightens us about breakthroughs in science, medicine, psychology, and education. We know now that virtually everything psychological is also biological and that the brain plays the leading role in the functioning of how it all plays out in our behavior and in our lives.

The Decade of the Brain gave way to the Century of the Mind. Teachers, psychologists, pediatricians, and neurologists are uniting in the search for exactly how the brain learns and operates and how better to facilitate these processes. The brain brings it all together in the body, and it is bringing us all together in the disciplines of knowledge as well. Do educators really have to become neuroscientists? Not entirely, but to better understand teaching and learning, we must all understand a bit about brain functioning. To do this, we need to know some of the terminology as well as some of the parts of the brain that are integral for understanding learning. We begin with a quick study in brain science (for non-neurologists).

Today, we know that the body is made up of cells. Some of these cells "talk" to each other, and the brain is the keeper of the keys to most all of the action. Most cells in the body have specific jobs that they are designed to accomplish. Hair follicle cells grow hair. Muscle cells build tissue with the ability to contract, relax, and grow muscles. The brain cells we are most interested in are called *neurons*.

Neurons are not the only cells found in our brains. In fact, of the trillion brain cells that reside there, neurons make up only about a tenth of them, or about one hundred billion. The rest are mostly *glial* cells, which is Greek for "glue." But the neurons exist for one very important purpose, to communicate. They do this through a complex system of electrical and chemical signals from cell to cell. This occurs on the microscopic level. The overall combined function of these cells in the brain is to receive information from the environment and from all parts of the body through the senses, interpret it, and then decide on and execute responses to it. This is accomplished through an unfathomably complex network of neurons.

The adult human brain weighs about three pounds and is roughly the size of a large grapefruit or cantaloupe. It is a fragile mass that is found at the top of the spinal column. It is surrounded by membranes that serve to protect it and is enclosed in the skull for even greater protection. The brain of an adult resembles the texture of Jell-O, while the brain of an infant more closely resembles custard. As any Jell-O and custard connoisseur knows, jarring custard can be much more shape altering than giving a good jolt to Jell-O that has been set in the refrigerator. Both substances will wiggle and jiggle, but only custard will change beyond recognition when disturbed. This is one reason we should never shake a baby. Permanent brain damage and even death may be the result.

SEEING BRAIN CELLS

Galileo developed a magnifying device with a convex and concave lens in the early 1600s, and Robert Hooke is credited with viewing cells under a rudimentary microscope in the 1660s. However, it was a few centuries later before actual brain cells were first observed under a microscope and Louis Pasteur finally put to rest the theory of spontaneous generation, the prevailing theory that microbes could spontaneously generate in a sterile environment. The microscope of those days magnified cells up to around 1,500 times.

It wasn't until the birth of the electron microscope in the 1930s, and its development into the 1960s that magnified viewing up to eighty thousand times that scientists were actually able to see the details of brain cells. Today's transmission electron microscopes can magnify an object around two million times, and through even more advanced and sophisticated functional imaging such as EEG and MEG, we can view activity in live brains. All of this is to say that we have a much clearer idea of brain function based on the tremendous advances in technology that are continually being developed, giving us a better idea of what is going on in our brains. So complex is the organ that the more we find out, the more we learn that we do not know or at least cannot yet explain.

By most accounts today, it is generally agreed that an average baby is born with over a trillion brain cells (give or take a few billion), although some scientists speculate that it could be more. Perhaps the most important type of brain cell for our discussion is the neuron. At birth, each neuron is ready and waiting to be developed through its connections with other cells. To help imagine the size of a neuron, consider this—approximately one hundred thousand of these neurons can fit on the head of a pin.

Neurons are the critical actors within the brain and the entire nervous system of the body in the transmission of data or information. Neurons differ from other cells in the body in that they can grow to have upward of tens of thousands of branches emerging from them. These branches are called *dendrites*, after the Greek word for "tree." Dendrites receive communications via electrical impulse from other neurons and send them on to yet other neurons through axons.

Typically, each neuron has only one axon, a long fiber surrounded by an insulating myelin sheath that extends off the neuron like dendrites but

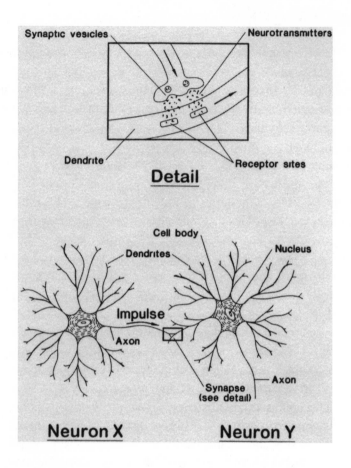

Portrait of a Neuron.

without the branching. The myelin sheath is important because it protects the axons from other cells and speeds the transmission of the electro-chemical impulses that pass through it. In people with multiple sclerosis, the myelin sheath degenerates and results in the eventual loss of muscle control. Presently it is believed that the majority of the myelin sheath forms during the first year of life.[1]

In a normal brain, there are tiny breaks along the axon in the myelin sheath that help facilitate the impulses, the "action potential," to skip along down the axon at incredible speeds of up to 250 miles per hour. In addition, since there are typically thousands or even sometimes tens of thousands of dendrites relaying messages, the cells end up combining and averaging all of this input to one output to send on to the next neuron through an axon.

The dendrites and axons of neurons communicate with one another without ever actually touching. Information travels away on the axon to a neighboring dendrite, and there is a tiny space between these microscopic strands that is roughly a millionth of an inch wide. This miniscule area, where data is transferred from one neuron to another, is called a *synapse*. *Synapse* is Greek for "to join together."

Normally, a neuron collects information from other neurons through its dendrites, which have connected with neighboring axons through synapses. To send on the signal, the neuron shoots out electrical impulses through its axon toward a neighboring neuron's dendrite, and they meet at the synapse. In this very small space of the synapse and for a very brief time, the electrical message from the neuron becomes chemical.

The message impulse interacts with other chemicals called *neurotransmitters*, which are stored in tiny sacs at the ends of the axon called *synaptic vesicles*. As neurotransmitters are then released, they either stimulate or inhibit the connecting neuron's dendrites or spines to receive the information. This transfer of data between the axon and the dendrite at the synapse is a critical moment.

In its simplest and most basic definition, "learning" occurs when neurons communicate with other neurons through synapses. The actual process becomes tremendously complex—certainly more than can be explained in this book. Simply put, however, all that we think and feel boils down to trillions of alternating electrical and chemical transmissions between networks of neurons at the synapse, and if synapses are not firing, learning is not taking place. There are a plethora of different videos to be found online to help display this synaptic action as well as views of brain areas.

NEUROTRANSMITTERS AND HORMONES

Neurons use oxygen and glucose for fuel to fire messages between neurons. Glucose can be found in natural sugars, not processed sugars; fruits are a good source, but processed sweets are not. The more the brain works, the more the cells fire, and the more fuel it burns. Water is also absolutely essential for the brain to function at its best. Water helps move neuron signaling throughout the brain. This is why a big glass of water (or two), movement, and a healthy breakfast in the morning are all essential for the brain to operate optimally each day.

There are some additional chemicals that affect cell firing that should be considered as their role in brain function increases with our knowledge of them. Neurotransmitters are molecules that act as chemical signals that are released from the presynaptic terminal of the axon into the synapse. They then bind to specific receptors in the receiving dendrite, consequently changing the electrical property of the receiving cell. The distance a neurotransmitter travels to act is tiny, less than a micrometer.

Over recent years, these important agents or neurotransmitters have been found to be critical in the balance of normal brain functioning similar to the use of gasoline or oil in your car. They are necessary for brain functioning, and the type or quality or quantity of these agents can have a direct impact on performance. The first neurotransmitter was actually identified around the time of World War I, but scientists were then focused on studying how chemicals affected other organs, such as the heart, rather than how they worked in the brain. That first neurotransmitter identified and named was *acetylcholine*.

Noradrenaline is another neurotransmitter, which is released in the brain to increase arousal. Drugs such as cocaine boost the availability of this particular neurotransmitter. Noradrenaline is made from a chemical called *dopamine*. People with Parkinson's disease are lacking in dopamine, while in patients with schizophrenia, there appears to be too much. A miniscule amount of imbalance in a neurotransmitter can have dramatic results on thought and behavior.

Another example that reflects the importance of neurotransmitters in our brains is the fact that acetylcholine is deficient in the brains of most patients suffering from Alzheimer's disease.[2] Neuroscientists have not yet concluded why these states exist, but testing and other research is ongoing.

Other chemicals that also produce action but travel beyond the brain throughout the body are called *hormones*. Consider adrenaline. When we are especially afraid, adrenaline is released from an adrenal gland into the bloodstream where it ultimately causes the heart to beat more rapidly, breathing to accelerate, and sometimes palms to sweat. Since the chemical causes a full body response that travels over much distance in the body, it is generally referred to as a *hormone*.

Some hormones, however, can also act as neurotransmitters, including adrenaline. One example is oxytocin. This chemical is released from the pituitary gland but also acts as a neurotransmitter at several synapses in the brain as well. So both neurotransmitters and hormones are chemical messengers that are released and are designated to carry a signal to a target cell somewhere in the body. If the target is in the brain, it is called a neurotransmitter. If it is elsewhere in the body, it may be a hormone. Both affect brain chemistry, which affects brain function.

Most important for new parents or caregivers to be familiar with in regard to young children are the big three: adrenaline, cortisol, and norepinephrine. These are the three major stress hormones that when constantly present in abundance over time can have a debilitating effect on the brain development of young children, ironically when they also have an effect on their caregivers. These chemicals are usually automatically released when we encounter danger and the need to "freeze, fight, or fly."

The amygdala, a part of the brain which will be discussed shortly, perceives fear and instantly sends a message to the hypothalamus, which notifies the pituitary gland to release another hormone that tells the adrenal glands to let it fly! The short story is that fear and stress are conducive for survival. This probably originally evolved for surviving in the wild and steering clear of flesh-eating animals.

However, rather than a flash of fear followed by a quick release of stress chemicals occurring once every few weeks or months, in today's world we find ourselves with looming deadlines or ongoing stressors that can cause the body to release stress hormones continuously over time with little letup. This can lead to suppressed immune systems, acne, obesity, and other unhealthy states for adults and can actually be dangerous for the brain development of young children.

The more we learn about neurotransmitters and hormones, the more we know we need to relax, take a breath, and take up yoga or decaffeinated tea in the morning rather than racing through traffic trying not to spill a latte. You wouldn't be reading this book if you didn't care about the brain development of young children, so if there is one message to take away to improve both your and your children's brain health, it would be to seriously limit ongoing stress. Drink more water, eat more fruits and vegetables, and most importantly, relax!

NEURAL NETWORKS

Clusters of neurons that work together by firing repeatedly over time are called *neural networks*. There are neural networks already in place when a baby is born that tell the body to breathe, the heart to beat, and so forth. Babies do not need to be taught how to do these things. However, the vast majority of the quadrillion possible synaptic connections that a baby's billions of neurons could produce only come together through experience, through stimulation from their environment.

For example, language is not hardwired at birth, but when a child repeatedly hears language over time, neural networks will form that will ultimately provide the connections necessary to produce spoken language. Neurons repeatedly connect to the same or similar nearby neurons, creating pathways or networks. Experience and repetition lend greater strength to these clusters of firing neurons, forming a faster neural network through which signals flow.

Stimulation from the environment holds the key to the cognitive development of the newborn brain and, to a somewhat lesser but still significant extent, to the brains of adults as well. The reason for this is that the brain is not unlike most other parts of the body. If we want our muscles to be stronger and bigger, we must stimulate them by lifting weights or challenge them with strenuous activity. If we want our heart to be stronger and more efficient, we must challenge it with aerobic exercise and support it with proper nutrition.

Likewise, if we want our brain to be stronger, have more capacity, and operate more efficiently, we must exercise it, too. We do this by challenging the brain to increase neural networks through exposure to new information from the environment. Building more of these neural networks and building larger, more complex tapestries of networks earlier in life gives children a broader foundation upon which to build more knowledge throughout life. Every kindergarten teacher can tell you which children came from environments that were enriched with multiple varieties of developmentally appropriate stimulation and which came from stress-filled or neglectful homes. The bottom line is neural networking.

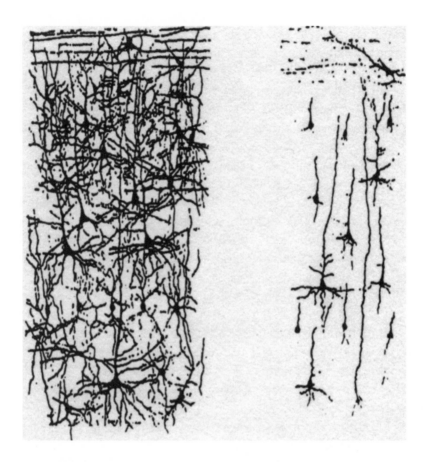

Neural Networks.

OTHER IMPORTANT PLAYERS

To complicate matters further, neurons aren't the only fish in the brain's complex sea. For every hundred billion neurons, there are at least a trillion cells called glial cells—ten times the number of neurons. *Glial* comes from the Greek word for "glue," which basically describes what these cells do in the brain: stick to neurons and take care of them. They perform the housekeeping tasks of maintaining a healthy chemical environment around each neuron. They help scavenge from injured neurons and act as sponges to clean out excessive toxins of any kind around them. Thus, they have become known as the "Cinderella cells."[3] Some glial cells actually wrap around neurons and protect them. Loss of these protective glials can cause gradual paralysis and other symptoms such as those present in patients with multiple sclerosis.

More recently scientists have found some neurons in the front of the brain that fire just before someone enacts a planned movement of some kind. Interestingly, these same neurons are fired when that person sees someone else enact the very same movement. For example, if a person sees someone prick their thumb on a rose thorn, the same neurons fire in their brain as those in the person actually trying to pick the rose. These cells have been named *mirror neurons*.

Scientists now believe that mirror neurons may allow us to decode intentions and predict the behaviors of others. Some are studying the role of mirror neurons and empathy. Interestingly, some autistic children do not appear to have the same levels of mirror neuron activity as those without the disorder, although this is still inconclusive as this is a new line of research for neuroscientists.

BRAIN STEM SUPPORTS SURVIVAL

The oldest part of the brain is the brain stem. This area is located just above the spinal column and is often referred to as the *reptilian brain*. It is believed that the brain stem evolved over five hundred million years ago, and eleven of our twelve body nerves that go up to the brain end here. The brain stem harbors the functions of heartbeat, digestion, respiration, and body temperature—functions vital to the survival of the organism.

The brain stem is generally believed to be a part of the brain that is hardwired at birth, and as mentioned prior, the neural networks are already established for these survival functions. Thus, babies are born with the capabilities to breathe, eat, and excrete without ever being taught how to perform these functions. These important yet low-level functions are completely controlled and monitored automatically through the brain stem and occur without any conscious effort on our part. They are, nonetheless, subject to damage such as that caused from shaking a baby when the other brain areas are not so hardwired or neck muscles are not sufficiently strengthened. This is also why parents and caregivers of infants are informed that the baby's head must be supported at all times until the neck muscles have strengthened sufficiently to support the child's head.

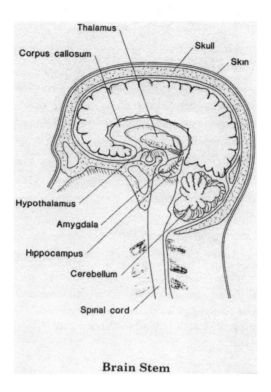

Brain Stem

The Basic Brain.

CEREBELLUM AND COORDINATION

The cerebellum is a brain part located just behind the brain stem and below the back of the cerebrum in the back of the head. This "little brain," as it is often called, coordinates every movement of the body without initiating any of them. Again, the tasks of the cerebellum are automatic; whether we are awake or asleep, it keeps managing our life-sustaining functions as needed. The cerebellum controls balance, coordination, and movement. Thanks to a well-developed cerebellum, you can usually slice and butter a warm muffin and bring a teacup from the saucer to your lips without spilling a drop. It is also considered responsible for automating much of our more mundane movements such as tying shoelaces or riding a bike.

The cerebellum is a particularly interesting and important brain part. It is a highly organized, deeply folded structure that while consisting of only about 10 percent of the brain's weight, it contains more neurons than all of the rest of the brain combined. Recent research suggests that it is also involved in more complex cognitive processing including mental rehearsal, which can result in allowing the rest of the brain to focus on other tasks while the cerebellum takes care of the more automated tasks.

Development of the cerebellum is going on as children play on swings, seesaws, merry-go-rounds, and learn to ride bikes. Hopscotch, jump rope, and most play movements are important for developing this brain part. Children should be encouraged to try to walk on a straight line, balance, spin, and jump. As infants, the less time babies are transported from stroller to car to home in one seated position for extended periods of time, the better for the cerebellum.

Since the cerebellum involves interplay between the senses and movement, it is associated with actions that are initially learned, such as driving a stick-shift car. However, once learned, the skill becomes almost effortless. Patients who have suffered damage to the cerebellum cannot coordinate complicated sequences of movement and may thus appear clumsy. They find it almost impossible to play a song they once knew on the piano or walk in a straight line.

Recently, some doctors are prescribing a movement-based regiment for treating problems such as lack of concentration or inability to focus, based on studies involving the cerebellum.[4] The more we learn about this brain part, the more important it becomes, and for the early years, movement and play provide key developmental experiences for improving the efficiency of later learning involving the cerebellum.

HIPPOCAMPUS AND SELF-CALMING

Hippocampus is the Greek word for "seahorse." Early researchers who thought this part of the brain was shaped like a seahorse called it that, and the name stuck. This little area in the central base of the cerebrum plays a critical role in the functions of memory and learning. It is also critical in the making of meaning, and so it is important for educators and parents to have a basic understanding of its function. The hippocampus works in conjunction with the next brain part in our study, the amygdala, to develop parts of memory.

For example, a two-year-old may believe that there is a monster under his bed. He perceives it, and his amygdala signals fear! This message travels immediately to the hippocampus to check prior experiences. It takes repeated reinforcement through the years of us showing the toddler that there is no monster under the bed to convince him that this is in fact true. In time, when the amygdala projects fear again at the thought of this scenario, the neural networks between the amygdala and the hippocampus will become established and the hippocampus will assure the amygdala that it has nothing to fear. This process in infants is often referred to as the development of "self-calming" skills.

For infants to develop self-calming or self-soothing skills, there must first be a regular routine and a regular consistent bedtime. Perhaps following a routine bath, book reading, and a few moments of cuddle and comfort, after which the caregiver lays the baby in bed awake but drowsy. Oftentimes, they will doze right off to sleep. If, however, older babies are used to being rocked to sleep, it may take some time to establish the new routine. Over time, the amygdala will not trigger fear or the hippocampus will not register out of the ordinary, and a new routine will be established incorporating the self-soothing. Much like the young child who never learns to crawl because his body is never given enough time on the floor to learn, we can assist with the development of self-calming skills through developmentally appropriate routines from early on.

In the meantime, caregivers need to calmly and cheerfully reassure the terrified toddler by looking under the bed until the time comes that the fear subsides without help. Parents (perhaps more likely fathers) find humor in scaring their child by jumping out from a closet or hiding behind a door. This behavior is only delaying the time it will take for the hippocampus to become more convincing to the amygdala that there is nothing to fear, and as well it bathes the brain in stress hormones unnecessarily and should be avoided.

Because the hippocampus harbors portions of our memory storage, adults whose hippocampus is removed or damaged through surgery can remember everything that happened to them prior to surgery but nothing afterward. In fact, without a properly functioning hippocampus, any information coming into memory is lost within seconds. It just doesn't stick. Understanding this and the important fact that the hippocampus must be properly developed should be established in the early years. If the young child is exposed to too much stress in their early environment, some research suggests that malfunctions of the hippocampus may be a factor leading to depression or even schizophrenia later on.[5] It is important that patience and calm explanations are the appropriate responses to a child's imaginary fears instead of ridicule or increased stress. Remember, the monsters in the closet are real to children until repeatedly proven otherwise. On the other hand, imagine what happens to the hippocampus of the child who really does have just cause for fear in their home environment.

AMYGDALA AND EMOTIONAL DEVELOPMENT

Also possessing a Greek name, this one meaning "almond," the *amygdala* is a combination structure attached to the hippocampus. These two small, almond-shaped brain parts, one each in the left and right hemispheres, play a critical role in decoding emotional messages. When stimulated electrically, the amygdala can cause us to feel tremendous fear, rage, or any of a wide range of other aggressive emotions.

Research suggests that emotions play a critical role in cognitive processing, which makes sense since the amygdala is attached to the important meaning maker, the hippocampus. Additionally, when we recall an experience that was replete with intense emotions, the memory alone can cause us to relive the emotions of the experience, even the actual physiological ones. Past lovers didn't actually break your heart, they simply moved your amygdala. However, the phrase "You broke my amygdala" just doesn't resonate!

Recent research shows that children with larger amygdalae have more problems with anxiety.[6] The children in one study also showed greater connectivity between the amygdala and other brain regions responsible for attention and self-regulation compared to children with lower levels of anxiety and smaller amygdalae. It is unknown whether increased stress causes an enlarged amygdala or whether the preexisting larger amygdala leads to increased anxiety. Either way, less stress is better for young children than more stress, and this is the salient point for parents and caregivers to keep in mind.

HYPOTHALAMUS, REWARD, AND REGULATION

This interesting structure has been pinpointed as one of the brain's primary pleasure centers as it is located along the circuit that is informed in the presence of rewards. It is located just above the amygdala and below the thalamus, which monitors information coming in from outside of the body. The hypothalamus monitors the internal system and acts on the pituitary gland right beside it as well as several other areas that affect behavioral responses. The hypothalamus regulates body temperature, hunger, thirst, sleep, and pituitary hormones.

Early experiments found that by setting up an environment in which rats could stimulate their hypothalamus on their own by pressing a pedal for stimulation the rats would do so up to seven thousand times an hour—usually until the point of exhaustion. Some researchers believe that addictive disorders may be related to the possible dysfunction of this brain part.

The hypothalamus plays an important role in our response to stress by causing the release of hormones that travel throughout the body and not just in the brain. If a person is trying to stop smoking, for example, their hypothalamus may send out stress hormones that can in turn create additional stress. They are thus termed *relapse triggers* as increasing stress typically also leads to relapse.[7] In other words, when the addict tries to stop, they get a double whammy of stress, making it even harder to stabilize this brain area.

Hormones and neurotransmitters play important roles in brain chemistry and will be addressed later. For now, keep in mind that these brain parts are like a variety of vegetables in a salad bowl; when combined differently, the salad tastes different, even if only slightly. But when dressing is added, the taste and even the texture change as well.

CEREBRUM: THE "FACE" OF THE BRAIN

The area that most folks think of as "the brain," that pale gray, wrinkled area that is the first visible part of the brain inside the skull, is known as the *cerebrum* or *neocortex*. Its weight makes up about 80 to 85 percent of the overall size of the brain, and it helps direct critical functions such as speech, muscular movement, and thinking, and it has some role in memory. It coordinates movement with input from the senses. (A different brain area, the *basal ganglia*, is involved in more primitive types of movement such as the spontaneous acts of standing up and sitting down.)

One large fissure spans the top center of the brain, dividing it into two cerebral hemispheres: the left and the right. The left hemisphere controls the right side of the body and the right hemisphere controls the left. Contrary to the faulty assumptions of the "left-brain, right-brain" theorists of decades ago, the nerves in the left and right hemisphere do talk to one another. In fact, they are constantly communicating through the corpus callosum, a thick, cablelike structure made up of over 250 million nerve fibers that connect the two halves of the cerebrum.

People, animals, and even insects generally do have a hemispheric preference, and certain functions are found specifically in either the left or right hemisphere within the cerebrum, so there is some truth to the hemispheric preference debate. Both hemispheres, or the entire outer skin of the cerebrum, are covered with a barklike layer called the *cortex* (which means "the bark of a tree"), which has a surface area of about two square feet. It is made up of a thin layer of thousands of miles of connecting fibers where most of the action of the brain takes place. To summarize, the cerebrum is covered by the cortex and is what you generally see when you view a picture of a brain.

PREFRONTAL CORTEX AND HIGHER-ORDER THINKING

This area of the brain, located behind the forehead, is believed to be the most recently evolved area of the brain for humans. The behaviors associated with the prefrontal cortex include imagining, predicting, planning, organizing, and creating; in other words, higher-order thinking skills. Also associated with this area of the brain are insight, introspection, empathy, reflection, intuitive thought, and formulation of our sense of purpose. This part of the brain houses our most complex thoughts and behaviors and regulates all of our other brain parts. It is our executive control center, and it is not believed to be fully developed until the mid-twenties. An immature prefrontal cortex is one reason why it is thought that teens are more prone to making decisions based on emotions rather than reason.

Scientists say that our prefrontal cortex is approximately twice the size that it would need to be for a primate of our size and overall body weight.

Since it is the last part of the brain to come to fruition, it is thought to be the most susceptible to environmental factors. Also, because its development is greatly dependent upon the environment that developed other parts of the brain, it is arguably the most important body part of high-level critical thinking, and much greater attention and scientific research is now being focused on the development of the prefrontal cortex.

There are few studies addressing the early childhood environment and its relationship to the maturation of the prefrontal cortex in the teen years and later. Research at this point would imply, though, that the level of enrichment in the earliest years could directly affect the eventual development of the prefrontal cortex. This is an enormously important area that needs further study.

Damage to the prefrontal cortex can result in a condition called *source amnesia*, in which a patient can recall an event but cannot remember a frame of reference for it. An example would be the sensation in dreams of being unable to place experiences into a specific time or location.

A BRIEF HISTORY OF BRAIN SCIENCE

The scientific approach to understanding the brain is roughly a century and a half old. Throughout most of civilized history, those curious about the structures and functions of the brain explored every dissectible feature and tried to explain what they found. They were limited to working on the brains of the deceased, since this was the only legal and certainly the only humane way to study what was inside the human skull. Over time, as was customary in the sciences, Latin or Greek names were given to most parts of the brain, thus the terms *cerebrum, corpus callosum, hippocampus, amygdala*, and so on.

Some of the earliest explorers labeled parts of the brain by actual location—forebrain, midbrain, and hindbrain. Only a few decades ago, Paul MacLean explained the brain in relation to the stages of evolution: reptilian, paleomammalian, and mammalian.[8] His model is a simplified explanation of looking at brain structure and works well for those interested in early childhood in particular based on the function of areas.

THE TRIUNE BRAIN: REPTILIAN, MAMMALIAN, AND HIGHER-LEVEL THINKING

Explaining brain functioning can be simplified by approaching this complex structure as three brains in one. Over time, the brain has evolved, adding ever more mass to the front of the brain as its capabilities have become more and more complex.

As noted earlier, the survival-related activities, such as breathing and heartbeat, are controlled by what MacLean refers to as the reptilian brain or the old brain. This lowest part of the brain, the brain stem, involves no emotion or thinking beyond what is deemed by it to be necessary for survival (such as assuring that we breathe and that the heart beats). It

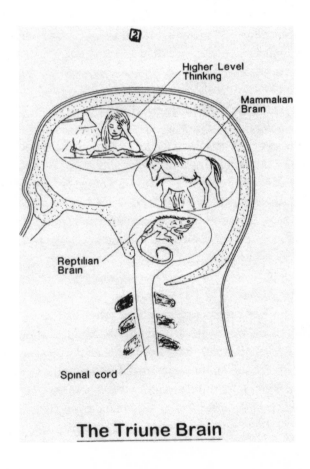

Triune brain.

resembles the functioning of the current brains of reptiles. All processes revolve around physical survival.

An appropriate visual image for the functioning of this part of the brain is a lizard or turtle. Eggs are laid, and the mother leaves the area. When the young reptiles are eventually hatched, these baby reptiles are basically self-sufficient. They are not dependent upon the mother for survival in any way. Consequently, the reptilian brain is termed the *survival brain*.

The second section of the brain to evolve was the mammalian brain. This section is also referred to as the *limbic system*, a term coined by Dr. MacLean as early as 1952. The mammalian brain includes structures involving basic emotions that are also linked to survival, only in mammals. It is found above the reptilian brain and houses the amygdala and hippocampus, among other structures. If a mammal finds itself starving, there is a fear that survival has been jeopardized. Anger, rage, and emotions associated with that fear arise in the amygdala.

Mammals have several critical attributes that distinguish them from reptiles; they have fur and are warm-blooded animals. Most importantly, for the triune brain theory reasoning, is that mammals (with the exception of the platypus) do not lay eggs as reptiles do. They give birth to live baby mammals that are dependent upon their mothers for survival. Mammal mothers nurse their young (with mammary glands) or their young do not survive. This is the level at which attachment occurs, a type of survival attachment, which is different from reptiles. The visual image here is a mother kitten or monkey with its babies quite literally attached to a mammary gland on their warm, furry body. (Very different from the cold-blooded lizard.)

The third section of the brain to evolve was the cerebrum. This is the largest of the brain areas and is the one wherein "thinking" occurs. Over time and with proper development, this thinking can be strong enough even to delay or subdue the natural emotions and actions that normally occur with respect to survival as perceived by the reptile brain or mammalian brain.

Consider a common scenario, for example. Two very young children are at a picnic table with their lunch bags. If one child reaches over and takes half of another child's sandwich, the lower-level reptilian brain of the victim might automatically respond by grabbing it back and perhaps striking out at the thief. It is the survival instinct in the lower brain that is triggered and demands immediate action for the sake of survival.

However, as the brain develops (around age five or six, for example), the higher-level cerebrum area of the brain once neural networks have developed and connected can offer the child some alternative options. "There are several considerations for me here. I can ask that child why he took my food and request that he return it. I can go tell the teacher what happened and probably get it back that way. I can look at what else mom has packed in my lunch and determine if I really need that half sandwich anyway. And tomorrow at lunch, I won't sit near him."

The primal concern for survival is subdued and delayed by thought and consideration of options—ultimately, a plan of action or reaction. This is a result of increased neural networking or brain maturity, and depending on the environment in the early years, it may not be operable until the teen years, if then.

The last area of the brain to develop over time, both evolutionarily speaking and in individual human development, is the prefrontal cortex. This is the area where visualization, planning, imagining, and reasoning take place. This is regarded as the place in the brain where our most advanced thinking occurs and is not networked or developed in babies. Many neurologists believe that this area of the brain is largely dependent upon experience for development.

As previously stated, babies arrive in the world already hardwired to breathe, and they are born breathing. We do not have to teach them how. Other functions necessary for survival are also already networked at birth in the reptilian brain. On the other hand, the majority of neural networks in the brain are formed with considerable influence from experiences after birth. Babies are born with the capacity to learn to speak a language. In fact, they are born with the capacity to learn every nuance of all of the languages of the world. However—and this is a crucial "however"—they may never actually learn any language if they are not exposed to it in their early environment. Language is not hardwired at birth, but the potential to learn language is in most babies. Furthermore, studies show that babies will learn language much faster and more completely if they are born into an environment in which they hear lots of language. [9]

Clearly, simply studying brain regions and neurons does not begin to tell the entire complicated brain story, which some believe is just in the "once upon a time" stage of revelation. However, the more we know, the more we realize we need to know. The more parents and caregivers know, the more they will be able to bring all of this exciting research to its place of meaning: their connections with developing young minds.

SALIENT POINTS

- Neurons connect with other neurons creating neural networks, which increase the efficiency of communication within the brain.
- Dendrites on neurons branch and grow when stimulated, creating more potential communication between neurons.
- Neurons connect at the synapse where important brain chemistry takes place while transferring messages from neuron to neuron.
- Reducing distressful experiences throughout childhood helps to reduce the stress hormones in young children that can interfere with development.
- Children need developmentally enriching environments throughout early childhood to increase neural networking without overly inducing stress.

NOTES

1. S. E. Poduslo and Y. Jang, "Myelin Development in Infant Brain," *Neurochem Research* 9, no. 11 (November 9, 1984): 1615–26.

2. Enrique J. Rivera, Alison Goldin, Noah Fulmer, Rose Taveres, Jack R. Wands, and Suzanne M. de la Monte, "Insulin and Insulin-Like Growth Factor Expression and Function Deteriorate with Progression of Alzheimer's Disease: Link to Brain Reductions in Acetylcholine," *Journal of Alzheimer's Disease* 8, no. 3 (2005): 247–68.

3. Susan Greenfield, *Brain Story* (London: BBC Worldwide, 2000), 32.

4. Edward M. Hallowell and John J. Ratey, *Delivered from Distraction* (New York, 2005).

5. O. Agid, B. Shapira, J. Zislin, M. Ritsner, B. Hanin, H. Murad, T. Troudart, M. Block, U. Heresco-Levy, and B. Lerer, "Environment and Vulnerability to Major Psychiatric Illness: A Case Control Study of Early Parental Loss in Major Depression, Bipolar Disorder, and Schizophrenia," *Molecular Psychiatry* 4, no. 2 (2000): 163–72.

6. Shaozheng Qin, Christina B. Young, Xujun Duan, Tianwen Chen, Kaustubh Supekar, and Vinod Menon, "Amygdala Subregional Structure and Intrinsic Functional Connectivity Predicts Individual Differences in Anxiety During Early Childhood," *Biological Psychiatry* 75, no. 11 (2014): 892. doi: 10.1016/j.biopsych.2013.10.006.

7. A. Tom Horvath, Kaushik Misra, Amy K. Epner, and Galen Morgan Cooper, edited by C. E. Zupanick, *Stress Regulation and Withdrawal: Addictions' Effect on the Hypothalamus*, Sevencounties.org.

8. Paul MacLean, "A Mind of Three Minds: Educating the Triune Brain," in *Education and the Brain: The Seventy-Seventh Yearbook of the National Society for the Study of Education*, part 1, edited by J. Chall and A. Mirsky (Chicago: University of Chicago Press, 1978).

9. Betty Hart and Todd Risley, *Meaningful Differences in the Everyday Experience of Young American Children* (Baltimore: Brookes Publishing, 1995).

3

HOW WE KNOW WHAT WE KNOW

At birth nearly everyone is programmed to be phenomenal.
—Barbara Clark, *Growing Up Gifted*

It has not been uncommon to read in literature on child development that the behavior and thinking skills of young children simply "emerge."[1] To conclude this, the focus was on behaviors, and the brain of the developing child was rarely mentioned. However, recent technology has dramatically changed the way we view child development largely because it has changed the way we view the brain.

The last two decades have brought incredible technological advances that allow scientists to view the live brain in action. Prior to the mid-1990s, our view was stagnant, like a still photograph, and prior to the 1990s we mostly knew about brains through observing behaviors or dissecting cadavers. And after two decades of newer technology in use, perhaps the most startling concept to come out of the research laboratories is the critical importance of nurturing the brain properly in the first few years of its life.

Positron emission tomography (PET) scans, functional magnetic resonance imaging (fMRI), electroencephalography (EEG), and magnetoencephalography (MEG) have catapulted the study of the live brain into warp speed, and remarkable findings are published in scientific journals monthly. Some of these findings have been gradually making their way into the popular media, if not quite the headlines, perhaps because interpreting these neurological studies is still no simple task. In fact, despite rapid advances in technology, communication between neurologists, psychologists, educators, and parents has only made the new information slightly more accessible. While politicians today warn of a problem between the haves and have-nots referring to socioeconomic factors, the gulf between those in the know and those who need to know represent an even more ominous problem. Left alone, the learning gap only widens.

The earliest brain research took place on cadavers. Many of those studies of brains suggested that there was a direct link between a person's brain health and the work that a person did throughout life. As soon as high-powered microscopes allowed us to observe cells and the dendritic branching of neurons, scientists were able to prove that changes in the environment altered the communication between cells and consequently changed our minds. Studies showed that the more complicated the cognitive demands of a person's particular occupation, the more branches on dendrites were found on that person's neurons over time. In other words, by consistently increasing the complexity of our vocabulary, skills, and thoughts or ideas on a regular basis over time, we are actually stimulating our dendrites to grow and branch out and changing our brains physiologically.[2]

When a baby is born, most of her brain cells have only first- or second-level dendritic branches. The more the child sees, hears, smells, tastes, and touches in a developmentally nurturing environment, the more her brain cells will talk about that environment with other neurons in her brain. The more those neurons are exercised (talk to each other), networked (talk to each other regularly), and used in increasingly complex ways, the more branches develop along the dendrites and the more possible connections emerge.

Imagine a tree. The more the limbs branch out, the more leaves will grow and overlap and the more shade it will be able to produce. A dendrite that has formed additional branches now has a multitude of additional possible connections between its neuron and others. Research on Albert Einstein's brain matter revealed seventh-level dendrite branching.[3] No wonder he could imagine himself riding on a beam of light!

Experience, neural networking, and brain development are directly related and affect each other in physiological ways. Marian Diamond writes that neurologists can now "connect the four month-old's ability to focus and see at a distance for the first time with the surge of synaptic connections in the visual cortex." Neurologists can also "link the growing coordination between eye and hand movements, like picking up a rattle and bringing it to the mouth, with connections between the visual cortex and its counterpart in the motor cortex."[4] What this shows is that experience begets neural connections, and the more neural connections, the greater and more complex the capability of an infant's level of activity and behavior.

ALL TOGETHER NOW

Perhaps the most important finding of recent brain research is that while we tend to explain parts of the brain and its functioning in terms of regions, those regions are far more involved with one another than had previously been thought. No one single brain area is completely responsible for a single mental activity per se. When mental activity occurs, entire constellations of brain areas are activated at different times, depending on what a person is doing. Consequently, it has become more challenging (and risky) to pin a precise function to a particular brain part.

In addition, we now know that when we build or improve the operation of one area or brain system, it often leads to unforeseen changes in other areas of the brain. Among other phenomena, this may someday help explain the as yet undefined but obvious connection between math performance and music performance in so many children and adults.

TECHNOLOGICAL TALK: TEACHINGS PET

While the brain makes up only a small fraction of our total body weight, it uses up oxygen and glucose at a far greater rate than any other organ in the body. Technology enables us to see just what areas of the brain are using that oxygen and glucose. PET scanning shows in brilliant color which brain areas are most active in burning fuel during different activities. For example, PET scans show a tremendous difference in brain glucose burning between active learning and passive learning.

Sitting still, being quiet, and listening to the teacher are almost the equivalent of sleeping when it comes to brain activity. Or perhaps worse, since it has been shown that sleeping is necessary for new information to be encoded and stored in memory. On the other hand, getting up and conducting an interesting experiment reveals activity on the opposite end of the brain activity continuum. Much more glucose is being used when active learning takes place.

Unfortunately, while the PET scan is a phenomenal tool for studying brain activity, the nature of the process limits its use to within the medical and scientific community. PET scans involve the injection of a slightly radioactive solution of oxygen and glucose into the body. It is the concentration of the radioactivity that the scanner picks up to portray the colorful image. Because of the small health risk from exposure to this radioactivity, the PET scan is not a technology that can be used indiscriminately to investigate brain activity; it is usually only used to study patients with severe problems.

Another technological tool, functional magnetic resonance imaging, or fMRI, also monitors brain energy use. This scanner is able to measure oxygen levels in the brain by detecting faint radio signals that are emitted by hemoglobin in the blood, enabling differences to be measured when people undertake different mental activities. An advantage of this technology over the PET scan is that this technique requires no injection of a potentially harmful radioactive solution.

But a problem that both the PET and fMRI share is that in terms of brain activity, both are very slow. They tell the brain story in seconds instead of the milliseconds in which the brain really works. Because of the amount of brain activity that can take place over the several seconds needed to produce fMRI or PET scan results, we end up with a somewhat imprecise picture of mental activity, albeit a far better picture than was heretofore available. Unfortunately, an awful lot of brainwork can be lost in one second!

A third technological tool is the magnetoencephalography, or MEG, scanner. This scanner is an outgrowth of the earlier EEG, or electroencephalography, scan. Whereas the PET and fMRI pick up increased blood flow in parts of the brain that are particularly active, MEG can detect magnetic fields produced from activity around brain cells themselves. Unfortunately, MEG can only pick up signals from around the outer cortex. It loses touch with signals as one tries to look more deeply into the brain. So whereas PET and fMRI are too slow but do show the big picture, MEG shows us the finer tuning but on a much more limited scale. Despite the drawbacks of these three important technological developments, they have greatly advanced brain science. [5]

The act of observing babies in their natural environment, while cumbersome, is still the method of choice for many researchers. The use of videotaping has enhanced this method considerably. However, much of this type of analysis can simply result in highly educated guesswork if we are not careful.

Just what do non-neurologist researchers consider evidence of infant understanding? Most studies assume that infants pay greater attention to some stimuli than to others, thus revealing their ability to distinguish the difference in the stimuli. Heart rate, breathing, sucking, and visual engagement are the primary behavioral changes that can be observed, helping scientists in their attempts to understand infant thinking. Alan Slater explained in 1994 that for an infant to recognize a new stimulus as different, the baby had to be able to recall the initial stimulus. It has only been since the early 1980s that researchers have recognized an infant's ability to develop such memory capabilities. Previously, it had been assumed that infants had no such memory ability for this. Once again, faulty assumptions overshadowed our understanding of the infant's complex capabilities.

A BRIEF HISTORY OF PSYCHOLOGY

A scientific understanding of the brain and its relationship to the mind and body is relatively recent in the perspective of human history. Advances in the biological sciences around the turn of the twentieth century made it plausible for theorists to suggest that the brain and the mind were, in fact, housed in the same part of the human body, the brain. Prior to this the two were seen as separate entities and were believed to be found in different and distinct areas of the body. Similarly, the old view of the mind and heart as separate is reflected in the famous quotation attributed to Blaise Pascal, "The heart has its reasons which reason does not know."

In the 1600s, philosopher John Locke presented his famous metaphor of the child entering the world as a tabula rasa, or blank slate. Children who, because of their age, operated solely through intuition or emotions (from their reptilian or mammalian brains) were seen as irrational and uncivilized. The younger the children are, the less they were regarded as capable of any intellectual activity. This faulty assumption managed to survive (and is still evident in the belief systems of a few educators today, although their numbers are quickly decreasing through retirements and the spread of new knowledge).

The blank-slate notion of childhood reasoning is quickly being replaced with developmental research that depicts babies and small children as observant, thinking, reasoning little scientists. "The scientist in the crib" is how the psychologists Alison Gopnik, Andrew Meltzoff, and Patricia Kuhl suggest that we view infants.[6] To understand how this previous view of babies as a blank slate was established and came to be accepted for so long, we must look briefly at the history of behavior and brain science.

DEVELOPMENTALISM DEVELOPS

The view of babies as unteachable little beings gradually began to change in the early part of the last century. In the 1930s the well-known Swiss biologist Jean Piaget began to record his observations of infants and young children. His subjects were his three children, Jacqueline, Lucienne, and Laurent. The voluminous Piaget diaries record the behavior of his babies in incredible detail. With the assistance of his wife, Valentine, Piaget developed the theory that the baby's world is as highly structured and as complex as that of an adult, just different. The Piagets watched as their babies grew and made sense of their worlds through experience, enabling them to alter their understanding of reality in a manner, the Piagets argued, that was as natural for them as eating. While Piaget's Stages of Cognitive Development theory was initially ignored, it eventually became well accepted and was incorporated into textbooks in the second half of the century.

The first period of life, Piaget said, is the sensorimotor period, lasting from birth to around two years of age. During this period, a baby differentiates himself from other objects and seeks stimulation. Meanings such as object permanence are defined largely through manipulations of objects. The baby gradually discovers that he is a separate entity from the rest of the world. His hands, feet, fingers, and toes belong to him and are connected to him.

Object permanence can be understood by considering a ball rolling across the floor. If the ball rolls under the couch, does it cease to exist? Or is there actually a ball under the couch? One explanation for why many babies appear so fascinated with television programs is the abrupt changing of scenes. Where did those people go? Where did those new ones come from? And how do they fit into that small box? The sights seen on a TV screen are illogical to a child in this stage of development (and, many would argue, developmentally inappropriate).

An area that Piaget seemed to overlook, however, was the role of adults in the child's environment and their influence on child development. Since recent advances in research have proved that environment does matter and we are not simply playing out the blueprint of some genetic plan set in stone at birth, the role of adults in shaping a child's environment becomes critical. While some of the biological changes in a child are caused largely by genetically programmed instructions in DNA, even these changes are influenced by, and therefore, dependent upon, the kind of care and nourishment that the child receives in their early environment.

Piaget observed that during the sensorimotor stage of cognitive development, before babies have discovered object permanence, out of sight appeared to mean out of mind. Piaget suggested that when an older infant continues to look for a ball that had rolled under the couch, this behavior is an indication that object permanence has matured. More recent research, however, suggests that infants as young as three months may know that the ball is still under the couch; they simply do not have the motor skills to show us that they know. They may or may not be lacking the memory skills to hold on to the memory of the ball. Researchers continue to debate this concept.

INFANT MEMORY

What do you recall from your days in the crib? Probably nothing. Psychologists have termed this state *infantile amnesia*. Most people are not able to recall much from their lives before the age of three or three and a half. Sigmund Freud was one of the first psychologists to attempt to describe this phenomenon. He suggested that infants were probably trying to suppress painful memories. However, his theory seemingly falls apart when we consider that five- and six-year-olds can and do recall traumatic experiences without repressing them.

Some researchers have suggested that children younger than five just don't have the neural circuitry in place yet to hold on to memories over a long period of time. But even this theory breaks down in light of more recent research. In 1990, Eve Perris, Nancy Myers, and Rachel Clifton at the University of Massachusetts found that a six-month-old baby remembered an experiment involving flashing lights and noisemaking toys in their dark lab two years later.

In the first experiment, the baby was shown a noisy toy. Then the lights were turned out to see if the child could find the toy by hearing it even though it could not be seen in the dark. The child could. Two years later, in the same lab, when the lights went out, the child reached for the toy, indicating that there was still a memory of the earlier experiment from infancy hiding somewhere in the brain. This astounding finding has been successfully replicated several times.

Linda Acredolo and Susan Goodwyn, in their book *Baby Minds*, share some fascinating insights gleaned from this experiment. Rather than being afraid in the lab when the lights went out, the two-year-old child that was the subject of this experiment was actually interested in the possible toys to be found in the dark. This observation led Acredolo and Goodwyn to conclude that "by providing children with lots of varied experiences, parents can help them feel at ease in a wider range of circumstances down the line."[7]

So exactly which neural networks are set at birth? In his 1998 textbook, *Psychology*, author David Myers summarizes, "Researchers believe that Piaget and his followers underestimated young children's competence."[8] Not completely shedding the old paradigm of the blank-slate baby, Piaget did not believe that infants—or even young children before the age of two—could think. More recent research is suggesting otherwise. The work of Andrew Meltzoff and his colleagues has helped forge the notion that infants are actually discovering their worlds much as scientists conduct research: through constant experimentation and learning from successes and failures. In fact, their research demonstrates that babies come into the world as thinking machines.

Unfortunately, most current authors, including Meltzoff, stop short of drawing the logical conclusion from all of the current data: the failure to provide an enriched environment for babies and young children prevents them from realizing their full potential later on. It limits their potential to fully develop cognitively and become whatever they could have become in life with an enriched environment. It takes away choices they other-wise could have made. In effect, it ultimately denies them full exercise of their right to "life, liberty, and the pursuit of happiness."

THE MONTESSORI SCHOOL

One of the most fascinating aspects of studying the past is discovering the early insights of those who went before us; though, regrettably, their genius often went unacknowledged during their lifetimes. Maria Montes-sori (1870–1952) was one such woman. After becoming Italy's first fe-male physician, she devoted her life to education. In 1907, she opened the Casa dei Bambini (Children's House) in a poor section of Rome. There she educated the children of beggars, unemployed laborers, criminals, and prostitutes, among others.

Her results with their children were so successful that news spread and she became well known in her lifetime. Unfortunately, her ideas were too far-fetched for the broader education system of the time. That, and the birth of an illegitimate son, caused her to retreat from the limelight. Though she continued her work and continued to conduct studies with children, by 1920, she was almost forgotten by all but her most fervent followers.

Four decades later, her theories were rediscovered, and today Montes-sori schools enjoy popularity throughout the world. Basically, the Mon-tessori philosophy of education states that children are naturally eager to master certain tasks during sensitive periods of their development. Work-ing extensively with developmentally delayed children, Maria Montessori found that all children have an inner drive to master tasks; they simply need the appropriate environment and methods to do so. Children do not necessarily understand the need to know what most adults think they should learn—how to read and write—but they do desire to learn and will naturally follow their own interests if allowed or encouraged to do so.

Montessori found that children need objects to stimulate their senses and concrete tasks that permit their physical activity and interaction. In her view, the adult's job is rather simple: to be a facilitator of the environ-ment. The adult must be especially watchful for evidence of the child's inner maturation. As this maturation becomes apparent, the adult should simply assist it.

For example, if a baby shows a particular interest in a flower while strolling in the park, the adult should pause at the flower to allow the baby to explore it more thoroughly. The Montessori curriculum today includes specially designed manipulatives such as pegs of ascending size to be placed sequentially into appropriate holes in a board. A Montessori classroom typically includes groupings of children of different ages involved in tasks such as pouring from a pint-sized pitcher into bowls or cups, folding napkins, and shining shoes. Dolls and trucks aren't typically found in a Montessori classroom. Maria Montessori's studies showed her that young children actually prefer to practice and learn about reality—the activities they see their families engaged in, such as sweeping or cooking. Interest in the fantasy world, she believed, evolved later on. Early childhood educators attest to seeing toddlers pretend cooking in a child-sized play kitchen. However, they don't begin to pretend they are superheroes or fairy princesses until around age three or four.

ENTERING THE PROXIMAL DEVELOPMENT ZONE

Lev Semenovich Vygotsky was born just three months after Jean Piaget. The son of a banker and a teacher, Vygotsky grew up in a house filled with people: his parents and seven siblings. The family is said to have loved extensive conversation, and by his teens, Vygotsky was so obviously bright that peers called him the "little professor." He had the misfortune of being born Jewish in Russia in the year 1896 and of only living thirty-eight years.

Miraculously, Vygotsky won one of the few lottery spots allocated for Jews to attend the University of Moscow. After starting out in medicine, obtaining a law degree, and then discovering an interest in psychology and obtaining a doctorate in the subject, he discovered that he had tuberculosis. He didn't let this bad news slow him down intellectually, however. He proceeded to write seven books and over a hundred journal articles before his death in 1934.

Vygotsky became a professor of psychology. His students reportedly packed the halls to hear what he had to say.[9] Unfortunately, in the late 1930s psychology as a field of study became politicized in Russia, and the Stalin government only acknowledged certain psychologists. Vygotsky experimented with intelligence tests, and since the Communist Party condemned such tests, Vygotsky's work was suppressed until the late 1950s.

Vygotsky had actually criticized IQ tests and was exploring new ways of using them, but authorities misunderstood this.[10] As a result of the repression of his writings, the West had to wait for a thaw in the Cold War before it could learn of Vygotsky and his fascinating theories. Since the late 1970s, Vygotsky's writings have been available in an English translation. However, even though we live in the information age, it still takes time to get the word out when theories such as Vygotsky's emerge. Increasingly today, the majority of books on psychology, educational psychology, gifted education, and related fields include Vygotsky's name. Over time, however, this astonishing young man's theories of development have taken root and are influencing the design of early childhood curriculum.

Vygotsky basically argued that since human development occurs in a particular cultural context, and since that context has such a profound effect on child development, development cannot be explained apart from that cultural environmental setting. For example, some Indian girls in southern Mexico learn extremely complicated weaving patterns at very young ages. They learn this skill from the adults in their environment.[11]

While outsiders might consider it impossible to perform such complex work at such an early age, the cultural norms of these girls' particular societal setting make it possible. In another tribe, it is common to find men running in excess of seventy miles in a single day. For most cultures, this, too, sounds impossible, but it is commonplace where expected. In Western Europe, many children learn at least two and often three languages in elementary school. A culture that expects more from its children may, in fact, get it.

Vygotsky referred to cultural tools that play critical roles in cognitive development. Some are actual tools (e.g., the printing press) while others are symbolic tools (e.g., our numbers system). To quote Anita Woolfolk's classic textbook *Educational Psychology*, "Vygotsky emphasized the tools that the culture provides to support thinking. He believed that all higher-order mental processes, such as reasoning and problem-solving, are mediated by (accomplished through and with the help of) psychological tools, such as language, signs, and symbols." She goes on to point out that children learn these tools by watching adults in their regular day-to-day experiences.[12]

When we find a text today that references Vygotsky's work, the concept most commonly attributed to him is that of cognitive development as a socially mediated process. Following the Marxist view, Vygotsky believed that human development cannot be separated from its social context. The values, beliefs, and customs of a particular cultural group are transmitted to the next generation through interactions among the adults and the children of that culture and in turn shape everything about the information, including the way in which it is transferred.

While Piaget did not consider the direct teaching of adults to be of importance in the development of young children in their care, Vygotsky saw the process as critical. In addition, Vygotsky did not accept Piaget's view of the stages of development. He believed that once a child acquires language, the child's much increased communication ability leads to great and continuing changes in thought processes and, consequently, behavior. He said that without mastering language, a child cannot master logic. Thus, a second principle of Vygotsky is that language plays a central role in the mental development of a child.

Like Piaget, Vygotsky believed that children construct their own knowledge through their experiences; it is not imparted to them. However, unlike Piaget, Vygotsky believed that genuine learning always involves more than one human being. In addition, while behaviorists believe that no structural distinction exists between learning and development, Vygotsky saw a complex relationship. He claimed that learning can actually lead development. This is a sometimes overlooked piece of his theory and is perhaps that most critical with respect to parents and caregivers and the definition of developmentally appropriate practices.

Vygotsky observed and worked with many different groups of children, including the handicapped and children of displaced refugees from differing cultures. He saw that there is a distinct difference between what a child can accomplish unassisted and what a child can accomplish in an environment deliberately structured to provide assistance. He labeled the tasks that a child can perform completely alone as the Level of Independent Performance. If a teacher or other adult then intervenes, giving the child a few hints or clues, the second level of performance is the Level of Assisted Performance. The difference between these two levels of performance he termed the Zone of Proximal Development. He saw that adults could intentionally set up a particular learning environment that would enable children to display knowledge they could not otherwise display.

For example, when asked to count as high as he can, a young child may only be able to count to six. However, if a teacher or adult sets up a row of fifteen blocks and points to each one as the child counts, the child may actually be able to count up to fifteen. All that is needed for the higher level of performance is slight assistance from someone who is at the next level; that someone could even be an older child, or one of a similar age who has already achieved this level of knowledge.

Consider, for a moment, standardized testing, a method of assessing knowledge that has increased significantly in the recent decade and is also being administered to younger and younger children. This type of testing is intended to assess the individual performance of a child; however, the administration uses no hints or clues or intervention of any kind, in some cases even at the risk of serious consequences. In the counting example cited above, which performance best represented the actual knowledge of counting by the child? Clearly the second session revealed his true knowledge. Standardized tests only tell us the first, and yet the American education system is using them more with each passing decade.

Vygotsky found that the Zone of Proximal Development shifts continually in children, and as it moves, children are constantly able to learn more complex concepts and skills if developmentally appropriate interventions are made. The implication of his theory is that children know more than they can reliably express. By waiting for a child to show unassisted evidence of a particular skill or knowledge to then present new knowledge, we could actually be hampering the learning process, slowing it down unnecessarily. Should a caregiver wait to speak to a child until the child can speak? Of course not. Having the right caregiver with the right assistance at the right time can dramatically change the learning of the child at that moment and consequently improve the cognitive development of the child.

On the other hand, boredom has also been shown to affect the brain. In the absence of stimulation or enrichment that leads to positive development, the cortex of the brain thins out. Marian Diamond, in her more than four decades of brain research, has looked closely and extensively at the brains of rats. "A boring environment had a more powerful thinning effect on the cortex than an exciting environment had on cortex thickening. Young rats are obviously very susceptible to losing mental ground when not challenged."[13]

If this is true for the brains of children as well, it has profound implications for education today. This idea will be discussed in-depth in chapter 7. Meanwhile, today we know that a more specific description of child "development" can be synthesized and described more fundamentally as increasing neural networking in a child's brain and the resulting changes that occur as a result. Enrichment makes a positive difference.

WINDOWS OF OPPORTUNITY

In 1977, neurobiologist Tim Teyler stated, "It has been shown that brain processes present at birth will degenerate if the environmental stimulation necessary to activate them is withheld. It appears that the genetic contribution provides a framework which, if not used, will disappear, but which is capable of further development given the optimal environment stimulation."[14]

HEARING

More recent studies have proved Teyler's point. We now know that a normal baby is born with the capability of learning all of the languages of the world. Unfortunately, after the first six months to a year of life, babies actually lose the ability to hear many of the subtle sounds of different languages that they have not been exposed to in infancy. If the sounds were not present in the infant's environment, the neural circuitry in the brain necessary to hear those sounds does not develop. If the connections within the brain do not form in the first year of life, research suggests that they never fully do.

Yes, children and even adults can learn different languages, but it usually takes much longer and they rarely learn to speak with the accent of a native speaker. This is because of the failure of the brain to develop the neural networks to hear subtle sounds unique to a specific language after the critical window of opportunity has closed.

If, on the other hand, the subtleties of the language are present in the infant's environment, the infant's brain does form the neural circuits needed to hear and speak the language, even if the child doesn't actually take up learning the language until later in life. For example, when many people from some Asian cultures learn the English language, they sound out the letter *r* as if it were an English *l*. *Rice* often sounds like *lice*. This is because there is no *r* sound in many Asian languages, and speakers have lost the ability to hear that sound on a neurological level after not having heard the specific sound in infancy. For an excellent explanation of this research, listen to Patricia Kuhl's presentation in 2010 on TED Talks titled "The Linguistic Genius of Babies" (http://www.ted.com/talks/patricia_kuhl_the_linguistic_genius_of_babies?language=en).[15]

Hearing affects the brain profoundly, particularly in the first year of life. Hearing affects the organization of the brain, and it also affects the ability of a child to learn language, and, ultimately, the ability to learn to read. An inability to hear in the first years of life can be a life-altering situation that may not be corrected or compensated for by a greatly enriched environment later on if not detected and corrected early on.

Unfortunately, it is also the most prevalent congenital birth defect.[16] This represents a window of opportunity and an important piece of evidence in the case for environmental intervention with complexity early on. If parents want to enhance children's ability to speak multiple languages more quickly and authentically with minimal or no accents in their adulthood, they should repeatedly expose their babies to the sounds of those languages right from birth.

Research findings suggest that children with hearing impairments, even chronic ear infections in the first two years of life, usually suffer delayed speech and often have other language-related problems throughout their lives, including difficulties learning to read. The ability to hear, especially in the early years, is critical to the reading process. The brain needs the complex data brought to it through the ears to tool up and lay a foundation for later learning. Different sounds cause the formation of different neural networks. In the absence of sound, those connections simply do not form.

Jane Healy points out that children with difficulty hearing generally fail to develop fundamental language concepts. Their delayed speech and later reading difficulties can compromise the foundation upon which higher-level thinking depends.[17] Marianne Meyers, a neuropsychologist at the Wake Forest University School of Medicine, states that students who are poor readers in third grade rarely catch up to their peers.[18] Roughly 15 percent of this group drops out of high school. She also says that half of all young adults with criminal records have difficulty reading, as do half of youths with a history of substance abuse.

The U.S. Department of Corrections claims that roughly 82 percent of prison inmates do not have high school diplomas, mostly due to reading difficulties. Clearly, hearing problems in early childhood can create a lifetime of struggle and certainly a lifetime of unfulfilled possibilities if not detected and corrected as soon as possible in early childhood.

Doctors have had the technology to test the hearing of newborns at birth for many years. Some hospitals do not offer those tests because of the high cost, largely resulting from the false positives that the tests occasionally produce. Follow-up testing is even more expensive. However, given the known life-changing effects of hearing impairments, including difficulty with learning in school and related social consequences later in life, one may ask if hospitals should be required to give these tests to every newborn free of charge, especially for at-risk births.

An economic argument may come into play. Statistics show that for every dollar spent on high-quality early childhood education, society may be saved approximately $17 spent on future social services. If every pediatrician was mandated to order a hearing test for infants at six months, how many millions of dollars might be saved on social services later in life?

Researchers appear to be unanimous that the earlier the interventions for problems can be carried out, the more the resulting damages can be reduced. Some state policymakers recognize this fact. Fourteen states now mandate hearing tests for all newborns, and others are considering this critical legislation.

Another faulty assumption is that hearing many different languages confuses babies. Some studies have shown that babies hearing two or more languages in their homes occasionally start to speak slightly later than others. However, when they do speak, they are bilingual or trilingual and often catch up rapidly to the single-language learners. Speech experts guess that the brain is simply sorting out the increased complexity of multiple languages.

What is remarkable is the ease with which young children are able to acquire other languages and the difficulty that is encountered when teens attempt the very same task. By adolescence, the brain is significantly more hardwired and less plastic; it just isn't set up for the complex task for which infants are born ready and waiting to take on. Learning a new language after the brain is wired is like building a skyscraper and, upon completion, deciding to change the internal plumbing throughout. What could have been accomplished easily at the outset becomes an almost insurmountable challenge later on. Studies of immigrant children learning second languages found that what mattered most was not how long a child had studied the second language but how young the child was when instruction in the new language began.

This research has been available for almost two decades. One has to wonder why so many school systems continue to ignore it. Typically in the American education system, world-language-acquisition training does not begin until the middle or high school years, well past the ideal window of opportunity for learning language. If we genuinely value improved communication and high-level thinking (which is proudly professed by many school mission statements), why do we not introduce second-language learning in the earliest primary grades? Many other countries do this and enjoy a multilingual society.

Linguists such as Steve Pinker of Harvard University note the evidence of another possible window of opportunity: grammar capacity in children. Around the age of three, children begin to put words together in a meaningful order. However, often pronouns are used incorrectly, as in the statement, "Me go potty." But by age four, most children have picked up enough grammar from their environments to correct this to "I need to go to the potty." Children are able to accomplish this with no lessons on verbs, subjects, prepositional phrases, or sentence diagramming from their parents or caregivers. They come to understand the complex grammar of a language quite naturally—if they hear it.

Evidence of a window of opportunity for grammar comes from children who, for whatever reason—perhaps hearing impairments, perhaps a socioeconomically challenged society—are not exposed to proper grammar in their early childhood years. Many of these children are never able to develop correct grammatical structure even with intensive intervention in later years. This even seems to hold true for deaf children and sign language. If these children are diagnosed early and begin to learn sign language before they are six, they become much more proficient signers than children exposed to sign language after the age of six.

SIGHT

A more obvious window of opportunity appears in the study of vision. Neurologists have discovered that synaptic activity for vision multiplies rapidly in two-to-four-month-old babies. This activity continues until around eight months of age. Daphne Maurer of McMaster University in Hamilton, Ontario, and psychologist Terri Lewis discovered what happens when the brain is deprived of visual stimuli. They studied children born with a cataract in one eye and none in the second eye. In their study, they found that if the cataracts were not removed before age two, the children would be forever blind in the affected eye.

Many of the children in the study were less than seven months old, and in 100 percent of the cases, sight loss had begun before the sixth month of life. In children with a cataract in one eye, neural networks formed normally in the unaffected eye. However, in the case of the other eye, neural networks began forming at birth, apparently expecting to receive data from the affected eye. But when, because of the cataract, the receptors did not receive data stimulation from the outside world, vision was not able to be restored.[19] According to Jane Healy, if the cataracts were not removed before six months of age, normal vision had little chance of escaping impairment.[20]

Vision develops continuously throughout the first year of life. The eyes send the data they receive to key cortical areas in the brain, and over time and through interaction with the environment, sight develops. Clearly there is a crucial window of opportunity for the development of sight, and there are life-altering consequences if the needed stimuli are not present. The good news is that the earlier the problem is detected, the greater the possibility that the child will enjoy normal sight.

What is actually going on in the brains of young children exposed to a rich, stimulating learning environment? Marian Diamond and Janet Hopson, in their wonderful book, *Magic Trees of the Mind*, wrote, "The answer is sculpting the brain by preferentially reinforcing connections within and between certain neural circuits."[21] The more circuits that are strengthened, the more the brain is physically changed. Children who are not exposed to enrichment and are in fact impoverished or abused do not show this brain activity and never catch up to their peers whose neural networks were nurtured.

Whether children have the opportunity to learn correct grammar or multiple languages easily, or whether they have sight or sound capabilities at all, may sound like radically different questions. However, they all lead to the same answer. Experience in early childhood affects children's lives in many dramatic ways. The environment in the earliest years of a child's life matters critically for optimal brain development, whether we are focusing on giving sight to those who cannot see, giving sound to those without hearing, or simply maximizing children's potential. Through nurturing neural networks in the earliest years, we are maximizing learning potential for later on in life.

SALIENT POINTS

- The resurfacing of the work of Italian physician and educator, Maria Montessori, helped to inform scientists and society that intelligence quotients (IQs) are not fixed at birth and that young children are "educable."
- The translation of the Social Development Theory of Soviet psychologist Lev Vygotsky into English and other languages helped bring to light the importance of the environment on learning. His research suggested that child development was at least partially the result of the interplay between children and their social environment.
- Determining hearing ability at birth is critical for proper development.
- Determining eyesight at birth is critical for proper development.
- While it is important to learn about different brain areas and their functions, it is also important to recognize that the brain is like a committee of experts with no one single brain area as completely responsible for a single mental activity; rather, the brain parts all work together in the operation of every thought and movement in which the body engages.

NOTES

1. Marian Diamond and Janet Hopson, *Magic Trees of the Mind* (New York: Plume, 1999), 112.

2. Bob Jacobs, Matthew Schall, and Arnold B. Scheibel, "A Quantitative Dendritic Analysis of Wernicke's Area in Humans. 2. Gender, Hemispheric, and Environmental Factor," *Journal of Comparative Neurology* 327 (1993).

3. Diamond and Hopson, *Magic Trees of the Mind*, 118.

4. Diamond and Hopson, *Magic Trees of the Mind*.

5. Susan Greenfield, *Brain Story* (London: BBC Worldwide, 2000), 23.

6. Alison Gopnik, Andrew N. Meltzoff, and Particia K. Kuhl, *The Scientist in the Crib* (New York: Morrow, 1999), 201.

7. Linda Acredolo and Susan Goodwyn, *Baby Minds* (New York: Bantam Books, 2000), 65.

8. David Myers, *Psychology* (New York: Worth, 1998), 89.

9. J. V. Wertsch and P. Tulviste, "L. S. Vygotsky and Contemporary Developmental Psychology," *Developmental Psychology* 28, no. 4 (1992): 548–57.

10. William Crain, *Theories of Development* (Upper Saddle River, NJ: Prentice Hall, 2000), 215.

11. C. P. Childs and P. M. Greenfield, "Informal Modes of Learning and Teaching: The Case of Zinacanteco Weaving," in *Advances in Cross-Cultural Psychology*, 2nd ed., ed. N. Warren (London: Academic Press, 1982), 269–316.

12. Anita Woolfolk, *Educational Psychology* (Boston: Allyn & Bacon, 2001), 45.

13. Diamond and Hopson, *Magic Trees of the Mind*, 31.

14. T. Teyler, "An Introduction to the Neurosciences," in *The Human Brain*, ed. M. Wittrock (Englewood Cliffs, NJ: Prentice Hall, 1977), 23.

15. Patricia Kuhl, *The Linguistic Genius of Babies*, TED Talks, 2010, http://www.ted.com/talks/patricia_kuhl_the_linguistic_genius_of_babies?language=en.

16. Heidi Toth, "Hearing Loss Most Common Birth Defect in U.S.," *Daily Herald*, October 11, 2009, http://www.heraldextra.com/news/local/hearing-loss-most-common-birth-defect-in-u-s/article_dc41c731-2ff5-5320-aad4-9b332ab17223.html.

17. Jane M. Healy, *Your Child's Growing Mind* (New York: Doubleday, 1994), 36.

18. Marianne S. Meyer, "What We Have Learned from Reading Research: Implications for Teaching Struggling Readers," paper presented at Mineral Springs Elementary School, Winston-Salem, NC, October 5, 2000, 1.

19. Greenfield, *Brain Story*, 57.

20. Healy, *Your Child's Growing Mind*, 36.

21. Diamond and Hopson, *Magic Trees of the Mind*, 173.

4

NURTURING OUR NATURE

Long-lasting effects occur as a result of experience. The more complex the experience, "the richer" the environment, the more complex the brain.

—Richard M. Restak, *The Infant Mind*

We never have more neurons in our brains than in infancy. While most of the cells in our body's organs, such as the stomach or liver, are continuously being renewed, almost no nerve cells in our brains are generated after early childhood. Neurogenesis, or the growing of new nerve cells, has been shown to occur in the hippocampus sometimes throughout life. However, while dendritic branching is increasing connections between neurons and ultimately increasing our brain capacity over time, the brain also decreases the number of neurons along the way.

Some purposeful pruning of neurons is called *apoptosis*, and this is genetically programmed at birth. Apoptosis goes on throughout our lives to a degree. However, some time around the age of nine or ten, the brain undergoes a much more rigorous pruning process than at any other time in our lives, killing off many millions of neurons that have not been routinely used.[1] The conclusion of the brain may be that if certain cells have not yet been particularly needed, they must not be needed in the future. The brain does continue to grow slightly in size and weight after adolescence, but this is the result of dendritic branching, not from an increase in the number of cells.

Scientists debate whether or not the pruning process can be slowed or stopped, or even whether this would be a healthy prospect for the brain or its function. After all, caterpillars need the apoptosis process to turn into butterflies. Only time and technology will tell. Meanwhile, the preponderance of evidence from available neuroscience and related research is that if we don't use it, we lose it, meaning our neural networks. We all know this to be the case with other physical capacities such as muscle strength. It seems only logical that it would be true with the brain as well.

Children are born with the capacity for speech but don't learn it unless they hear it. To learn speech, children must be spoken to. Parents or caregivers who do not speak to the child in their custody are probably denying that child the possibility of ever enjoying the richness of a life with well-developed speech and language abilities. According to Lev Vygotsky, they could be subjecting the child to permanent deficiencies in determining the reason or the logic of any matter.

Research also shows that the more speech and the more complex speech patterns that the child is exposed to, the more words and more complex speech patterns he or she will learn. The child may even speak sooner than children denied this enrichment. These scenarios are true because of the neural networks that the environment creates in the brain. Learning equates with the building of neural networks, and we can alter the cognitive development of a child by altering his or her environment, positively or negatively, especially in early childhood.

THE ROLE OF ADULTS: BABY TEACHERS

Babies learn, and to a great extent their future learning depends on the understanding by the adults in their world that they are baby teachers. As Alison Gopnik, Andrew Meltzoff, and Patricia Kuhl state about babies, "They are designed to learn about the real world that surrounds them, and they learn by playing with the things in that world, most of all by playing with the people who love them."[2]

Unfortunately, some parents who abuse and neglect their children also claim to "love" them. Yet language such as "no" or "stop" delivered in a harsh tone can send stress hormones racing through their brains. Repeatedly bathing brain neurons in neurotransmitters that warn the brain to be on guard or watch out or downshift for survival rather than explore new boundaries and investigate new learning deter deeper learning. Consequently, this language should be used very sparingly and for emergencies only. We have all seen toddlers whose primary vocabulary consists of "no." It is obvious what that child is hearing repeatedly in their environment, and "no" in many cases means "no learning."

Does this mean that we should *never* use the words *no* or *stop*? Of course not. There are situations in which these words are appropriate and can even keep a young child from being injured or in danger. However, as baby teachers we need to structure our own language to redirect our infants in positive and meaningful ways.

Instead of "Don't climb on that chair!" we can say "feet are for floors" while gently placing their feet back on the ground and directing climbing interests in a more safe direction. Instead of saying, "Stop crying!" from across the room, we can walk over to the baby, get down on his or her level where we are much less threatening with our physical presence, and calmly talk with the baby.

Notice, in this scenario, we do not comfort by picking the child up automatically (although this may be needed, too); instead, we calmly reassure the infant with our mere presence, thus calming the baby and encouraging the baby to develop their own self-calming skills though the use of language, which also serves to continue to stimulate their brain development, language development, sight, and hearing. All of this is accomplished through one simple interaction rather than simply administering a harsh verbal directive or, at the other end of the care continuum, picking up the child at every cry. Be a truth seeker, an investigator, and calmly communicate with the child to find a solution to their tears.

Parents who park their newborn in a restrictive seating device in front of a television set with a proposed educational video being displayed as Classical music plays in the background represent the other end of the misunderstanding. Humans are complex. Human interaction is probably the most complex interaction between infants and their environment of all. Babies will learn from that interaction and, for better or for worse, that learning follows them into adulthood.

What do we want them to learn? If they are mistreated by the humans in their environment, their brains will develop differently than if they are not. If their parents or caregivers simply stare at them, their brains will develop differently than if their parents or caregivers talk to them. How the parents talk to them will determine how they themselves will talk. Do we not have a responsibility to see that all children are nurtured in an enriched environment, one in which they can learn more than they will learn lying in a crib in a room with no stimulation whatsoever?

Environment matters. It matters because it determines the complexity of the construction of neural networks or provides obstacles to their formation. A more complex and richer environment creates a brain with more neural networks, more and better speech abilities, and ultimately more and higher-level thinking abilities. Do we not want this for all children? Do they not deserve this, each and every one?

GENES

All of this complexity is, first of all, based on a genetic blueprint. Genes are located inside the nucleus of every cell, including brain cells. The genetic blueprint generally determines the predetermined organization of the brain and the basic functions of the many complex parts. It commissions the cells and sends them on their various complex journeys. But even before birth, the complexity and interdependence of the interaction between genes and the environment become evident.

Genes may direct cells to divide, but their ability to grow depends on many variables, including the availability of certain chemicals in their immediate environment. Factors that play a role in how neurons connect to one another and grow in the brain are called *epigenetic*. An obvious example is the nutritional intake (or lack thereof) of the mother. Smoking, alcohol, and drug use can change the course of the genetic blueprint even before birth. Lack of one or another nutrient can result in serious problems, such as spina bifida, a birth defect that prevents a baby's spinal cord from developing properly.

On a more microscopic level, neurologists have proved that translations of gene messages from DNA to RNA can be different than intended. DNA, or deoxyribonucleic acid, is a sort of blueprint of the biological instructions for all living organisms to follow and is where genes are found. RNA, or ribonucleic acid, is the helper for carrying out these blueprint guidelines. Some substances, such as hormones, have been found to cause genes to translate differently. Perhaps the most important discovery was Rita Levi Montalcini's remarkable finding of a protein called nerve growth factor (NGF). This important epigenetic substance helps dendrites and axons grow and can also prevent neurons from pruning themselves. This breakthrough won Montalcini and her research partner, Stanley Cohen, the 1986 Nobel Prize for Medicine and Physiology.[3]

As presented earlier in this chapter, the pruning of cells from the brain is called apoptosis, a process that is critically important in other forms of life as well as humans. Tadpoles lose their tails and become frogs through apoptosis. Researchers are still studying the dramatic apoptosis in the human brain that happens around the age of nine or ten or the onset of puberty. Some theorize that this pruning not only happens to cells that the brain has not yet used but also to those that the brain believes it will have no more use for in the future. According to Jane Healy, "The brain selectively 'prunes' itself into an efficient information processing system. . . . Scientists are excited about the finding that the growth of these networks—and thus the ultimate quality of an individual's thought—is responsive to environmental influences."[4]

In one study, Bernard Devlin and his colleagues at the University of Pittsburgh School of Medicine analyzed the IQs of identical and nonidentical twins. They found that identical twins reared apart had similar IQ scores. Initially, the finding was attributed to identical genes. However, after reanalyzing the data from the nonidentical twins reared apart (those with different genes but the same prenatal experience), they found that a significant proportion of the identical twins' IQ scores may have actually been the result of their common prenatal experience and not genetics.[5]

It must be noted that genes are now attributed to a higher percentage of overall IQ than was accepted just two decades ago. In fact, some estimates from research summaries show the similarity in IQ between twins raised apart to be upward of 75 percent even into adulthood. That same research also suggests, however, that a safe, healthy, and nurturing environment "enables people to maximize their genetic potential so that the only variation left is innate."[6]

In addition to all of the research on speech, language use, and sight, it has been found that in the brains of people who are blind and regularly read Braille, larger parts of the areas involved with the sense of touch are developed. In June 1999, a six-year-old boy named Harrison had nearly the entire left side of his brain removed in an attempt to control epileptic seizures. Amazingly, soon after the operation he was able to walk and talk and the seizures disappeared. The miraculous recovery is attributed to the fact that Harrison's brain had compensated for the seizures earlier in his young life. Years prior, the right side of his brain had compensated for the damaged left side. This scenario has played out many times in the last two decades and reveals the plasticity of the early developing brain.

Since the human brain is wonderfully plastic, it can adapt by refining and improving and learning within even the most challenging environments. However, because the majority of studies from medical science need to be as noninvasive as possible ("first do no harm"), it is still difficult for neurologists to determine what every change means on a cellular level. In addition, it is virtually impossible to completely control enough of the variables in the environment of humans to determine a direct cause-and-effect result.

Fortunately, research involving the observation of rats has helped to more closely connect environment and neural networking. In particular, the study of "Riley's rats" in the late 1940s helped move the faulty paradigm of fixed intelligence further along. Donald Hebb, a Canadian psychologist, found that rats that enjoyed a cage filled with interesting toys and the company of other rats—those who enjoyed the "life of Riley"—had longer dendrites and more complex neural networks than rats left to a solitary, unstimulating environment. This was evidenced after only four days! [7]

A more recent study by Dale Purves of Duke University Medical Center in North Carolina found that the cortical areas of rats that involved the sense of touch grew more as they were used more. More important, he found that the enlarged areas used up energy more quickly and had a more extensive supply of blood than other parts of the brain. This was direct evidence that the hardest-working areas of the brain do in fact grow more neural connections. [8]

BEGINNING BEFORE BIRTH

We know that the prenatal environment is critical for setting the stage for the beginnings of child brain development. Evidence has mounted to the point of becoming accepted fact that the prenatal stimulation of babies does make a difference, a positive one. Since the late 1970s, sensitive ultrasound, fetal heart monitors, and fiber optic cameras have helped researchers look at life in the womb more closely. Prior to these technological advances, life before birth was mostly a mystery.

As with early brain science, most early fetal studies have been behavioral or developmental rather than neurological in nature. However, the number of neurological studies has been increasing, and findings from these studies support the theories of the developmental psychologists. Researchers have observed changes in rates of sucking, heart rate, movement, and anything else observable in the fetus.

Starting at around six months in utero, the normal fetus can hear, and it is definitely listening. Anthony DeCasper, a psychologist at the University of North Carolina at Greensboro, studied babies less than two days old. Working with colleagues, he invented a device that monitors the sucking of a baby. DeCasper was able to differentiate a fetus's reaction to its own mother's voice from its reaction to that of a stranger, and the evidence shows that Mom's voice is preferred.[9]

Even more interesting, in the first two days of life, an infant would rather hear his or her mother's voice as it sounds in the uterus than as it sounds traveling through the air. The infant would rather hear a recording of Mom's heartbeats than other voices, even another relative or caregiver. (Don't worry, Dads, they prefer your voice in a few weeks.) Also, the infant would rather hear Mom's voice speaking in her native language than anyone, even Mom, speaking in another language.[10] In short, infants prefer what they have become comfortable with or are familiar with, which is ultimately a result of the developing neural networks in their brains. Change represents a challenge, even for infants.

Another experiment by DeCasper showed that the fetus is not only hearing while in utero, it is also learning. He had sixteen pregnant women read Dr. Seuss's well-known book *The Cat in the Hat* twice a day in the last month and a half of pregnancy. After their babies were born, DeCasper used his sucking device to determine the infant's preferences for stories. The babies were read a different children's story, *The King, The Mice and The Cheese*, and then read *The Cat in the Hat*. Their sucking patterns made obvious to the researcher that they had listened to, remembered, and preferred the familiar Dr. Seuss.[11]

Further evidence of prenatal learning has come through studies with rats. William Smotherman at Oregon State University taught rats to hate a particular taste and smell even before birth. He injected a small amount of apple juice into the rat mother's amniotic sac and followed this up immediately with a dose of lithium chloride, a substance that causes mammals to become violently sick. Even after the rat pups had been born and were very hungry, they turned and ran from their mothers if her nipples were coated with apple juice. They had clearly learned to associate the smell and taste of the apple juice with the lithium chloride. Again, this "learning" was a result of the neural networking that resulted from environmental intervention, even before birth.

One of the best-known proponents of baby teaching to date is Rene Van de Carr, an obstetrician in Hayward, California, and author of the book *Prenatal Classroom* (1996). Van de Carr first came upon this concept in the late 1970s and started teaching classes on the subject in the 1980s. He says he noticed that a fetus reacts quite differently depending on whose hand is laid on the mother's abdomen. He saw distinctly different reactions by the fetus when, say, the mother or father touched the mother's abdomen and then, immediately following, Van de Carr touched the same spot. He was certain that the fetus could detect the different set of hands and instantly froze and stopped responding. It was almost as if the fetus was suddenly asking, "Whose hand is that?"[12]

Van de Carr has claimed for decades now that the differences in stimulated babies versus nonstimulated babies are "Startling! Apparent! Major!"[13] In behavioral descriptions, the stimulated babies have better muscle control and a better attention span. Their motor capabilities develop faster, speech develops sooner, and they begin verbalizing sooner than nonstimulated babies. The stories from Van de Carr's three thousand patients are intriguing. Most are convinced that the early stimulation produced babies that were more alert, more aware, and more self-confident.

Some parents claim their stimulated babies grow to be more sensitive and more polite, have better memories, and are more caring with respect to the needs of others. And all of this comes from stimulation just twice a day for a few minutes according to his research. The resounding message from the Van de Carrites is, "If you don't believe it, try it and see for yourself!"[14]

Another study giving evidence of learning in the womb and its lasting effects came from a former music professor at the Eastman School of Music, the late Donald Shetler.[15] Shetler had been administering the school's Talent Education Program for many years and was interested in finding and encouraging children who showed signs of having musical gifts. He then had an idea on how to generate this gift in the first place.

Shetler solicited help from thirty pregnant volunteers, who were willing to play Classical music to their fetuses twice a day for no more than five minutes at a time. The women played the Classical music of Handel or Beethoven in the morning and Bach or some other Baroque composer with a tempo of sixty beats per minute (the pace a mother's heart generally beats) in the evening. These women, along with a control group not playing the complex music, checked in with Shetler every six weeks. They then brought their children in to visit with him every couple of months for over a decade. During each visit, Shetler interviewed the parents and the children and videotaped their singing or playing.

Shetler found that children stimulated with complex music were talking, on average, three to six months earlier than the unstimulated children. Upon entering school, the stimulated children were further developed in several cognitive areas, and many skipped grades in school. Most amazing to Shetler were the musical abilities of the stimulated children. They picked up singing and playing naturally and could memorize musical notes quickly and easily compared to his control group.

Shetler ultimately became convinced that prenatal musical stimulation heightens and speeds up not only musical abilities but also language skills. Like Van de Carr, Shetler was adamant that he was not trying to create superbabies. "We were trying to see if getting the brain to function at a higher level would enhance a child's chances of reaching his or her fullest potential." He believed it did. [16]

Many researchers, such as Thomas R. Verny, author of *The Secret Life of the Unborn Child*, Beatriz Manrique of Venezuela, and others have contributed to the concept that prenatal stimulation increases cognitive development, language development, hand-eye coordination, and even central nervous system maturity and problem-solving abilities. [17] Manrique, who tracked children for six years, found that the stimulated children averaged fourteen IQ points higher on the Stanford-Binet scale than children who were not stimulated. [18]

THE IMPORTANCE OF PROPER NUTRITION

Have you ever wondered why human babies grow so much more slowly than other mammal babies? Their pace of bodily development is more closely matched to a tortoise than a hare. New research suggests this may be because the brain of a baby dominates our body's metabolism in infancy, and energy is rapidly funneled there in the early years.[19] Kuzawa, Leonard, and other researchers from Northwestern's Weinberg College of Arts and Sciences participated in the first study to pool existing MRI and PET scan data on the rates of glucose burning in brains, which showed the rate of development to be more energy intensive in early childhood.

This supports the theory that babies grow slowly and are dependent on the care of others for such an extended period because of the amount of resources needed to develop the human brain. So much is needed in the early years of brain development that less is available for the growth of their bodies. So while their bodies are growing more slowly, the brain is growing most rapidly, usually up to around ages four and five according to the study. Once they reach this age, the brain grows more slowly and the body takes off.

There is probably no one in America or any other developed country that hasn't heard that proper nutrition is critical for proper brain development. We have also heard that breakfast is thought by many to be the most important meal of the day. Food is absorbed into the body and converted into glucose to provide the power for the body, particularly the brain, needed to function and grow. Study after study has shown that children in elementary school who regularly skip breakfast usually also have poorer school attendance and increased tardiness, less verbal fluency, and exhibit more behavior-related problems. (Many elementary educators know all too well that one of the best ways to calm a raging kindergartener in the morning is to keep a stash of healthy snacks in their desk drawer.) So to be a champion, we need the breakfast of champions. But what is that for babies and young children?

A healthy diet for babies begins before birth. Mothers are highly discouraged from inhaling or ingesting any toxins such as cigarette smoke, alcohol, or drugs. All of these categories have been shown to be harmful to brain development and increase the possibility of learning issues later on. Research has shown that the baby's brain is developing even faster during the nine months in the womb than any other time in their lives, so it is critical that whatever going into the mother's blood system be helpful and not harmful. This includes the chemicals produced by too much stress or anxiety in the mother.

A dozen or more research studies have shown that mother's breast milk is best for babies if this arrangement is possible. Breast milk contains hundreds of nutrients such as lactose and taurine that cannot usually be replicated in a store-bought formula. It also contains just the right proportion of cholesterol and specialized fats to promote brain growth, necessary products for cell growth and communication.

Not only is the breast milk usually the healthiest and cheapest choice, it also generally comes along with the ancillary benefit of increased holding, warmth, and nurturing close to Mom's body. This has also been shown to produce increased responsiveness in babies and have a powerful influence on a child's development both physically and intellectually. In addition, studies have shown that the content of a mother's breast milk actually naturally changes as the baby gets older and the needs of the baby change. This is impossible to replicate in a "one size fits all" formula purchase. So the ideal choice for babies is mother's breast milk for as long as possible.

As babies are able to master the pincer grasp between their thumbs and forefingers generally around nine months, they will soon discover that they can get items into their mouths all by themselves. This is also the time to be especially vigilant, observing exactly what in the child's environment is now accessible to them as motor skill development will soon have them on the move on their own. Carefully keep close watch on objects on the floors or within reach of this curious new creature as he becomes able to explore on his own.

And explore he should! Create an environment that is safe and healthy for the toddler so as to avoid the startling "no" response by caregivers as much as possible. Save those important, albeit stress-inducing directives for emergency situations and instead, encourage movement around and throughout the safe environment. Remember, learning what should go in the mouth and what shouldn't is not innate.

It turns out that the *type* of food young children eat in the morning is as important as whether or not they eat at all in many cases. A breakfast high in sugar inevitably results in a midmorning crash and interferes with sustained energy. So grocery store managers who keep the brightly colored boxes of sugary cereal available on the shelf most easily reached by young children in the shopping cart seat should be informed that we do not appreciate their lack of respect for developing young minds.

A healthy breakfast for a young, growing brain is one that is protein and fiber rich. Oatmeal or granola over Cocoa Puffs, and yogurt with fruit over Froot Loops. Plenty of resources are available to parents, such as the WebMD website that includes lists of toddler-friendly foods (proteins, fruits, vegetables, and grains) and for other healthy feeding tips for very young children. There are also healthy choices for "on the go" families such as organic, low-sugar yogurt tubes. And scrambling an egg takes about ninety seconds, so pop that egg in a whole wheat tortilla and you have a healthy breakfast in two minutes!

Not only is proper nutrition important for normal development, it can also serve as preventative medicine for later in development. Researcher Dr. Kathi Kemper, author of *Addressing ADD Naturally*, has found that proper nutrition can sometimes even ward off or eliminate attention deficit disorders.[20] Clearly, nutrition in the earliest years and throughout childhood are an important environmental factor that impacts brain development, and it needs the attention of parents and caregivers.

TRAGIC CONSEQUENCES OF POOR NUTRITION

While most readers of this book are already aware of the importance of proper nutrition for brain development, few may be familiar with the depth of the debilitating results of improper nutrition and other early childhood adversities. Psychologists and educators have been reporting for decades that poverty can affect a child's academic achievement level; new research from the neurosciences is showing us exactly how factors from poverty interfere.

The Adverse Childhood Experiences study (ACE) is an ongoing research project between the Centers for Disease Control and Prevention in Atlanta, Georgia, and Kaiser Permanente, a large health maintenance organization (HMO) in San Diego, California. Researchers analyzed questionnaire results from almost twenty thousand adults, many of whom who had experienced adverse childhood experiences such as psychological, physical, or sexual abuse, living in a household with violence or substance abuse, or any number of other adult risk behaviors including lack of proper nutrition.

Each adult was assigned a score depicting the number of risk factors that each had experienced as a child. As expected, people with higher

ACE scores were more likely to experience a plethora of health risks, including early pregnancy themselves. One of the lead researchers, Dr. Felitti, reported that the number of traumatic childhood experiences was directly proportional to a person's risk of a wide variety of major social, cognitive, and medical problems later in life. Most alarming was the finding that "time does not heal some of the adverse experiences we found so common. . . . One does not 'just get over' some things, not even 50 years later."[21] This makes the urgency of understanding the concept of teaching babies, rather than just caring for their basic needs, even more crucial.

TOO MUCH OF A GOOD THING, OR PUTTING SPEED IN PERSPECTIVE

Some people ask if overstimulation should be a concern. Policy number one in medicine is, as it should be in education as well, "First do no harm." In utero, normal stimulation appears to do only good. But studies have been conducted with animals that suggest that unnatural interventions could be harmful. For example, researchers in Virginia made small openings in the shells of quail eggs to expose the developing chicks to light to see if they could speed up visual development. Normally, the quail chicks would not encounter direct sunlight until after hatching. Early exposure to light in these cases disrupted the newborn chicks' ability to detect their mother. It is emphasized that this was an unnatural and developmentally inappropriate invasive intervention.

This dysfunction is similarly represented in problems that some premature babies exhibit. The theory that complex data introduced earlier will enhance neural development in a way that will be evident in more advanced behavior and brain development comes with a developmental component. If babies are born early, they are exposed to more complex stimuli by the world outside the womb than babies taken to term. Why are they not, then, more intelligent and faster to develop than full-term babies?

The answer lies in the *developmental appropriateness* of the stimuli within the developmental continuum. Since the senses do not all come to fruition simultaneously, some senses in premature babies are not ready for the stimulation of the world outside the womb. If a proper foundation of neural networking is not laid, it cannot be built upon, any more than the roof can be placed on a house after a foundation is made yet before the walls are erected. It just won't hold up.

On the other hand, research has shown that *developmentally appropriate* increased stimulation of premature babies can actually help them considerably. One such area is that of touch. Many studies have shown that premature babies who are stoked and massaged gain weight faster than their peers. In one study, such babies gained 47 percent more weight than premature babies who were not massaged from birth.[22] What happens when a baby is gently massaged? The skin cells send messages to the brain, and the neurons connect in a way that somehow signals other cells to respond and develop accordingly. Again, the environment creates the brain activity that affects the development of the child, for better or worse.

It is important for parents and caregivers to conscientiously consider the issue of precisely when a particular behavior emerges with children and not always assume that sooner necessarily means better. Consider the multiple-language learners. The increased complexity in a dual-language environment actually appears to cause the brain to take a little longer to orchestrate the neural circuitry in some cases. However, most would agree that the first utterances of multiple-language children are worth the wait. After all, Albert Einstein barely spoke a word before his fourth birthday!

As is always the case, if parents or caregivers ever have concerns about the development of a child in their care, these should be discussed with the child's pediatrician. In addition, enhancement programs of any kind should only be carried out under the supervision of a qualified children's doctor. But consider this: If a fetus can somehow determine the difference between his or her mother's hand on her abdomen and someone else's, then they are sure to pick up any anxiety or concern over their development. Relaxed parents typically have relaxed babies. Enough cannot be said for remaining calm, and soothing and nurturing complex neural networks with at least as much patience and optimism as worry and skepticism. Your baby will know the difference.

SUMMARY

Nature and nurture work together along a continuum. As Susan Greenfield writes in *Brain Story*:[23]

> In very simple animals, behavior is more genetically programmed than the product of interaction of the environment. The price paid for this inflexibility is that all the members of a species have similar behavioral repertoire and lifestyle; it seems to us that goldfish, let alone sea slugs, don't come with a wide range of personalities. In animals with more sophisticated brains, however, more emphasis is placed on learning than acting out the mindless dictates of genes. Cats, for example, have far more personality and individuality than goldfish. And in more complex creatures still, such as humans, that shift from nature to nurture is even greater.

The external factors that interact with nature begin even before a child is born. From the perspective of a parent, caregiver, or any other educator, the realization that environment matters critically is of utmost importance, particularly in the early years of life. Everything we do and say to and with babies alters their brains biologically and neurologically and ultimately changes their lives. This is an enormous responsibility, not just for parents but also for society as a whole.

We have the capacity to help build brains that can learn to build their own capacity for learning throughout life. Barbara Clark, internationally known expert on gifted children, stated,

> We have not properly appreciated the ability of our organism to expand or decrease as it interacts with the environment. . . . By the environment we provide, we change not just the behavior of children; we change them at the cellular level. In this way gifted children become biologically different from average learners, not necessarily at birth, but as a result of using and developing the wondrous, complex structure with which they were born.[24]

SALIENT POINTS

- Through the process of apoptosis the brain prunes millions of neurons, particularly at the onset of adolescence.

- While a number of neurons are reduced in the brain over time, dendritic branching can be increased over time, which can result in an increase in brain size and function.
- Dendritic branching increases the number of potential synapses between neurons in the brain, providing the possibility of more connections resulting in more complex thinking.
- Developmentally appropriate stimulation and enrichment in the environment can cause increased dendritic branching and more and more varied synapses between neurons and is the cellular basis for "learning." This can begin before birth.
- Proper nutrition is critical for optimum brain development, particularly in early childhood and especially in utero.
- The more complex the living organism, the more dependent it is on environmental interaction for development; human babies are the most complex of all.

NOTES

1. Rafael Yuste and Tobias Bonhoeffer, "Genesis of Dendritic Spines: Insights from Ultrastructural and Imaging Studies," *Nature Reviews Neuroscience* 5 (January 2004): 24–34. doi:10.1038/nrn1300.

2. Alison Gopnik, Andrew N. Meltzoff, and Particia K. Kuhl, *The Scientist in the Crib* (New York: Morrow, 1999), 201.

3. Rita Levi-Montalcini, *In Praise of Imperfection* (New York: Basic Books, 1988).

4. Jane M. Healy, *Your Child's Growing Mind* (New York: Doubleday, 1994), 19.

5. Michael Daniels, Bernie Devlin, and Kathryn Roeder, "Of Genes and IQ," chapter 3 of *Intelligence, Genes, and Success*, eds. B. Devlin et al. (New York: Springer-Verlag, 1997).

6. Matt Ridley, "Is IQ in the Genes? Twins Give Us Two Answers," *Wall Street Journal*, June 22, 2012.

7. Richard E. Brown and Peter M. Milner, "The Legacy of Donald O. Hebb: More Than the Hebb Synapse," *Nature Reviews Neuroscience* 4 (December 2003): 1013–19. doi:10.1038/nrn1257.

8. D. Purves, W. T. Wojtach, and R. B. Lotto, "Understanding Vision in Wholly Empirical Terms," *Proceedings of the National Academy of Sciences* 108, no. 3 (2011): 15588–95.

9. Anthony DeCasper and Melanie J. Spence, "Prenatal Maternal Speech Influences Newborn's Perception of Speech Sounds," *Infant Behavior and Development* 9 (1986): 133–50.

10. DeCasper and Spence, "Prenatal Maternal Speech Influences Newborn's Perception of Speech Sounds."

11. DeCasper and Spence, Prenatal Maternal Speech Influences Newborn's Perception of Speech Sounds."

12. Rene Van de Carr and Marc Lehrer, "Enhancing Early Speech, Parental Bonding, and Infant Physical Development Using Prenatal Intervention in Standard Obstetric Practice," *Pre-and Peri-Natal Psychology* 1, no. 1 (1986): 20–30.

13. F. Rene Van de Carr, *While You Are Expecting: Creating Your Own Prenatal Classroom* (Atlanta: Green Dragon Publishing Group, 1997).

14. Van de Carr, *White You Are Expecting.*

15. Donald Shetler, "The Inquiry into Prenatal Music Experience: A Report of the Eastern Project, 1980–1987," in *Music and Child Development: The Biology of Music Making, Proceedings of the 1987 Denver Conference*, ed. Frank R. Wilson and Franz L. Roehmann (St. Louis, MO: MMB Music, 1990).

16. Shetler, "The Inquiry into Prenatal Music Experience."

17. T. Verny, and P. Weintraub, *Nurturing the Unborn Child: A Nine-Month Program for Soothing, Stimulating, and Communicating with Your Baby* (New York: Delacorte Press, 1991/2000).

18. B. Manrique, M. Contasti, M. A. Alvarado, M. Zypman, N. Palma, M. T. Ierrobino, I. Ramirez, and D. Carini, "A Controlled Experiment in Prenatal Enrichment with 684 Families in Caracas, Venezuela: Results to Age Six," *Journal of Prenatal and Perinatal Psychology and Health* 12, nos. 3 and 4 (Spring and Summer 1998): 209–34.

19. Christopher W. Kuzawa, Harry T. Chugani, Lawrence I. Grossman, Leonard Lipovich, Otto Muzik, Patrick R. Hof, Derek E. Wildman, Chet C. Sherwood, William R. Leonard, and Nicholas Lange, "Metabolic Costs and Evolutionary Implications of Human Brain Development," *Proceedings of the National Academy of Sciences*, August 2014.

20. Kathi J. Kemper, *Addressing ADD Naturally: Improving Attention, Focus, and Self-Discipline with Healthy Habits in a Healthy Habitat* (www.Xlibris.com, 2010).

21. Sarah D. Sparks, "Scientists Trace Adversity's Toll," *Education Week*, November 7, 2012.

22. Jodi M. Beachy, "Premature Infant Massage in the NICU," *Neonatal Network: The Journal of Neonatal Nursing* 22, no. 3 (May/June 2003): 39–45.

23. Susan Greenfield, *Brain Story* (London: BBC Worldwide, 2000), 63.

24. Barbara Clark, *Growing Up Gifted* (Columbus, OH: Merrill, 2012).

5

ARTS SMARTS

I am not a historian. I happen to think that the content of my mother's life—her myths, her superstitions, her prayers, the contents of her pantry, the smell of her kitchen, the song that escaped from her sometimes parched lips, her thoughtful repose and pregnant laughter—are all worthy of art.
                              —August Wilson, Pulitzer Prize–winning playwright

For almost two decades, important brain research has suggested that more and more emphasis be placed on the significance of the development of the brain in children from birth to age three. Beginning with a *Time* magazine cover story on February 3, 1997, that opened with the sentence "Environment matters," it was reported that "of all of the discoveries that have poured out of neuroscience labs in recent years, the finding that the electrical activity of the brain cells changes the physical structure of the brain is perhaps the most breathtaking."[1] Young children need love, language, healthy foods, and all of the wonderfully stimulating experiences that our natural environment in conjunction with developmentally appropriately designed environments have to offer through interesting and complex opportunities and experiences.

Along with the important question of how we teach babies and young children in developmentally appropriate ways comes the accompanying choice of what, exactly, do we teach them? We know that babies are born to learn. They will absorb whatever their environment presents to them, and it is in the careful design of that environment that we, knowingly or unknowingly, nurture neural networks or not.

One important area that can greatly enrich the insatiable quest for learning by the infant brain is any content area that we call "the arts." Be it exposure to visual, auditory, or tactile and kinesthetic varieties of stimulation, as long as the engagement is developmentally appropriate, experiences in the arts will generally be a welcome addition to the baby's world. In fact, they create it on their own!

In 2005, a Harris Poll reported that 93 percent of Americans believed that the arts are an important part of a good education, and another 86 percent believed that a good arts education improves their children's attitudes toward school overall.[2] In 2006, the National Assembly of States Arts Agencies commissioned a report, "Critical Evidence: How the Arts Benefit Student Achievement," and virtually all of the research on arts and education show that arts participation has significant benefits across many academic spectrums.[3]

In 2004, the Rand Corporation published "Gifts of the Muse: Reframing the Debate about the Benefits of the Arts."[4] The Rand Corporation is a nonprofit research organization that provides objective analyses regarding challenges facing the public and private sectors worldwide and has no vested interest in arts education in any way. Their report, commissioned by the Wallace Foundation, pointed out many individual, private, and public benefits of arts participation.

Some findings are that children who regularly participate in arts programs have improved test scores, more positive perceptions of school in general, more respect for others, better self-esteem, and overall better attitudes and behaviors than those not involved in arts programs. The jury finally appears to be in, and the decision is unanimous! From Head Start to No Child Left Behind to Common Core education policies, participation in some kind of arts education is encouraged and even mandated within K–12 education. Unfortunately, however, most of these views travel through a PK–12 telescope, completely overlooking the importance of the arts in the earliest childhood environments. So just what are arts for babies?

VISUAL ARTS FOR BABIES

Babies' natural curiosity about their world is obvious as they dig their fingers into a bowl of spaghetti on their highchair tray or push a square of wiggly Jell-O around in a bowl. What spreads? What doesn't? What happens to the colors of the sauce as the noodles are smeared across the flat surface? It is interesting to babies to watch the process as well as to observe the resulting effect of colors, textures, shapes, anything that changes in their view, particularly when they are the impetus of the changes.

What we may call a mess is simply a science experiment for a young child, and in some respects, a visual arts experience. To add a tactile component, watch as the young child works to find his mouth and feels the interesting sensations of the miss. For the baby, core content areas are naturally intertwined and connected as they actually exist in the real world, unlike as in a hundred years of separating them out into subject areas such as math, science, and so on as traditional schooling has done.

Most importantly, this curious behavior should be encouraged rather than discouraged as long as the child is safe. The value of learning what happens to the sights and textures is much more important in this natural art lesson than trying to teach a very young child to be "neat." They will eventually learn as they observe that adults do not smear their food around the table, just as they will eventually learn to use tools to scoop it up such as forks and spoons.

A disheartening and exhausting activity for new parents or caregivers who are feeding young children in high chairs may be termed the Gravity Game. In this scenario, the infant repeatedly and deliberately drops food items off the high chair tray to delightedly watch them fall to the ground. The completely natural human tendency would be to respond with a frustrated, "No!" thus startling the baby.

Why does a baby do this? Doesn't their developing brain teach them, after a few tries, that the item will always fall? What is going on in their mind that they continue to drop food off the tray?

Think about what we have learned about infant brain development. If a child has not developed object permanence, they may literally be surprised every time the object disappears, even if they know it still exists. They may enjoy, and be learning from, the texture of the food squishing through their fingers and then the sound of it splattering on the floor. Or, they may just really not like the green beans on their plate and want to get away from them. The adult role is to sit back, relax, and enjoy watching your baby experiment and learn. And it might be a great idea to invest in a good "splat mat" under the highchair to make cleanup easier and to salvage the floors.

We deprive a young child of an important physics lesson when we put the lid on a sippy cup and allow them to believe that liquids do not spill out when the container is moved in particular ways or tipped to certain angles. Of course, there is a place for sippy cups and a time to eat neat. However, the developmentally appropriate approach attempts to minimize restrictions to natural curiosity and to seek ways to meet that interest and take it even further.

Art for babies and toddlers may be defined as an approach to communicating ideas and feelings through some visual form. This broad definition allows an infinite number of opportunities for young children to engage with and learn from art throughout their normal day with an insightful parent or caregiver. Fingers, hands, toes, and feet can all interact with colors, papers, play dough, or noodles to create masterpieces whenever they may get the chance.

Be prepared for cleanup afterward but relish the nurturing of neural networking that will occur as babies let their own curiosity and creativity lead the way. (Sponges can be used for the artwork as well as the magical disappearance of the messes during cleanup!)

Entrepreneurs have jumped on opportunities to help parents and caregivers with this type of teaching. There are bathtub paints available for young children to see what happens when red and blue or yellow are mixed together. Taping a large piece of paper onto a floor and letting your one-year-old become a budding designer provides plenty of opportunity for creativity, either with crayons, toxin-free paints, chalk, or any number of instruments that produce opportunities to explore color.

These activities all need close supervision. In particular, never ever leave a young child alone in or near water, and we must always be on the lookout for what the curious little mind may want to taste. But the possibilities are nearly endless as the parent or caregiver acts as facilitator with sights, sounds, textures, or other opportunities for the young brain to engage using their own creativity.

High-priced sensory toys are not necessary. An occasional stroll through a fabric store provides plenty of interesting data for the young researcher to experience and consider. Weekly field trips to the produce sections of our local grocery stores provides a plethora of opportunities to observe shapes, sizes, colors, textures, and even smells, and this should not be overlooked as they are excellent opportunities for encouraging neural networking.

These types of everyday free activities provide a plethora of opportunities to develop the complex vocabulary of the child. We should not feel self-conscious explaining every little detail of the differences between a lemon and a lime, an orange and a tangerine, or iceberg and romaine lettuces. And don't just explain, let them touch, feel, taste, and respond wherever possible and appropriate. It's a rare mom or caregiver that I see with the self-confidence to have an ongoing conversation with their infants in public places, but when I do see them, I shower them with accolades for their caring and understanding of enriching brain development. We should all be nurturing this behavior when we find it if we care deeply about our future generations of students.

Another simple and inexpensive visual arts opportunity for babies and toddlers is interacting with paper. It can be crinkled up, thrown, folded, and unrolled. It can become a hat, a bib, an airplane, or even turned into a whistle. How many times have we seen toddlers chastised for their fascination of how a toilet paper or paper towel roll unwinds? It can be fun to try to wind it back up on the roll as well, or it functions just fine unrolled in a box on the floor or counter, and anyone who has cared for young children would understand its state.

The point is, opportunities exist around the house that will intrigue the young children in your care without having to travel to a museum and incur possible entrance fees (although museum visits can be beneficial, too). Just seek and seize opportunities as you find them. Speaking of museums, many have become much more user friendly for young children, allocating specific times and encouraging caregivers to bring infants or toddlers to come visit. As an example, the Toledo Museum of Art in Ohio invites the community to Toddler Time or Baby Tours and even provides some multisensory opportunities to engage with selected artwork. Search the web for local museums in your area and ask them what they are doing to enrich neural networks while starting early to develop future arts patrons.

MOVING FOR MINDS

Dance is another common area of the arts, but what would that entail for a young child that hasn't fully identified his or her arms and legs yet? Dance involves movement and usually music. Like the visual arts, it involves expressing ideas, only this is accomplished through motion in time and space. Research on these two arts areas has recently become so compelling that both are working their way into traditional core curriculum.

What would be considered "dance" for babies? Their first experience with dance would be visual, watching others move. We know that on one level this experience is critical for proper development to take place, including visual and spatial brain development. (So again, visual arts and movement are intertwined.) Babies learn to crawl, roll, reach, turn and later walk, skip, and run. It takes neural networking for this to occur. Dance also typically involves music, which is another category of arts education. The research on music and cognitive development is so powerful that it has earned its own chapter in this book.

Once a baby can crawl, they can move away from or toward noise or music. They can place some distance between themselves and the floor and then come to fully distinguish which is their body and which part of their environment is not connected to them.[5] They also develop better vertical eye tracking. This skill of horizontal and vertical eye movement will later become essential when learning to read a book, and it is through moving around their early environment that this skill begins to develop.[6]

Consequently, leaving young children in car seats that can become baby carriers that can become high chairs without so much as a single muscle movement by their little bodies and little more than a forty-five-degree sight angle is robbing the child of critical opportunities for development of important school skills later on.

While it is understandable that modern conveniences, such as the ability to move an infant from a restrictive car seat into a stroller base is helpful for a busy caregiver, it is actually detrimental to a young child's development. Parents and caregivers, whenever possible, should allow children the freedom of movement needed to develop motor skills and motions. Keep arms and legs free to move and provide plenty of opportunities for them to interact with the floor. Socks and long sleeves or pants can be slippery and deprive your baby of important tactile connections needed to develop motor skills. Get down on the floor with them and describe what is going on. Everybody's gotta move, from cradle to grave, and movement throughout life helps ward off that final resting site.

While these observable behaviors are happening, an infinite number of other actions are taking place within a child's body and brain that we do not see. As with language, the more complex the environment, the more enriched the stimulation for all sensory neural networking. If your home or care facility is simple with few rooms, take your young child to bigger, more complex places such as the mall or library on a regular basis. This will broaden their vision, literally, on more complex possibilities for spaces.

Put on music and dance with your baby. Use a variety of music, such as waltzes in three-four time, faster music, and slower music. This adds a layer of complexity as well as providing opportunities for pattern recognition. Emphasizing the beat and rhythmic experiences through your body enriches spatial-temporal perception development as you and your baby both sway and swing and rock and turn to the music, not to mention the joy and laughter this bonding activity can produce. The Children's Music Network provides a wonderful sharing site for all types of children's music, and much of it matches efforts to move beautifully.

The U.S. Center for Disease Control and Prevention recommends that children should be involved in at least sixty minutes or more of physical activity each and every day.[7] This federal organization has come to that conclusion based on many studies establishing the importance of movement for physical and cognitive development over time. More active children have not only greater strength and endurance and healthier bones and muscles, they also have higher academic achievement, better psychosocial functioning, and better all around cognition.[8]

Individual researchers and support from practitioners abound enforcing the importance of movement from the earliest years on, and much of it is quite compelling. Carla Hannaford's book, *Smart Moves*, is one that shares amazing stories of healing brains through specific cross-lateral moves such as "cross-crawls" and "hook-ups."[9] (I have purchased the book for every PE teacher my children have ever had in their schools, and all have remarked how much it helped them in their jobs and gave increased value to their work.) Indeed, one of the hardest physical tasks that an infant can master is cross-body motion, so seek opportunities to help them work it out.

Perhaps John Medina spells it out most clearly in his best-selling work, *Brain Rules*: "One fact that every paleoanthropologist on the planet accepts can be summarized in two words: We *moved*."[10] He goes on to point out that "the human brain became the most powerful in the world under conditions where motion was a constant presence."[11] We must be vigilant about making movement a regular part of every child's (and adult's) life, starting with our own. If early childhood movement in turn creates a ballerina or a ball player, the important part of this art-smart tactic is that we maximize movement whenever and wherever possible.

DRAMA QUEENS (AND KINGS)

No survey of the arts would be complete without making mention that all the world of a young child is definitely a stage—a stage upon which they both observe and perform. Babies and toddlers are born actors and actresses; they mimic what they see, recreate events through storytelling, and eventually engage the imagination seedbed of the brain through creating their own original plots. Therefore, encourage verbalizing, storytelling, story embellishment, and anticipation. One of the most developmentally stimulating questions that we can ask a young child while reading a book to them is, "What do you think will happen next?" This is an easy yet powerful way to stimulate higher-level thinking and verbalizing skills.

Typically an outgrowth of play or simply an imitation of life, dramatic arts in early childhood can be brief, spontaneous, and fragmentary events that emerge any time of the day and in any setting that may grab a child's imagination. Perhaps most importantly, reinforcing these skills rather than discouraging them can lead to the better-developed higher-order thinking skills that all educators aspire to see emerge in their students in school later on.

As with the other arts areas, research has shown that dramatic play and participation can lead to the development of many important school skills. The Project Zero meta-analysis of 2000[12] as well as the Rose and Parks reanalysis of this project in 2002[13] both found that participation in drama clearly had a positive and robust effect on verbal outcomes, reading achievement, reading readiness, writing, and storyline comprehension.

Further research findings have not been limited strictly to investigating students taking drama classes or participating in school plays. One study integrating dramatic arts into English classes in middle school found that the treatment group not only experienced improvements in English language arts and mathematics performance and school engagement, but they were also able to sustain their gains the following year as measured on state standardized tests.[14] There was also an increase in overall student engagement and a reduction in absentee rates.

Based on these studies, some local theater groups have reached out to this younger clientele. As examples of this, the Toledo Museum is working to increase the exposure of young children to the visual arts, and the Applause Performing Arts program in New York caters directly to people from babies to adults. Their mission is to foster an appreciation and love of the arts for babies and families to enjoy together. Building the brains of those babies is just an ancillary benefit.

The earliest known curriculum, that of Greek civilization, included arts education as a mandatory component. The history of education in the United States has not necessarily included the arts at the same level of urgency as say, math or science. Based on the research of the 1990s, the Decade of the Brain, the passage of No Child Left Behind (NCLB) in 2001 actually mandated that the arts be treated as a core curricular area (and therefore be assessed) by the year 2014 (a good intention, albeit a bit behind). Inclusion of the arts as a core curricular area is evidence that the research on arts smarts was significant enough to result in its inclusion in the Act.

Ironically, the increased emphasis on math and reading test scores in the early 2000s brought on by NCLB resulted in an erosion of arts classes over time to make room for more test prep in the daily school schedule. So the very legislation that intended to help the arts in fact hurt them. In addition, arts programs in schools can be expensive, and as budgets were crunched in the late 2000s, arts budgets were slashed even further, and many classes were cancelled altogether. As this book goes to press, it is hoped that the arts, which strengthen neural networking brainwide and improve cognitive skills in multiple areas in and out of schooling, will find their important role not only among the other core subject areas but integrated within them as well.

SALIENT POINTS

- Children must be encouraged to move their bodies throughout their development.
- Engagement in the arts can be aesthetically pleasing and help reinforce bonds between children and adults.
- Engagement in the arts helps build neural networks that develop important school skills later on, such as reading and mathematics and teamwork.
- It is important to expose young children to many and varied types and styles of music. (Many free options are available through websites and music-sharing programs such as Pandora or Spotify.)
- Arts programs should be preserved in schools as well as integrated into other core curricular areas and should be mandatory in all teacher preparation programs from babies to twelfth grade.

NOTES

1. James Collins, "The Day-Care Dilemma," *Time*, February 3, 1997, 58.

2. Americans for the Arts, "New Harris Poll Reveals That 93% of Americans Believe That the Arts Are Vital to Providing a Well-Rounded Education," 2005, http://www.artsusa.org.

3. National Assembly of State Arts Agencies, "Critical Evidence: How the Arts Benefit Student Achievement," http://www.nasaa-arts.org/Publications/critical-evidence.pdf.

4. Kevin F. McCarthy, Elizabeth H. Ondaatje, Laura Zakaras, and Arthur Brooks, "Gifts of the Muse: Reframing the Debate about the Benefits of the Arts," http://www.rand.org/content/dam/rand/pubs/monographs/2005/RAND_MG218.pdf.

5. Bette Lamont, "Learning and Movement," *Pathways: Creative Dance Center Newsletter*, Seattle, WA (Spring 1996): 4–5.

6. Anne Green Gilbert, *Brain-Compatible Dance Education* (Reston, VA: NDA/AAHPERD, 2006).

7. Division of Nutrition, Physical Activity and Obesity, National Center for Chronic Disease Prevention and Health Promotion, Atlanta, GA, November 9, 2011.

8. Caitlin Lees and Jessica Hopkins, "Effect of Aerobic Exercise on Cognition, Academic Achievement, and Psychosocial Function in Children: A System-

atic Review of Randomized Control Trials," *Preventing Chronic Disease*, 2013. doi: http://dx.doi.org/10.5888/pcd10.13010.

9. Carla Hannaford, *Smart Moves: Why Learning Is Not All in Your Head*, 2nd ed. (Salt Lake City: Great River Books, 2005).

10. John Medina, *Brain Rules: 12 Principles for Surviving and Thriving at Work, Home, and School* (Seattle: Pear Press, 2008), 10.

11. Medina, *Brain Rules*, 11.

12. Ellen Winner and Lois Hetland, eds., "The Arts and Academic Achievement: What the Evidence Shows," *Journal of Aesthetic Education* 34, no. 3–4 (Fall/Winter 2000).

13. Dale Rose and Michaela Parks, "The Arts and Academic Achievement: What the Evidence Does (and Doesn't) Show," *Grants in the Arts Reader* 13, no. 3 (2002).

14. E. Walker, C. Tabone, and G. Weltsek, "When Achievement Data Meet Drama and Arts Integration," *Language Arts* 88, vol. 5 (2011): 365–72.

6

MUSIC MATTERS

Music is a more potent instrument than any other for education.

—Plato

How we teach babies, knowingly or unknowingly, is important, and what we teach them, particularly complex language, is important. More recent research also shows us that music matters in the lives of young children, too, on multiple levels. In fact, the inroads made toward understanding the potential roles of music in cognitive development have increased at least as rapidly as advances in other areas of child development, and some might argue, even more so. Listening to music causes a response of electrical activity in the brain, resonating to enhance learning, and probably laying the neural pathways that create a better foundation for learning a multitude of skills normally associated with cognitive skills.

Just what is the magic of music? How does it affect us? Our children? Exactly what music is best for babies and young children to cut their teeth on? This chapter and the next address research involving music and its relationship to neural networks and the resulting development of cognitive skills. Some researchers believe that selecting the appropriate auditory stimulation for babies and toddlers could be as important as exposing them to language and print—perhaps even more so.

The social and emotional effects of music with respect to young children are easily observable in the short term and have been well documented. Whether it's a resounding "Happy Birthday to You" at a party, the "Star Spangled Banner" at a ball game, or a solemn hymn in a church, children and adults generally enjoy music, and music helps them to build a sense of community or social cohesion within a group. It deepens feelings, helps establish ritual, and has an ability to communicate beyond that which is possible solely through words or pictures. [1]

MUSIC AND OUR MINDS

Most people with normal hearing today have seen a variety of music performed and heard music played throughout their lives. Music is often referred to as the universal language. It has spanned all cultures throughout known history. There are musical artifacts on the cave walls and in the burial sites of the earliest of civilized humans, and it is speculated by some that musical expression preceded speech. [2]

Regardless of what language we speak or culture we were raised in, music affects us. Music can make us feel elated or terrified or reduce us to tears, all without using a single word or picture to help elicit the emotion. How does it do this? Scientists are using new technology discussed in earlier chapters in seeking an answer to this question through research of what goes on inside the brain.

We have known since the beginning of our knowledge of civilization that music affects human emotions. Emotions, ancient philosophers and thinkers believed, were harbored somewhere in the heart. For centuries, it was believed that the heart and mind were located in different places and were often at odds with each other. Both were considered to be powerful forces, but they were seen as operating separate and apart from each other. (Which was another faulty assumption.)

Now we know that it is the amygdala in the limbic system of the brain that holds our heartstrings as it is acted upon and subsequently acts upon other brain areas. So the heart of history past is actually housed in the mind; the two are in fact one. Since music affects our emotions, and since our emotions are lodged in our brains, we can safely conclude that music affects our brains, and it does. However, beyond the emotional level, how can music affect us? What is music, anyway? How does it differ from speech or other sounds? How does it affect the physiology of our brains? Perhaps most importantly, how can it affect brain development in young children?

While studies of the physiological effects of music on the brain were somewhat limited in scope and few in number only a decade ago, there has been a resurgence of interest in this area, and with it, increased funding for research. Most people don't need a researcher to tell them that music can bring them pleasure or make them feel sad, but fortunately now we have that scientific research to help us understand why and how.

As early as 1980, a study was published that gave credence to a connection between music and feeling on a physiological level. Avram Goldstein injected one group of volunteer listeners with an opiate-receptor antagonist called naloxone. This is a material that covers a pleasure receptor, preventing it from being stimulated. Another group of listeners was injected with saline. After listening to their favorite music, the group injected with the saline reported much greater listening pleasure than the group injected with the naloxone.[3] The implications are that, somehow, music is able to cause the release of endorphins that stimulate the opiate receptors in the brain.

Another study, by Hajime Fukui in 1996, showed that the testosterone levels of undergraduate students who listened to their favorite music decreased compared to those of students listening to no music. The decrease was apparent proportionately in both male and female students. Since testosterone has been associated with aggressive behavior, perhaps music actually does soothe the savage breast.[4]

Neurophysiologist Walter Freeman suggests in his 1995 book, *Societies of Brains*, that oxytocin is released when humans listen to music. Oxytocin is a hormone that is associated with ecstasy and can even have amnesic properties. Men and women both release it after sexual orgasm. Freeman and cognitive musicologist David Huron offer this property as evidence of how music helps to bring about or influence social bonding.[5]

MUSIC THEORY 101 FOR NONMUSICIANS

We are born with incredible potential for learning. While we are not born knowing how to speak, we are born with the potential to learn language. And many people do learn to speak even though they never learn to decode letters and read or write. Fortunately, throughout history, literacy has been found to be an efficient way to communicate widely, and the invention of the printing press dramatically changed society. It changed communication forever and greatly accelerated the need and desire for high levels of literacy worldwide.

Society responded. We became a society of written laws that based behavioral expectations on written documents rather than on oral traditions based on selective memories. Organized public school systems were set up and laws were passed compelling children to attend. The widespread literacy that resulted not only changed the world, it also changed our brains.

We are also born with the potential to make music. Many people can hum a tune but never learn to decode notes and read or write music. Some argue that reading music is more complex than reading words, primarily because it is so multidimensional. To read words, we need to know the sounds of symbols called letters. The letters appear one after another in groups known as words. Words are grouped to make sentences that are specifically put together to give a meaning beyond what is expressed by a collection of individual words or letters. Words give meaning to letters; sentences give meaning to words.

To read music, we need to know much more than just the linear sounds of the notes. There are also "rests" in music, which are times of silence, carefully organized within music. As in spoken language, a pause can completely change meaning. For example, "Let's eat, grandpa!" and "Let's eat grandpa!" communicate completely different meanings based on an extraordinarily brief comma pause. In music, the patterns of pitches and pauses are even more complex. So as a baseline knowledge, we need to know both the time values of notes and rests and the pitch of notes, or their sound. *Pitch* is the word that stands for placement of whether a note is high or low. So each note in music has both a time element, known as rhythm, and a sound element, known as pitch.

There is also a dynamic quality to music that involves whether a note is loud or soft or performed gently or abruptly. *Tempo* is the term for whether a piece of music is fast or slow, and much music also speeds up and slows down within songs. Tempo and timing in music is much more carefully organized and complex than timing in language. Notes are usually organized to form a melody or a musical sentence.

To complicate the matter even more, music usually involves several notes sounding at the same time. We never see two or three letters on top of each other on a page, requiring the reader to discern their meaning vertically as well as horizontally, but this is the norm in music reading.

Notes added vertically to a melody are generally referred to as harmony. In addition, the musical notes sounding simultaneously can be produced by a wide variety of different-sounding instruments all at the same time as when a symphony plays. While in language we hear different-sounding voices, we do not have to decipher language coming from other species. But in music we hear pitches from flutes, violins, and voices, and for the brain to process music, it must deal with the combination of all of these many complex components.

Language and music have an important commonality: both are received and translated by the ear. But the ear hears and processes groups of words and groups of notes differently. If you are in a room filled with talking people, you can only listen to one speaker at a time. You may hear the noise created by everyone talking, but you can only understand or make meaning from what one person at a time is saying. Just try to listen to a nearby conversation when someone is speaking directly to you. A similar sensation results from trying to read an email while talking to someone on the phone. The brain only wants to process language one word at a time.

Music, on the other hand, comes at the brain many notes at a time. A band or orchestra may be playing notes from upward of forty or fifty different instruments, and somehow the ear comprehends it and makes some sense of it all. Somehow the data from all these notes reach our brain and, more amazingly, our brain understands the message. The groups of notes can excite us, depress us, terrify us, calm us, even in the absence of words.

To be defined as music and not just cacophony, notes cannot just be randomly thrown together. The notes of music are actually selected to be played together in a very organized way that can be partially explained by the language of mathematics. Our ears hear pitches the way they do because of the vibration of the sound wave of the pitch. An action or force causes air waves to vibrate. As those vibrating waves reach our eardrums, they are then translated into messages our brain can decipher. A sound wave of molecules bombarding one another is transferred into mechanical energy by the eardrum. This mechanical energy speeds along the auditory nerve, and neurons respond. The result is hearing.

Depending upon the number of waves per second in a sound wave, we hear notes as different—higher or lower. For example, the ear hears the pitch A above middle C the way it does because that A vibrates at 440 cycles per second. This is called its frequency. The A note an octave, or eight notes, higher sounds or vibrates at 880 cycles per second. Consequently, our ears hear it as higher. The more vibrations per second, the higher the note, and vice versa. This matches the length and thickness of the string or pipe or whatever is providing the sound. Just look inside a piano at the length and thickness of the strings that play lower notes and the strings that play higher notes. The smaller or shorter or thinner the string or pipe, the higher the sound, and vice versa.

Other notes sound either right or wrong to our ears (consonant or dissonant) when played simultaneously with that A because of the mathematical relationships of the vibrations per second of the other notes to the A. Two notes played together form an interval. The combination of the vibrations from each note played together can create in us a sense or rest, or consonance, or it can cause us to feel unsettled, unresolved, or dissonant. For example, a perfect octave (A to A) or a perfect fifth (A to E) played simultaneously on an instrument sounds good or comfortable to our ears.

On the other hand, an A and a B flat do not create that same sense of comfort because of the fractions of their two vibration rates when played together. These mathematical relationships have some bearing on how the ear hears the notes and whether they are heard as pleasant or unpleasant. For example, when we hear the musical theme from a horror movie, it is almost always using a minor rather than a major mode and typically involves dissonance to create a feeling of unease to our ears. Likewise, music can warn us of impending doom in a scene through carefully contrived combinations of notes and rests, tempos and timbres.

Human beings can typically only decipher sound waves between 20 and 20,000 hertz. This represents approximately ten octaves. (A piano keyboard has a little over seven octaves.) Other animals, such as dogs, bats, and dolphins, have a much different hearing range. They can hear sounds that humans cannot. Therefore, conceivably, there is an entire "other world" of sound vibrations out there that happens without our conscious hearing (or brain) realizing it.

A BRIEF HISTORY OF MUSIC

Many thinkers have pondered the origin of music and music making. Unfortunately, much of the result remains mere speculation. We do have two notable artifacts to help guide the search. In 1995, paleontologist Ivan Turk discovered a flute made from a bone. The flute, known as the Neanderthal flute, was found in Divje Babe, Slovenia, in a burial ground roughly forty thousand to eighty thousand years old. It had been devised out of the bone of a now-extinct bear. A wooden flute of this kind would certainly have disintegrated by now. This flute is likely the earliest instrument found to date, but there is obviously no way of determining whether it was the first or five-thousandth instrument actually constructed.[6] Also significant is that this is a tonal instrument rather than a simpler rhythm instrument such as a drum or rattle.

One of the earliest styles of music that we know of is termed *monophonic*, *mono* meaning "one" and *phonic* meaning "sound." This is simply one melody line of music, usually sung in unison. In the absence of recording devices, the earliest monophonic music that we believe we know the sound of is called Gregorian chant. This was music sung by the monks of the early Christian Church. Since the monks actually wrote down these tunes in a notation style quite similar to today's and the church kept good records, we are confident of the sounds of these simple tunes. The tunes were collected and codified during the reign of Pope Gregory around AD 600.

It is worth considering the question of why chanting was so important to monks in the first place. Some believe that before language evolved, our ancestors intoned or sang out their expressions of fear, joy, and other emotions. Language may now be the expression mode of choice, but we still have "tone of voice," which can define the major message sent in a series of words. And involuntary expressions of varying kinds still erupt oftentimes as simply a sound: "ahhhh" or "mmmm."

According to Robert Gass, author of *Chanting: Discovering Spirit in Sound*, many spiritual traditions purport that the "creation was a manifestation of sacred sound."[7] Chanting may have been our original, natural means of vocal expression. It may have helped our forefathers to achieve an access to a perceived God that they could not achieve otherwise.

Chanting is still widely exercised today through various religious practices and in activities such as yoga. In fact, medical research points to healing benefits from chanting as based in traditional Chinese medicine, specifically chi kung, over centuries.[8] Since sound is vibration that is energy that can be directed throughout the body through singing, and singing is regulation and control of breathing as it passes through the vocal cords in the throat, scientists have documented healing sounds and their history of enhancing health beyond just the aesthetic value of vocal music. Circling back to our earlier discussion of an infant's ability to perceive sound in utero, this may help to explain an infant's strong preference for its mother's touch and voice.

THE BIRTH OF A MORE COMPLEX MUSIC

Over the centuries, some music became more complex. Polyphonic music ("many sounds") emerged. This was carefully composed music that included many notes or melodies sounding simultaneously. Some of this polyphony evolved into extremely complicated systematic music throughout history. Early music such as Gregorian chant and much music from the Middle Ages for which we have written records today was strictly vocal music—music intended to be sung. Much of the music of the Renaissance included instruments with the sole purpose of accompanying the vocal lines.

Later, however, instrumental music without voices came into its own, and musical works were specifically written for instruments without voices. By the Baroque Era of music, roughly 1600 to 1750, we find two distinct categories of western music: instrumental and vocal. It is also important to note that music was evolving in the East in such countries as China in somewhat different ways. This book focuses primarily on western music—music that evolved from Western Europe, producing such geniuses as Bach, Mozart, and Beethoven.

Not all music from the past evolved into highly complex polyphonic music. Some songs remained simply a melody with a few accompanying chords to provide harmony. This style of music is generally referred to as *homophonic*. An example of homophonic music would be a vocal solo with accompanying guitar or piano chords. By contrast, a more polyphonic texture is created by the singing of a melody in a round, such as "Row, Row, Row, Row Your Boat." Instead of one melody with an accompanying harmony, a round creates a song out of many parts of a melody sounding at once. The texture is different than a melody with accompanying chords played beneath a melody.

Some music gained complexity in dynamics or instrumentation but remained structurally simple. In other words, some music can be grasped or understood by the brain upon one hearing while other music takes multiple hearings for the brain to pick up the increased complexity. (For an explanation of complexity and structure in music see "Unlocking Music with Neuroscience: Ardon Shorr at TEDxCMU 2012" on YouTube.)

Perhaps this concept is easier to grasp through a visual example. Consider the analogy to the Ansel Adams photograph mentioned in the introduction of this book. A detailed black-and-white photo of a tree can be immensely more complex than a black-and-white drawing of a tree by a young child. Both depict trees. Both use the same color scheme. However, in terms of complexity, they are dramatically different, and one requires significantly more neuron connections in the brain to comprehend.

It is possible that the first music had no tones at all. Cognitive musicologist David Huron has pointed out that, as far as we know, the hunter-gatherer societies typically only developed and used rhythm instruments rather than tonal instruments.[9] For example, Native Americans used drums and rattles. The artifacts of the agricultural societies reveal evidence of more complex instruments and more complex music. (We will return to the notion of complexity in music and musical instruments when comparing the music of Wolfgang Amadeus Mozart to that of Johann Sebastian Bach in the next chapter.)

Gregorian chant in the early Christian Church was unaccompanied vocal music. In a later era, keyboard instruments were added to the Christian liturgical service. At first, only the organ was acceptable, but eventually entire orchestras were incorporated into church music. Music was also used in royal courts. Church music and court music made up the vast majority of music written down until the Classical Period. So by the early 1700s, we have both instrumental music and vocal music as well as simpler or more complex harmonies within music.

THE CLASSICAL PERIOD

Although many people refer to any music written before the 1900s as "Classical," music history, like art history, is actually divided into periods based on the specific characteristics or qualities that distinguish it. The years between 1750 and roughly 1830 in the history of western music are designated by most musicologists as the actual Classical Period of music. This music was quite different from the music in the era that preceded the Classical Era, the Baroque, and the music that came after it, Romantic. It not only sounded different, but much of it was used for different purposes.

During the 1700s a middle class of people with an increased interest in music grew in size and influence in Europe. Public concerts became popular for the first time, and a few ambitious composers attempted to write music simply for the sake of writing music. Wolfgang Amadeus Mozart was one of the very first. Prior to this, musicians basically had only two career options: work for a church or work for a royal court. "Work" for a musician was defined as either playing an instrument, singing, composing, teaching, or all four. Composers wrote according to the demands of their employer for church services or royal events of some kind.

The general characterization of the music of the Classical Period was that of balance and well-organized form. The sonata form of instrumental music became popular for composers. The piano became a popular keyboard instrument, replacing the harpsichord of the Baroque Era. Textually, music of the Classical Period generally used the homophonic style of composing, with a clear melody line and supporting harmony. This was true of both vocal and instrumental music.

Today, Mozart is probably the best-known Classical composer. Born into a musical family, historians note that he was child prodigy at the keyboard and grew to discover within himself an adventurous spirit early on. His music expressed a wider range of emotion than that of composers of former periods. This stylistic difference between Classical music and

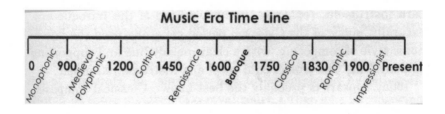

Music Era Time Line.

Wolfgang Amadeus Mozart.

the music that preceded it, Baroque music, will be discussed in more depth later.

Well-Known Classical Composers

Wolfgang Amadeus Mozart (January 27, 1756–December 5, 1791) Child prodigy composed a variety of works.
Ludwig van Beethoven (December 17, 1770–March 26, 1827) Dramatic composer who lost his hearing later in life but continued to write music. Added choir to his Ninth Symphony.
Franz Joseph Haydn (April 1, 1732–May 31, 1809) Father of the string quartet.

Mozart was a keyboard virtuoso, prolific composer, and the first real "entrepreneur" in the western musical composition world. By composing music simply for the sake of composing and not always within the framework of an employment request, he was ahead of his time. But he was never quite able to support himself with his craft. He died a pauper and was buried in an unmarked grave in 1791.

THE BAROQUE ERA

The era that preceded the Classical Period of music in western history was called the Baroque Era, lasting roughly from 1600 to 1750. During this time, music had begun to take on more organized forms than that of the Renaissance Period, which preceded the Baroque. This was the era in which opera became popular. Oratorio, a form of music similar to the opera but for performance in churches, was common. The first orchestras played a form of music called the *concerto grosso*, which later evolved and became known as the *concerto*. Thus, instrumental music without voices came into its own in the Baroque Era.

In the Baroque Era, for a composer or musician to earn a living at his craft, he generally had to be employed by either the church or some member of a royal court. Other jobs for musicians were scarce, and there were rarely public concerts. Musicians were not rated socially far above servants in those days. However, a few did achieve fame (if not fortune) by writing music and performing it.

> **Well-Known Baroque Composers**
>
> *Johann Sebastian Bach* (March 3, 1685–July 28, 1750). Wrote highly complex music primarily for the church.
> *George Frideric Handel* (February 23, 1685–April 14, 1759). Wrote the oratorio *Messiah*.

COUNTERPOINT

One particular compositional style of writing that became popular in the Baroque Era is counterpoint. Very simply put, *counterpoint* is more than one note sounding together. Recall that Gregorian chant, our best example of monophonic (one sound) music, was one note or one line of music played or sung at a time. In the Middle Ages, polyphony (many sounds) emerged and continued to grow in complexity throughout the Renaissance Period. Since the word *polyphony* means many notes or melodies sounding together, this term is often used interchangeably with counterpoint. However, polyphony refers more to a style of music and counterpoint more to a technique. *Grove's Dictionary of Music* explains that "polyphony is an end, counterpoint is a means."

More specifically, counterpoint is a tightly knit technique for composing polyphonic music that adheres to a strict, comprehensive system of rules. Those rules are ultimately based on mathematical principles since they are, in the most basic sense, driven by the equations of vibrations per second of various pitches of notes and their relationships. The polyphony of the Renaissance was simpler in its design. If one were to listen to a Renaissance vocal song and were then asked to sing the melody, they may not be able to recall it. The intermingling of notes, or polyphony in this era, does not necessarily involve distinct, recognizable melody lines.

In the Baroque Era, however, the melodies of the polyphony became more distinct, carefully designed, and developed so that the listener hears the melody repeated and repeated in a vast array of complex forms while maintaining its recognizability. In sum, with counterpoint music, the relationship between the different musical lines is that they are interdependent harmonically yet they can still be heard as independent in rhythm and contour. With repeated listening, this complexity becomes even more understandable.

While counterpoint can be extremely complex, some folks today may characterize this complex yet older style of Baroque music as rather unemotional upon first encounter. It has very little dynamic variety. In other words, there is generally little variation between the louds and softs within this era of music. For louder music, more instruments were added, and for softer music they did not all play together at the same time. This is generally how dynamic variation was achieved and was largely due to the makeup of the instruments of the time. Craftsmanship, however, began to change in important ways in the era that followed the Baroque, which also led to the change in the definition of the era.

MUCH ADO ABOUT MOZART

Now that we know the history of the development of musical styles, how do we apply this knowledge to brain development? We know that different music in different styles from different musicals eras makes us feel differently. Can it also make us think differently? Today, there is evidence that music does affect the brain beyond simply evoking our emotions, at least on occasion. This notion made its rather dramatic debut on the American scene through studies known as the "Mozart Effect" conducted in the 1990s.

The first study was published in the journal *Nature* in 1993, and then in *Neuroscience Letters* in 1995 by Gordon Shaw, Frances Rauscher, and a group of researchers at the University of California at Irvine. This study involved the music of Mozart and the mind. Specifically, the study involved Mozart's *Sonata for Two Pianos (K.448)*, a group of college students, and their spatial-temporal reasoning.

What is spatial-temporal reasoning? It is the brain skill (or intelligence) involved in working certain types of math problems, performing some types of music, playing chess, working puzzles, and calculating how to get a basketball through a hoop or a golf ball into a hole. Imagine that you are at the airport. Just how will you get all of those suitcases into the trunk of your car? Your success in this effort depends to a degree upon your own spatial-temporal reasoning abilities.

Spatial-temporal reasoning requires the mind to visualize different options of placement or organization, moving objects in space but not actually physically moving them. It is what enables you to rotate objects or flip them around within your own imagination. It allows you to consider different options for solving a problem by thinking about them before physically trying out the solutions, particularly those involving objects in spaces.

In the study, the college students were to be given three sections of the Stanford-Binet IQ test after a particular intervention. Before taking the test, the students were divided into three groups. One group observed ten minutes of silence directly before the test. One group listened to easy-listening jazz-style music. The third group listened to ten minutes of the Mozart sonata.

According to the UCI study, college students who listened to Mozart's music for ten minutes before taking the sections from the IQ test scored, on average, eight or nine points higher than students who listened to the relaxation music or observed ten minutes of silence before taking the test. This study received widespread media attention. The phenomenon from the study was termed the "Mozart Effect," largely by the media.[10]

Then in 1997, Rauscher, Shaw, and another team of researchers published the results of yet another study that could be said to involve Mozart's music—or at least so many members of the media thought. In this project, four groups of preschool children were exposed to various stimuli for ten minutes a day over an eight-month period to test for any change in spatial-temporal intelligence. One group had computer lessons, one group had singing lessons, one group had piano lessons (using some simple Mozart melodies as music), and the last group had no lessons.

After eight months, students in the computer lessons, singing lessons, or no-lessons groups showed no significance change. However, the children in the piano lessons group had experienced a 34 percent increase in spatial-temporal intelligence.[11] A detailed discussion of these studies is found in Shaw's book, *Keeping Mozart in Mind.* A CD of Mozart's *Sonata for Two Pianos* is included with the book.

Soon after the release of the first study, two major recording companies produced and marketed CDs designed to boost test scores. Advertisements included phrases like "Mozart makes you smarter" and "Hum your way to an A" under titles such as *Mozart for Your Mind.* The second study coincided with unusual media attention to the outpouring of research on babies' brains, and entrepreneurs rushed in to capitalize on applying the concept of the Mozart effect to young children.

The crafty entrepreneur who beat Shaw to the U.S. Patent and Trademark Office and secured the use of the phrase *the Mozart Effect* had nothing to do with the studies. Only a couple of pages in his book, *The Mozart Effect,* even refer to the study. With respect to the second Shaw study, few stopped to ask what Mozart music the three- and four-year-olds were actually mastering in their piano lessons and whether those little melodies ("Twinkle, Twinkle Little Star") were really the determining factor in the change in spatial-temporal reasoning. (Mozart wrote a wonderful theme and variations on the popular tune "Twinkle, Twinkle Little Star" for the piano. It was common in Mozart's time to take well-known melodies and compose music around them.)

Few reporters appeared to consider the possibility that it was the hand-eye-ear-mind skill combination that was responsible for the change in the preschoolers' spatial-temporal reasoning, not Mozart's melodies. After all, how much Mozart could a normal three- or four-year-old really master on a keyboard? The important difference was the multiple brain skills needed to manually play a keyboard translated from the symbols viewed on a sheet of music.

A more recent approach by Glenn Schellenberg and other researchers suggests that listening to music can affect cognitive performance because music arouses us and affects our mood, which in turn, affects our performance. He points out that while a causal link between listening and cognitive performance may not have been proven, music clearly changes a listener's emotional state, which can in turn affect their cognitive performance, and this does not make it any less meaningful.[12] Music affects our minds.

The point is, music is made up of patterns and relationships, and listening to complex music and learning to perform music has been shown to improve spatial-temporal brain performance. In an interview with the *Chicago Tribune* on May 24, 1998, Shaw is quoted as saying, "We first started working on a model of the brain that represents how we might think and reason. Music was the last thing on our minds. Physicists look for patterns and relationships. Our model was based on the idea that groups of neurons formed networks and that these networks eventually involved the whole brain."

Additional research has shown this to be true. The Mozart Effect study with listening has been replicated many times over with more successes than failures depending on the strategies employed and outcomes being investigated. Also, more and more evidence shows that connections exist between math ability networks and music as well as language-acquisition networks and music-listening networks within the brain.

Studies in the last decade have confirmed that piano lessons can dramatically improve spatial-temporal reasoning in elementary school–age children, whether or not they use Mozart melodies as the repertoire, and a whole host of other cognitive skills. Many school districts across the United States (that can afford it) have already mandated piano lessons in their K–5 curriculum, and others are considering movement in this direction. Much evidence suggests that music training develops mental flexibility in adults as well, strengthening the cognitive connections between music and other learning throughout a lifetime.[13]

IS IT MOZART OR IS IT MUSIC?

In another research approach since the Mozart Effect studies in the 1990s, researchers have taken a closer look at data they had already compiled involving music and the brain and found additional definite connections. It is necessary, however, to insert a word about research and babies at this point. As discussed in previous chapters, there are many different kinds of research, and research on babies is especially complicated.

Behavioral research involves observing behaviors. With respect to babies, we are basically observing sucking, breathing, heartbeats, and eye movement. Neurological research involves observing the activity of neurons within the brain and physiological changes in the brain to help discover how the brain learns and what strengthens the brain's operating capacity. This relatively new field of study is called *cognitive neurology*.

Many different types of research are going on simultaneously, and results can sometimes vary depending upon the interpretation of the data. The reader is cautioned to think carefully about the reports before drawing the same conclusion that, say, a marketing company might draw. On the other hand, drawing broad general conclusions from some research is criticized even when the outcome seems obvious.

For example, according to a study conducted by the National Center for Abuse and Neglect, 66 percent of institutionalized delinquents—offenders under the age of eighteen years of age, most of whom never go on to become hardened criminals—had a history of abuse and neglect as children. This information is considered in a profound book, *Licensing Parents*, by Jack Westman. The author makes a powerful case for considering early interventions of a more radical nature, including mandating parenting licenses before adults are allowed to take babies home from the hospital. After all, we need a license to drive, a license to teach, a license to build buildings. Which of these is more important than raising our children?

According to other research, over 90 percent of full-fledged prison inmates had a history of abuse and neglect as young children.[14] On the basis of all these data, can we say that child abuse and neglect creates criminals? No. But can we safely deduce that it is probably not a good idea to abuse and neglect children? Yes.

Clearly there is plenty of research revealing that there are strong links between abuse and neglect in childhood and achievement later in life.

However, there has been no study that I know of that has set up two groups of babies, nurtured and provided one group with an enriched learning environment, abused and neglected the other, and then checked back twenty years later to see which group had the most members grow up to become prison inmates. Hopefully, this study will never have to be conducted for us to conclude that abuse and neglect of young children can have disastrous effects. But without this type of study, how do we know for sure that this is true?

In many of my interviews with researchers and other scholars, inter-pretation of research results and willingness to then make recommenda-tions to educators has been overly conservative. Yes, "first do no harm." However, it would seem that some translation toward policy is possible, such as in the case with child abuse. No, we have not directly created a study to abuse children, however, enough anecdotal evidence exists to ban abuse. As in other fields, much of the study of music and the mind in the 1990s and 2000s had been just this type of research. Some of it was after the fact, and thus it is easily criticized as not proving conclusively that music helps improve the brain.

Consider the following information gathered by the College Entrance Examination Board of Profiles of College-Bound Seniors over decades. According to the College Board, high school students with coursework and experience in music performance and music appreciation scored higher on the Scholastic Assessment Test (SAT). These scores were fifty-one points higher on the verbal and thirty-nine points higher on the math test for music performance only, and sixty-one points higher on the verbal and forty-six points higher on the math test for music performance and appreciation compared to students with no music participation back in the 2000 to 2002 time frame.

In 2006, the College Board again published results showing that stu-dents with coursework and participation is music performance scored fifty-seven points higher on the verbal and forty-three points higher on the math on the SAT than students without these music experiences. In addition, students with coursework in music appreciation in addition to musical performance scored sixty-two points higher on the verbal and forty-one points higher on the math than those without. It certainly ap-pears that students with music training perform significantly better on the SAT than students without such training. But who can say for certain whether or not it is the music training itself that causes the higher scores?

One difficulty is proving these results are not only statistically reliable but also being able to identify and isolate other variables that could potentially invalidate the results.

The February 1999 issue of the *National Association of Secondary School Principals Bulletin* included an article giving other interesting evidence of the music-achievement connection. Records of medical school applications show that 66 percent of music majors who applied to medical school were admitted. This was the highest of any group, including biochemistry majors, of whom only 44 percent were admitted. The same issue of the publication points out that nations whose students consistently outperform the United States in tests assessing science achievement are the countries where music is a primary focus of the curriculum. In Grant Venerable's book, *The Paradox of the Silicon Savior*, he states that one of the most striking facts in the Silicon Valley industry is that "the very best engineers and technical designers are, nearly without exception, practicing musicians."[15]

An important music-mind-achievement connection for educators came on August 29, 2000, when the Harvard Graduate School of Education released the results of its Project Zero study. This meta-analysis, which included a comprehensive synthesis of 188 different studies, found convincing connections between music training and academic achievement. The researchers said they found three areas in which causal links could be demonstrated between the arts and achievement in a nonarts, academic area. These were listening to music and spatial-temporal reasoning; learning to play music and spatial reasoning; and classroom drama and verbal skills.

What about cognitive neurological studies? First, the Mozart Effect studies showed changes in spatial-temporal reasoning resulting from listening to and performing complex music. However, it should be noted that when the college students listened to the Mozart *Sonata for Two Pianos*, their improvement in spatial-temporal reasoning only lasted a matter of minutes. For a change to be considered long term, it must last more than twenty-four hours. The piano lesson studies with the young children were able to accomplish this.

Gottfried Schlaug, a Harvard Medical School neurology instructor, used magnetic resonance imaging (MRI) technology to examine the brains of musicians who took up their instruments before the age of seven, those who began later than seven, and nonmusicians. He found that certain regions of the brain, specifically the corpus callosum and right motor cortex, were larger in musicians who started their musical training before age seven. MRI was also used to find that musicians with perfect pitch have larger left temporal lobes than nonmusicians do.[16]

Susan Greenfield, in her book, *Brain Story*, states, "Expert violinists have a greater cortical area devoted to their left fingers than the rest of us, but they are not born this way—regular practice has stimulated the cortex to form complex new connections." She goes on to point out that "more than any other animal, we depended on experience—not genes—to give us the skills we need to survive. As we evolved and our brains became larger, the ability to form more neuronal connections, and hence to form more associations, gradually increased."[17] This reinforces our belief that a developmentally stimulating environment can physically change the brains of young children.

Drawing on our evidence from prior chapters on the impact of the early environment on a child's brain, we know the following: babies can hear even before they are born. The hearing sense comes to fruition between twenty and thirty weeks' gestation in the womb. We also know that what a baby hears can wire or rewire the brain for better acquisition of language skills and possibly even other skills. We could conclude, then, that listening to complex music and ultimately learning to interact with music needs to happen as soon as possible in a child's life. Therefore, we should be able to assume that listening to complex music in infancy, as with speech, can wire the child's neural circuitry in more complex networks.

Music affects more than simply our emotions and our SAT scores. Sometimes music rewires the brain and somehow improves other areas of learning. Will any music work? Perhaps not. Some studies indicate that the music must be complex. Singing simple children's songs daily was not found to improve brain functioning in Shaw and Rauscher's study.

In another study by Shaw and a large team of researchers, a Music Spatial-Temporal (MST) Math Program focused on teaching proportional reasoning, fractions, and symmetry to second-graders. These important concepts are sometimes introduced in the second grade in American schools but are not studied in-depth until the fourth or fifth grade. In their study, the researchers used the MST math curriculum to teach 380 second-graders from urban schools these complex skills. After completing the curriculum, the children performed at the same level on the Advanced

Math Concepts Test as fourth graders from a higher-socioeconomic school who did not have the training. In addition, the second-graders increased their scores on California's Stanford 9 math test dramatically (http://www.mindresearch.org/).

Shaw points out that our current education system concentrates on two basic types of reasoning. One is language-analytic reasoning skills. An example of this linear type of reasoning is solving an equation to get a quantitative result: two plus two equals four. The second type of reasoning is spatial-temporal. An example of this reasoning would be playing chess, in which the players have to be able to think several moves ahead and consider multiple possible solutions for various problems. This requires mental imagining within the brain.

Shaw and others have observed that the focus of the curriculum in our education system results in a majority of instructional time, particularly in early elementary grades, teaching language-analytic reasoning skills or linear thinking skills. Shaw argues that it is spatial-temporal reasoning that is critical to developing the skills needed for mathematicians and scientists and, somehow, music helps the brain gear up for this type of thinking. [18]

Peter Perret, former conductor of the Winston-Salem North Carolina Piedmont Triad Orchestra, decided that if young children could not come to the symphony, he would take the symphony to them. His objective was to test the theory that music training increases brain performance in some way. He selected a local elementary school made up of economically disadvantaged children; 70 percent were on free or reduced-price lunch. Perret and musicians from the orchestra met with the elementary school principal and teachers from the school, and together they designed a program now known as the Bolton Project.

The principal began piping Classical music through the school intercom system into the halls, library, and lunchroom. A group of orchestra members became resident musicians at the school, working three hours a day, three to four days a week, for sixteen weeks over three years. They did more than simply play complex music for the students; they worked with teachers to integrate music throughout the curriculum, and they taught music reading and skills.

At the end of the third year, when the students involved in the study took the state standardized tests to measure math and reading competence, a full 85 percent tested at or above their grade level in reading and

89 percent in math. The year prior to the music infusion program, only 40 percent of students were at grade level. The staff, students, parents, and orchestra members are convinced it was the music learning and listening program that helped boost the school's performance. There was, however, no control group in this study. Every child was given access to the enrichment.[19]

Another series of studies with control groups shows that music training can enhance both of the types of reasoning to which Shaw referred. In 1996, Martin F. Gardiner, a visiting scholar at the Center for the Study of Human Development at Brown University, studied first-grade classes using the Kodaly Method of singing training. To do so, six first-grade classes were divided into two groups. One group had regular classroom music and art instruction. The other group had Kodaly Method singing training. This method involves singing songs that are carefully sequenced in complexity.

The Kodaly Method uses a strategy called solfège (*do, re, mi, fa*, etc.), which uses syllables to identify different pitches and also includes hand and arm movements for each pitch of the scale. As the children master each song and corresponding arm motions, the complexity of the next song is increased. After seven months, students in the Kodaly group performed the same or better in reading but "zoomed ahead of their peers in math, even though they had started out slightly behind."[20]

This result was true of children in low, middle, or top achievement groups in their prior kindergarten classes. Gardiner stated, "If you develop one kind of mental skills involved in one area of learning, the brain can at least sometimes make learning easier through transfer." This study also shows that singing simple children's songs daily may soothe the soul but may not do much, if anything, to stimulate synapses, as those in the regular classroom music did not show academic improvements. Only by continually increasing the complexity of a task over time did cognitive performance improve. Once again, a developmentally stimulating and complex environment was shown to stimulate brain development in young children.

In the early primary years, children learn that the number one comes before the number two, two before three, and so on. The Kodaly Method of learning a major scale through singing that *do* is lower than *re*, and *re* comes before and is lower than *mi*, helps build a neural network that comprehends the concepts "less than" and "greater than" but involves the added complexity of the placement of higher and lower pitches or notes. By involving multiple facets of higher-level thinking, we add a dimension to the mental task. It involves more complex neural networks.

More recently, the cognitive effects associated with both music listening and music instruction have been further researched, and their results are even more compelling. The connections involve neural networking, the underpinnings of near and far transfer.

Transfer is what happens when learning in one context enhances a related performance area in a different context. It can be positive or negative. Positive transfer occurs when the learning in a specific context enhances the performance in another concept, and negative transfer results when the first learning experience actually undermines or creates an obstacle to a related performance in another context. Near transfer is the transfer between very similar contexts.

For example, one can guess that music training can affect auditory skills since music training requires listening. Correspondingly, since language learning also involves auditory skills, one could guess that music training could also enhance language development or vice versa. More recent research suggests even more strongly an underlying association of the basic auditory processing skills between music-reading and language-reading abilities and the proximity of the neural networking involved in these skills.

Many studies have shown a music and math relationship. However, there had been less research showing the effects of music training on reading skills. One meta-analysis of correlational studies that compared the reading performance of children with and without music instruction revealed that those with training scored significantly higher on tests of verbal ability and reading, however, causality could not be established due to the design of the study.[21]

In December 2011, the University of California Press published an issue of *Music Perception: An Interdisciplinary Journal* devoted entirely to reporting the best of recent research on the associations between musical training and nonmusical abilities with an introduction written by two important researchers in this field whose work was cited previously, Glenn Schellenberg and Ellen Winner.[22]

Schellenberg is widely cited for his ongoing research showing that musically trained subjects score higher than untrained subjects on both the IQ composite and a nonverbal subtest, and Winner was a primary investigator on the Project Zero meta-analysis mentioned earlier in the chapter. In summary, this issue shows a wide range of nonmusic skills that are associated with music training, producing many cognitive and educational benefits. In addition, making music involves several aspects of the motor domain, including controlling vocal chords, arms, hands, and fingers, and these motor functions must be integrated with the auditory system as well when playing music. (This could help explain the dramatic results of the Kodaly Method of music training mentioned above.) Several specific articles in this journal edition make a compelling case for increasing music instruction in learning environments, including in early childhood.

AUDITORY SKILLS AND READING

Music training in childhood has been shown to speed up the development of several specific skills related to auditory networks through near transfer. It has been shown that music training is associated with improving the skill of decoding words, which is an important skill for becoming a more proficient reader. Two researchers, Corrigall and Trainor, however, have gone beyond just reading skills. These researchers have shown that the length of duration of the music training by the children (normal-achieving six-to-nine-year-olds) predicted reading *comprehension* performance, even after they controlled for socioeconomic status, full-scale IQ, and the number of hours that the children spent reading each week. Their study showed a "strong association in our data—between length of time during which the student undertook music training and reading comprehension—is consistent with mechanisms involving transfer."[23]

In another study of even younger children (four-to-six-year-olds), Moreno, Friesen, and Bialystok found that a twenty-day intensive music-training program improved preliteracy skills. Their study involved sixty children, half receiving music training and half receiving instruction in visual art. Both groups of children improved in their ability to map unfamiliar symbols, but the music-training group's test scores were higher. The researchers' interpretation was that training in "note to sound" symbol mappings in music strengthened their use of symbolic representations and ultimately helped their ability to understand that a letter is an arbitrary representation of a sound. They also found that the general memory ability of the children was enhanced.[24]

In a study of nine-to-twelve-year-olds, Dege, Kubicek, and Schwarzer found that music lessons can have a positive influence on executive brain functions such as attention, planning, inhibition, and fluency, which in turn increases scores on intelligence tests.[25] Selective attention and inhibition were the strongest contributors to the mediation effect and showed that music training increased IQ indirectly through strengthening these executive functions and that in turn, enhances the successful completion of cognitive tasks overall.

The journal issue concludes with an updated overview by Frances Rauscher of the Mozart Effect fame on her work since those studies involving music and nonmusic benefits. Some of these benefits involve far transfer, and far transfer is a bit more complicated than near transfer. When a particular learning transfer appears to be remote or unrelated entirely to another learning context, however, applying the learning to situations that are different occurs. Rauscher and Hinton's work suggests that if the music instruction is begun before age seven, there is an even greater improvement in performance in some of the cognitive domains including mathematics. This reinforces the results of differences in brain development of the children who started playing the violin before age seven.

Compiling even all of these impressive studies does not yet allow us to make a direct, causal statement about music and cognitive development. However, Shore lays out the case in the National Head Start Association journal, *Dialog* (2010), suggesting that just like language, greater complexity in music listening in the early childhood environment could build a broader foundation for learning, creating more complex neural networks, and thus leading to more sophisticated and accessible higher-level thinking later in life. Language skills are easily observed in later years; thinking skills may be less obvious. However, this preponderance of research showing connections between music training and such a wide variety of other cognitive skills imply that such a connection is plausible.[26]

While this music and thinking ability phenomenon is not yet fully understood at a neuron-by-neuron level, empirical evidence suggests that in many cases, one somehow enhances the other. Thus, it follows that music may be even more powerful than language. Multiple studies show that regular exposure to certain types of music may speed up and enhance language acquisition. These studies imply that repeated exposure to complex music develops a close connection and that developing one set of complex skills may strengthen others. In these times of low-cost music playing devices, adding music to a baby's environment is probably one of the simplest enriching alterations a parent or caregiver can make. All that is required is strategically placing a playback device in the appropriate area with the appropriate music and pressing a button. Providing quality music instruction is a bit more involved, but it should be a component of any curriculum for the crib and beyond.

SALIENT POINTS

- Listening to music affects our emotions through triggering more or less neurotransmitters to be released in the brain; therefore, music affects our brains.
- Music training (and sometimes music listening) has been shown to enhance a wide variety of cognitive skills, including language acquisition and reading skills, possibly due to an underlying association of the basic auditory processing skills between music-reading and language-reading abilities and the proximity of the neural networking involved in these skills.
- Music must be complex in nature and structure to achieve the highest benefit to brain development.
- Older students with music training and performance experience often score higher on standardized tests than students without music training, and some students involved with group music experiences such as band, choir, or orchestra are better able to collaborate and work in teams.
- Early childhood environments, both structured and unstructured, should routinely expose children from infancy to complex and varying music compositions.
- PK–6 environments should place a budget priority on the arts in general and music education specifically, not only to develop enjoyment of the arts but also to enhance student performance on school skills.

NOTES

1. David Huron, *Sweet Anticipation: Music and the Psychology of Expectation* (Cambridge: MIT Press, 2006).

2. David Huron, "Music and Mind: Foundations of Cognitive Musicology," Lecture 2 of the 1999 Ernest Bloch Lectures at the University of California at Berkeley, September 24, 1999, http://www.musiccog.ohio-state.edu/Music220/Bloch.lectures/Bloch.lectures.html.

3. Avram Goldstein, "Thrills in Response to Music and Other Stimuli," *Physiological Psychology* 8, no. 1 (1980): 126–29.

4. Huron, "Music and Mind."

5. W. J. Freeman, *Societies of Brains: A Study in the Neuroscience of Love and Hate* (Hillsdale, NY: Lawrence Erlbaum Association, 1995).

6. Huron, "Music and Mind."

7. Robert Gass with Kathleen Brehony, *Chanting: Discovering Spirit in Sound* (New York: Broadway Books, 1999), 59.

8. Ralph Lorenz, "Health Benefits of Singing: A Perspective from Traditional Chinese Medicine and Chi Kung," *The Phenomenon of Singing* 9 (January 2014): 154–66.

9. David Huron, *Sweet Anticipation: Music and the Psychology of Expectation* (Cambridge: MIT Press, 2006).

10. Frances Rauscher et al., "Listening to Mozart Enhances Spatial-Temporal Reasoning: Towards a Neurophysiology Basis," *Neuroscience Letters* 185 (1995): 44–47.

11. Frances Rauscher et al., "Music Training Causes Long-Term Enhancement of Preschool Children's Reasoning," *Neurological Research* 19 (1997): 2–8.

12. E. Glenn Schellenberg, "Cognitive Performance After Listening to Music: A Review of the Mozart Effect," *Music, Health, and Wellbeing* (2012).

13. James R. Ponter, "Academic Achievement and the Need for a Comprehensive, Developmental Music Curriculum," *NASSP Bulletin*, February 1999, 108.

14. Sharon L. Kagan, Keynote Address at Kindergarten Readiness Conference, Winston-Salem, NC, October 21, 2000.

15. Ponter, "Academic Achievement," 108–13.

16. Debra Viadero, "Music on the Mind," *Education Week*, April 8, 1998, 25.

17. Susan Greenfield, *Brain Story: Why Do We Think and Feel as We Do?* (London: BBC, 2000).

18. Amy B. Graziano, Gordon L. Shaw, and Eric L. Wright, "Music Training Enhances Spatial-Temporal Reasoning in Young Children: Towards Education Experiments," *Early Childhood Connections* (Summer 1997): 30–36.

19. Peter Perret and Janet Fox, *A Well-Tempered Mind: Using Music to Help Children Listen and Learn* (New York: Dana Press, 2006).

20. Martin Gardiner, "Effects of Arts on Learning," *Nature* 384 (May 26, 1996): 192.

21. R. Butzlaff, "Can Music Be Used to Teach Reading?" *Journal of Aesthetic Education* 34, no. 3–4 (2000): 167–79.

22. Lola L. Cuddy, ed., *Music Perception: An Interdisciplinary Journal* 29, no. 3 (December 2011), University of California Press.

23. Kathleen A. Corrigall and Laurel J. Trainor, "Associations Between Length of Music Training and Reading Skills in Children," *Music Perception: An Interdisciplinary Journal* 29, no. 3 (December 2011), University of California Press.

24. Sylvain Moreno, Deanna Friesen, and Ellen Bialystok, "Effect of Music Training on Promoting Preliteracy Skills: Preliminary Causal Evidence," *Music Perception: An Interdisciplinary Journal* 29, no. 3 (December 2011), University of California Press.

25. Franziska Dege, Claudia Kubicek, and Gudrun Schwarzer, "Music Lessons and Intelligence: A Relation Mediated by Executive Functions," *Music Perception: An Interdisciplinary Journal* 29, no. 3 (December 2011), University of California Press.

26. Rebecca Shore, "Music and Cognitive Development: From Notes to Neural Networks," *NHSA Dialog* 13, no. 1 (2010): 53–65.

7

THE BACH EFFECT

What is this? Now, there is something one can learn from!
—Wolfgang Amadeus Mozart, upon hearing Bach's double-chorus
motet, *Singet dem Herr nein neues Lied*

In 1756 a baby boy was born in Salzburg, Austria. The boy was named
Johann Chrysostom Wolfgang Gottlieb Mozart and was called Wolfgang.
Wolfgang's parents were both musicians. His mother sang, and his father,
Leopold, was well known as a violinist, composer, and leader of the local
orchestra. Wolfgang also had an older sister, Nannerl, who showed remarkable talent as a musician, playing the keyboard with great proficien-
cy at an early age. Nannerl was five years old when Wolfgang was born.
Leopold was her music teacher. So infancy for Wolfgang was spent in a
crib surrounded by the sounds of the music of the time, from his father's
composing to his mother's singing and his sister's rigorous harpsichord
lessons.

Thanks to a 1984 Academy Award–winning film, *Amadeus*, most of
us know quite a bit about Wolfgang Mozart's life, even if we were not
music majors. For example, Wolfgang was considered a child genius and
began playing the harpsichord at age four and composing his own original pieces by age five. This movie helped catapult the adult life of the
child prodigy into a household story for millions. The name *Amadeus* is
the Latin version of one of Mozart's middle names, *Gottlieb*, which translates as "loved by God."

WHY MOZART? (A PERSONAL STORY)

My mother and father had an old piano in the garage when I was born. I showed interest in it at around five or six years old. So my parents began piano lessons for me in second grade. Thanks to several wonderful teachers along the way and the tenacity of my parents, I became a rather accomplished pianist, performing a Mozart piano concerto with my junior high school orchestra and later winning a young artist's award for piano in high school.

I enjoyed playing and singing, and while my talents in piano far exceeded my singing ability, I loved the choral experience. Being part of an activity that required a group working together toward a goal versus sitting alone on a piano bench appealed greatly to me, so I decided to become a choir director. My first university degree was in vocal music education, and I taught choral music for ten years.

I had heard somewhere long ago that playing Classical music for young children was "good" for them in some way. I had never researched why this was believed, but it felt intuitively right. Each night when I gave my young daughter, Lily, her bath, I played Classical music for her in the background. Since I knew the history of music, I was playing actual Classical music for her—that is, music written roughly between the years 1750 and 1830.

A little later, through my work in high school administration, I had become aware of the Mozart Effect research before it was even published. I recall attending a workshop for principals at the University of California at Irvine and hearing one of the other administrators mention it in passing. Some of the students in the pilot study were at this administrator's school.

I called lead researcher Gordon Shaw immediately, and he was kind enough to send me information on what had transpired in the study to that point. Since I had already been playing Mozart for my daughter, I thought to myself, "Aren't I the clever mommy?" But one morning when she was almost two years old, I woke up and wondered, "Why Mozart?" Why did Gordon Shaw and Fran Rauscher select the music of Mozart for their studies? What was so magical about the music of Mozart? And why this particular piece?

I proceeded to do what I thought any good mom would do: I called the researchers themselves on the telephone. When asked why they used Mozart's music in their studies, the researchers responded, "We chose

Mozart since he was composing at the age of four. Thus we expect that Mozart was exploiting the inherent repertoire of spatial-temporal firing patterns in the (brain's) cortex."[1]

In layman's terms, the researchers were wondering if listening to the Classical music produced by the mind of the phenomenal child prodigy, Wolfgang Amadeus Mozart, would have an effect on the brain of the listener. Could Mozart's complex music, specifically the *K. 448 Sonata for Two Pianos*, alter or enhance brain performance in some way? (For a much more in-depth, scientifically based explanation of this phenomenon, see Shaw's personal account in his book, *Keeping Mozart in Mind*, Second Edition. Serious scholars and academicians should be reading his words rather than mine regarding the Mozart Effect.)

Perhaps it is relevant that these researchers were not primarily musicians or education specialists; rather, they were scientists. They were neurologists and physicists, assisted by a psychologist who had played cello. However, having been a music teacher and education professional, and especially being a new mom, I wasn't as interested in what was coming out of Mozart as about *what was going in!*

MOZART WASN'T RAISED ON MOZART

Wolfgang Mozart was not listening to Wolfgang Mozart as he lay in his crib in 1756. In fact, it was not Classical music at all that he was hearing from birth to age three, it was Baroque. Exactly what is Baroque music? It was most certainly highly complex, mathematically organized Baroque counterpoint that he was hearing in infancy. This was the standard music pedagogy of the day. Mozart's older sister probably practiced it daily on the harpsichord, and it is likely that his father's other students practiced it at their lessons.

It is entirely plausible that Amadeus Mozart was literally surrounded each and every day by Baroque-style music. This systematically developed Baroque music surely helped to build connections in the mind of the child genius in his first three years of life. Because Mozart had a brain that possessed genius potential, this complex music stimulated his mental development to such a point that he began playing music at four and composing soon afterward. And as any trained musician can tell you, Baroque music is quite different from Classical in many significant ways.

The Baroque Era is characterized by much greater emphasis on the organization of the vertical combinations of contrapuntal complex harmonic, rhythmic, and textural structures and expression. It is brain music and appeals to the intellect over the emotions. (Bach enthusiasts would argue that the intellectual stimulation brings emotional pleasure, and research has shown this to be true.) Repeated listening to complex Baroque music reveals more of its intricacies and the brilliance that created it, and much like great literature, it becomes more revered with repeated consumption.

Generally speaking, the move from this Baroque counterpoint to Classical music was actually a move away from a high level of complexity and toward simpler harmonies. According to the *Harvard Dictionary of Music*, Classical composers "wished music to be developed in forms which should be more the free inspiration of the composer and less restricted in their systematic development." The move away from this Baroque counterpoint to Classical music was actually a move away from a high level of complexity and toward simpler harmonies.

According to *The New Grove Dictionary of Music and Musicians*, this move to a new style of music was partially necessary to satisfy the musical tastes of the new phenomenon of an emerging middle class of concert goers in the Classical Era. "Among the most striking features that distinguish harmony after about 1730 from that of the Baroque Era [is] the slowing down of harmonic rhythm. . . . It was necessary if the tonal outline of larger-scale form was to be accessible to a public comprising more ordinary music lovers than connoisseurs."[2] *The Oxford Companion to Music* states, "The phase that followed (the Baroque Period) was one of resimplification. In the music of Bach's sons, Haydn, Mozart . . . and others of that period, we do not find the complex polyphonic network of Bach. . . . Even Mozart, who greatly admired what he knew of the works of Bach, did not often emulate their depth and complexity."[3]

As a middle class developed in Europe and more people attended concerts, the appreciation levels of the average concert goers may have been reduced or simplified. Much like today, the billion-dollar pop music industry is made up of much simpler music that appeals more widely to the masses with no music training than the music aficionados or actual musicians or certainly classically trained musicians. The Classical audience had no "playback" option. They had no way of repeated consumption because they could not play it themselves and could most likely only hear music played live, a rare opportunity for most.

The dramatic differences in textures of the music in the Baroque and Classical eras could have been the result of other changes, including changes in the technology of the musical instruments themselves. The primary household keyboard instrument of the Baroque Era was the harpsichord. The pianoforte (*piano* meaning "soft" and *forte* meaning "loud") began to come into wider use in Mozart's day. The pianoforte, now just called the piano, could play louder or softer music simply by variations of touch on the part of the performer.

The mechanics of the Baroque harpsichord prohibited any dynamic changes from the touch of the performers' fingers. As a key on the harpsichord's keyboard was played, a quill plucked the string in the instrument's body. Whether the performer touched the key lightly or firmly, the plucking of the string was the same, causing the dynamic level of the note performed to be constant.

The new instrument, the pianoforte, made it possible to produce varied volumes of notes within a single piece of music or even a single motif. On a piano keyboard, when the performer strikes a key, a hammer hits the string in the body of the instrument to cause it to vibrate. If the performer touches a key lightly, the hammer inside the instrument lightly hits the string and a soft sound is created. If, however, the performer increases the force with which the key is played, the hammer's force is increased and the volume of the sound of the note generated is louder.

This difference in volume capacity offered performers, and consequently composers, the ability to more easily create music with much more dynamic variation within a single piece. This single technological advance accelerated the move away from the intellectually appealing Baroque music and toward the more emotional appeal of Classical and Romantic styles of music. While the piano reached its true legitimacy as an instrument at the hands of Beethoven (1770–1827), Mozart (1756–1791) played and composed specifically for the piano. Some sources state that he was the first to do so and that Mozart played the major role in popularizing this new instrument in Europe.

Leopold knew that he had something special on his hands with his young son, Wolfgang. Combining the talents of this child prodigy with the hottest new instrument on the market was sure to create a sensation throughout eighteenth-century Europe. Whether to take advantage of the situation or simply to share the uniqueness of his boy wonder, Leopold took Wolfgang on the road at an early age. (Leopold is often criticized today for this; some argue that these grueling road trips may have affected Wolfgang's already fragile health and contributed to his early death.) Regardless of the reason, Leopold took him and his sister, Nannerl, to perform for the masses, and they were a sensation.

Much to the dismay of Mozart worshipers, Leopold and Wolfgang suffered from a slight credibility problem. Because Wolfgang was a child performer, his advertised age was frequently a year or two younger than his actual age.[4] Since he was a sickly child and was much smaller than other children his age, this was easily believable. In addition, Leopold was thought to have "helped" Wolfgang with some of his early compositions.[5]

When Wolfgang was eight years old, his performances on the pianoforte were spectacular. However, Leopold realized that his son's initial compositions were "less than spectacular."[6] While he could play anything he heard or saw, Leopold didn't see writing music as Wolfgang's forte early on. Leopold moved the family from Paris to England in 1764 for several reasons, one of which was for Mozart to study counterpoint.

It was here that Wolfgang met his most beloved and influential mentor, Johann Christian Bach, the youngest son of the great Johann Sebastian Bach. Mozart scholars, including Teodor Wyzewa and Georges Saint-Foix, agree that "Johann Christian Bach became the only, true teacher of Mozart."[7] While this may sound a bit overblown, since obviously his father and sister had a tremendous impact on his musicianship, musicologists generally agree that five months under the close tutelage of J. C. Bach transformed Mozart's composing abilities.

In his book *The Mozart Handbook*, Louis Biancolli calls Mozart's early compositions "far from mature and sometimes positively faulty. There can thus be no doubt that the sonatas and symphonies of this period were extensively revised by Leopold, and some possibly by J. C. Bach. It does not, surely, detract from the miracle of the genius of a child approaching his ninth birthday to admit that he must have been helped in committing his ideas tidily to paper. What matters is that he did have ideas."[8]

Throughout Mozart's life, he frequently incorporated the work of his father, Bach, Handel, and an undeterminable number of other composers into his works. There are "startling similarities" between many of his symphonies and those of J. C. Bach.[9] However, this was not unusual in a time when printed books of music were a luxury, concerts were scarce, and recording devices and players were nonexistent.

Composers in this day regularly borrowed others' work, sometimes to pay tribute, at other times to improve on another's composition. In the case of J. C. Bach, Wolfgang was paying tribute. In his letters to his father, he repeatedly expressed his love for his mentor. On the other hand, he is thought to have also "improved" upon some of Antonio Salieri's work.

A BIT ABOUT BACH

For over two centuries, the Bach family produced a long line of successful musicians, so much so that the Bach name became synonymous with professional musicianship, as seven generations were "actively musical." Johann Sebastian was of the fifth generation. *The Oxford Companion to Music* states that "38 [Bachs] were known as eminent musicians but of the great majority of these, no music survives and of many of the others only 2 or 3 compositions are available in print."

As each new generation was born into another music-filled home, the Bachs' competencies and artistry escalated, reaching their peak with the complex work of Johann Sebastian Bach, or as he was called, Papa Bach. Two of J. S. Bach's sons, Philipp Emanuel and Johann Christian, actually became more famous as musicians during their lifetimes than their father, but this could be attributed to the change in status for musicians that came about during the Classical period. Johann Sebastian was known in his time more as an exceptionally talented organist than as a composer.

Over the last two centuries, however, appreciation of Bach's talents as a composer has grown steadily. This was largely due to the efforts of great musicians like Felix Mendelssohn, who recognized Bach's genius and began to spread the word about it. *The New Bach Reader* states that Mendelssohn "worked zealously and successfully for the cause of Bach" in the 1800s. Robert Schumann also repeatedly invoked the name of Bach. His often-quoted advice was, "Play conscientiously the fugues of good masters, above all those of Johann Sebastian Bach. Let the *Well-Tempered Clavier* [of Bach] be your daily bread. Then you will certainly

Johann Sebastian Bach.

become a solid musician. . . . We are never at an end with Bach, how he seems to grow more profound the oftener he is heard."[10]

According to *The New Bach Reader*, "What is true of the monumental proportions, the contrapuntal intensity, the rhythmic consistently of Bach's works is just as true of the cogency of his themes, the expressiveness of his melodies, the force and richness of his harmony, the diversity and logic of his orchestration. In all of them he brought seeds well germinated by his predecessors to fruition on a scale undreamed of before him."[11]

The Harvard Dictionary of Music notes that the contrasting style of true polyphony not only persisted but also reached its very pinnacle of perfection and greatness at the hands of the Baroque Period's best-known composer, Johann Sebastian Bach. *The World Book Encyclopedia* says he is "considered the greatest genius of Baroque music" and "the musician's musician." Richard Wagner claimed that Bach's works are "the most stupendous wonder in all music." Gioacchino Rossini stated that "if Beethoven is a prodigy among men, Bach is a miracle of God." Johannes Brahms claimed that the most important event to take place in the world during his lifetime was the unification of Germany. The second most important? "When all of Bach's surviving works were finally published."[12] No musician has been regarded by those in the field as more brilliant than J. S. Bach. *The International Encyclopedia of Music and Musicians* states, "It's hardly too much to say that he is the greatest musical genius the world has ever known."[13]

Fortunately, we have much evidence of Johann Sebastian Bach's brilliance today. This was largely due to the serious approach he took to his teaching. The typical teaching practice of the time was for beginning students to spend their first few years of study copying manuscripts. Bach wrote many works strictly for this purpose. These were circulated widely, and it is possible that Mozart was first exposed to Bach's counterpoint through these types of manuscripts.

In addition, it is plausible that Leopold and Nannerl Mozart may have used them for practicing in Mozart's home. Also, Leopold's duties as the town music master included Sunday church services. Counterpoint prevailed in the church services of this time and well into the Classical Era. It is likely that young Mozart heard this music regularly at church on Sunday as well as repeatedly in his home.

We don't know a lot about Bach's personal life, as he did not write many letters, in contrast to Mozart's hundreds. However, he was referred to as a solid citizen. He was a hard and dedicated worker and probably did not have time to write much beyond his vast library of musical works. Also, there is no doubt that the focus of Bach's life was spiritual—specifically, providing music for the services of the churches where he worked. He was a pious Lutheran and completely devoted to his duty to God and writing and performing music.

MELODY BY BACH

We have addressed monophonic music in an earlier chapter; that is, one line of melody without accompaniment. Polyphonic music is many melodies played together. To help with our comparison of Mozart's and Bach's music, we need to bring homophonic music back into the discussion.

Homophonic music is typically a melody line or theme or motif with an accompanying harmony of some kind. In homophony, there is clearly one important melody and the rest of the music simply supports or reinforces or highlights that melody in some way. By contrast, polyphonic music involves at least two or more melodies of equal importance. The song is the development or working out of the different melodies in part and in whole. The three textures of music may be represented visually.

Bach's counterpoint was unusually complex. According to the *New Grove Dictionary of Music and Musicians*, what other composers "saw realized in exemplary fashion in the music of Bach was the idea of music at once contrapuntal and full of character, at once strict and eloquent: Music in which the characteristic and the eloquent features of a contrapuntally differentiated texture were not forces on it from outside but were actually generated by it." [14]

Bach's fugues and fugal passages probably represent the best and most complex counterpoint compositions ever created. However, whether he was composing the giant *B minor Mass* or *Two-Part Inventions for the Keyboard*, Bach's work shows an attention to detail and genius in every respect that is unparalleled in most other contrapuntal works.

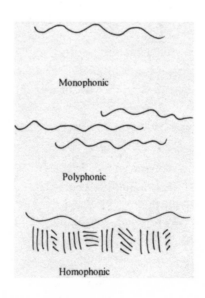

Monophonic

Polyphonic

Homophonic

Comparison of Three Musical Textures.

THE ART OF FUGUE

By the time Wolfgang Mozart was in his mid-twenties, we know that he was collecting the fugues of J. S. Bach. In a letter to his father in 1782, he reported that every Sunday he went to Baron van Swieten's house at noon to hear Bach's music performed. He then took five of Johann Sebastian's fugues from *The Well-Tempered Clavier* and *The Art of the Fugue* and created his own arrangements of them for strings. In his letter to his sister dated April 10, 1782, he wrote, "I am collecting at the moment the fugues of Bach." Then on April 20, 1782, he referred to the fugue as "this most artistic and beautiful of all musical forms." His first fugue was written for his beloved wife, Constanze. He wrote to his sister again, referring to the fugue he had written for his wife:

> I wrote down a fugue for her. So that is its origin. I have purposely written above it Andante Maestoso, as it must not be played too fast. For if a fugue is not played slowly, the ear cannot clearly distinguish the theme when it comes in and consequently the effect is entirely missed. In time, and when I have a favourable opportunity, I intend to write five more and then present them to the Baron van Swieten, whose collection of good music, though small in quantity, is great in quality. And for that very reason I beg you to keep your promise not to show this composition to a soul. Learn it by heart and play it. It is not so easy to pick up a fugue by ear. If Papa has not yet had those works by Eberlin copied, so much the better, for in the meantime I have got hold of them and now I see that they are unfortunately far too trivial to deserve a place beside Handel and Bach. [15]

Mozart was not alone in appreciating the genius of J. S. Bach. In March of 1783, a magazine article about eleven-year-old Beethoven reported that "he plays most of the *Well-Tempered Clavier* by Sebastian Bach, which Mr. Neefe has placed in his hands. Anyone who knows this collection of preludes and fugues in all the keys (which one could almost call the *non plus ultra*) will know what that means." [16]

Douglas R. Hofstadter's lengthy, Pulitzer Prize–winning book, *Godel, Escher, Bach: An Eternal Golden Braid*, shows how extraordinarily complex yet meaningful patterns can arise out of seemingly meaningless symbols. Hofstadter's examples of the ultimate depiction of these complex patterns include Godel, a brilliant mathematician; Escher, a unique and fascinating artist; and J. S. Bach—specifically, his fugues. [17]

Exactly what is a fugue? Answering this question for nonmusicians is no simple task. According to Paul Walker's book, *Theories of Fugue from the Age of Josquin to the Age of Bach*, "Bach's fugues are some of the most sophisticated and complex compositions in all Western music." [18] So before tackling the most complex type of musical pieces ever written, let us begin by considering a canon or a round.

In this type of song, a melody is devised that, by nature of its very construction, can be played with itself at later intervals within the song. The simplest examples of canons or rounds would be songs such as "Row, Row, Row Your Boat" or "Frere Jacques." When "Row, Row, Row Your Boat" is sung, one singer may begin alone and a second singer may begin the song later within the first singer's performance. Almost like magic (depending on exactly when in the song the second singer begins), the sound of the two singers performing the same song but starting at different times is consonant or sounds good to the ear.

For example, the first singer begins with "Row, row, row, your boat, gently down the stream," then the second singer begins the song as the first singer moves on to the second phrase, "Merrily, merrily, merrily, merrily, life is but a dream." The second singer finishes the song after the first singer. This simple song can also be performed in four parts with four singers. They would enter after each half-phrase. For example, when singer 1 begins with "Row, row, row your boat," then singer 2 can begin the song as singer 1 sings "gently down the stream." As long as all singers keep the same tempo, this seemingly simple little melody can be performed in a manner that makes it a much more complex piece by starting in different places within the piece by additional singers. (Try it in two groups, then four groups, then experiment with even more.)

A more complex canon would be one in which the main melody is repeated on a follow-up entry varying not only in the place in time where it enters but also in its pitch. Using the example above, when the main theme comes in for the second voice, it may enter on a different note instead of the identical note of the main theme. If the first note in "Row, Row, Row Your Boat" is C, the second singer may come in on a G instead. In this more complex form of canon, the harmonization of the tune remains the same, but different notes or harmonics are used.

Canons get more and more complex as the construction of the main theme gets more complex to accommodate the increased complexity. For example, instead of the second (or third or fourth) voice coming in simply on a different pitch, it may come in on a different pitch and be accelerated in rhythm or diminished in speed or even augmented. Bach wrote some themes that could even be played upside down and backward and still work to harmonize the main theme.

A phenomenal example of music in which most of these complex compositional strategies show up in the fugal sections is Bach's work, *Musical Offering*. Many consider this Bach's most outstanding accomplishment in counterpoint. Others, such as musicologist Charles Rosen, consider it to be the most significant keyboard composition in all of history. A simple web search can bring you the fascinating story of the composition of this work based on a theme given Bach by Frederick the Great, King of Prussia, as well as multiple recordings of the two ricercars, ten canons, and trio sonata featuring a flute (which King Frederick played).

A fugue is very much like a canon. It has a theme that recurs in different melodies or voices at different speeds and in different forms throughout the work. (The words *voices* and *melody* are used interchangeably, as most of Bach's fugues are not actually sung but are played on instruments.) It is somewhat less rigid than the canon, as it allows for free voices and some slight departures from the exact theme.

A fugue typically begins with a single voice, sometimes called a *subject*, or single line of music followed soon thereafter by a second voice of the same theme, only performed in a different place or different form within the work. The original subject continues as a countersubject to the second voice of the first. As the main theme is developed in all of its possible variations, the countersubject voices, exempt from the strict copying of a canon, continue expressing and developing whatever the composer wishes.

The key (no pun intended for trained musicians) is in the exorbitantly complex designs of Bach's melodies. For a melody to be manipulated so extensively within the fugal passages, its structure must be completely intentioned *from the start* to lend itself to such complexity. Bach didn't just write out a melody of which he liked the sound. He *engineered* it so that it could be developed into a complex fugue and still sound consonant.

In the *Musical Offering*, we find Bach presenting canonic puzzle after canonic puzzle in the fugal form. Bach's students worked hard to try to solve them. Bach even wrote in one section *quaerendo invenietis* (by seeking, you will discover). One of Bach's pupils, Johann Philipp Kirnberger, did solve the canon puzzles. However, Hofstadter wonders whether there could be even more solutions left to seek.[19] Bach's genius in complex composition seems to extend beyond mortal capabilities, according to some Bach lovers.

Bach included no dynamic markings on his solo keyboard or organ works. In fact, when the *Musical Offering* was delivered to King Frederick, there were no instructions whatsoever, not even in the order of preferred performance of the collection of the different pieces. It was not the style of the day to do so, probably because it was not yet possible to get dynamic variation within a piece of music on the individual instruments of the time. Markings such as *crescendo* (gradually get louder) and *decrescendo* (gradually get softer) did not come into use until Jommelli used them in Mannheim, Germany, much later. Bach used complexity of texture to express himself through his composing, not more emotionally appealing tactics such as the use of louds and softs.

On the personal side, Johann Sebastian Bach was truly the embodiment of what many now refer to as exemplifying "family values." He was an especially spiritual man, a devoted Lutheran, and he was employed as a church musician almost all of his long life. To Bach, whether music was sacred or secular, it had only one purpose: to honor God.[20] Bach inscribed the initials "J. J." at the beginning of many of his compositions. This stood for *Jesus jova*, or *Jesus help*. He closed most of his writing with the letters *SDG*, which stood for *Soli Deo Gloria*, which translates as "to God alone be the glory." Bach dedicated some of his keyboard works to Jesus, even though they were not composed for a church performance. (Some performers of Bach's vocal works often report a sense of spiritual transformation upon their completion.)

A PRESENT-DAY PRODIGY: THE KIT ARMSTRONG STORY

During the relatively brief period that I was fortunate to serve as principal of Los Alamitos High School, a multiple National Blue Ribbon award-winning high school in Southern California, I had one of those especially rare life experiences to encounter genuine genetic exceptionalism nurtured by a loving mother. May Armstrong came to the high school to meet with me regarding her unique problem: her seven year-old son, Kit, had completely mastered all of the math and science curriculum at the nearby elementary and middle schools in the district, and she asked if there were some way he could take any math or science classes at the high school.

She shared with me that Kit had seen a printed piano score around the age of four, seen the pattern on a piano keyboard, and began composing even before he almost instantly became an accomplished pianist when he started lessons at five. He immediately began winning awards, first state competitions (California Concerto Competition, both performing and composing at ten), and in the decade since, multiple international awards. He is a six-time winner of the ASCAP Foundation's Morton Gould Young Composer's Award, and his solo debut album released in 2013 by Sony Classical features the works of Bach, Ligeti, and those he has written himself.

Los Alamitos High housed the arts magnet for the area when Kit arrived in my office, and I was determined to help bring Kit to Los Al. The district administration agreed to be flexible with us, May quit her successful career to walk Kit from class to class across the 2,800-student high school, and Kit graduated at age nine and moved on to college. For more details of Kit's childhood, see the article "How Do You Raise a Prodigy?" in the *New York Times* by Andrew Solomon (October 31, 2012). For what Kit is up to these days, see http://www.kitarmstrong.com.

I stayed in touch with this amazing young man and his mother, and I asked him recently, "What do you think of the music of Johann Sebastian Bach?" Kit's reply was:

> I can say that there is no composer whose works move me like Bach's. For me, the most moving experiences in his works are not those where I feel that I am being spoken to, but rather the long moments where before me a worldview is revealed with depth and clarity. I had come to be especially aware of these after studying his works which combine text and music. Engaging myself with this music, I felt that as I started to understand it more deeply, I was opening myself to having and accepting thoughts of the eternal and of the sublime." (Email February 21, 2015)

A dedicated father, Bach had twenty children, ten of whom lived to adulthood, which was normal for this time period. Bach's first wife died after the birth of the fourth child. His second wife was a soprano in his church choir. Several of his children became musicians, and of those, we know that two had contact with Wolfgang Mozart. In fact, Mozart said of Carl Philipp Emanuel Bach's music, "His is the parent and we are the children."[21] Bach's devotion to family and God caused him to appear as somewhat of an anomaly among composers such as Mozart, Beethoven, Tchaikovsky, and many of the other great musicians with less focus on the divine or Judeo-Christian values.

Bach's music has steadily grown in stature over the decades. It was even included aboard *Voyager 1* and *2* as examples of the best that human culture has to offer.[22] J. N. Forkel, considered the father of historical musicology, referred to Bach as "the greatest musical poet and the greatest musical orator that ever existed, and probably ever will exist."[23]

BUILDING BRAINS WITH BACH

All of this knowledge of music and music history, combined with my intuition as a mother and educator, was not enough for me to completely jump with both feet into a Bach-versus-Mozart debate. Even though I had performed many works by both composers over the years and knew that Bach fugues were significantly more complicated for me to memorize and perform than Mozart sonatas or concertos, I was looking for more. I wanted specific research from experts that showed that the increased complexity of Bach's music could have a direct correlation to building brainpower in people who played and heard it.

It appears that the music of the Bach family affected the Bachs themselves. The Bach babies who listened to their music generation after generation grew into an unusual number of gifted musicians and, later, doctors and lawyers. But could this have been genetic? Somewhat, probably so. May Armstrong confessed to me that she was no musician, and she cannot recall Kit hearing any particular type of music in his infancy. She emailed me that

> Kit has immersed [himself] in the music of Bach since day 1. There is
> not a day that goes by without him playing/thinking about Bach. His

latest CD by Sony is a combination of Bach and Ligeti. Many musicians reckon that Kit will be remembered as the most important Bach player in his generation. Brendel once commented that Kit is the most natural Bach player he has ever encountered. (February 20, 2015)

From what we know today of the influence of environment on the developing brain, and of the role of increased complexity in language in development, it only served as reason to me that complex music could likewise build more complex neural networks. We know now that practice doesn't make perfect, it makes permanent. However, I decided to research my theory further. My theory hadn't panned out on the most gifted human I had ever met, Kit Armstrong, as he apparently did not listed to Bach in early childhood that his mother can recall. He did, however, recognize Bach's genius immediately upon being exposed to it. I decided to study the history of giftedness a bit more in-depth and see if there might be some clues or other enlightening information in that body of knowledge.

There was a lot, and yet there was nothing. There was plenty of evidence that gifted musical children became exceptional achievers, and vice versa. There was also a great deal of information to support the concept of an enriched childhood environment as a major contributing factor to giftedness or other forms of exceptionalism. However, in trying to differentiate between the music of Mozart and the music of Bach, I repeatedly ran into that familiar error: lumping all music written before 1900 into the category of "Classical." I found statements such as the following regarding exceptional children:

S. [names are protected in the texts] liked only Classical music performed by experts and had no interest in the music of contemporary composers. . . . He had no language before age 5 but was able to hum songs he heard on the radio or phonograph from an early age.[24]

N. P., an only child, had entered a residential home for long-term placement at age 17. He had almost no spontaneous speech, made little eye contact and displayed the obsessive and bizarre behavior patterns characteristics of autism. . . . He gave local concerts of popular music, hymns and his favorite, Classical pieces.[25]

[Erwin's father] reported that his son tried to sing before he was 1 year old; before 2, reproduced tunes correctly . . . by 8, he learned Beethoven sonatas and Bach fugues after hearing them three or four times.[26]

Where did Erwin hear Bach fugues? His father was a musician with the Royal Opera chorus in Budapest. The point is, there are stories of the profound effects of music on or involving gifted children. Unfortunately, the differentiation I was looking for between specific styles of music was not apparent.

As "unscholarly" as it sounds, almost as if led by the spirit of the Old Wig (as his sons called him) himself, I was able to come serendipitously upon some support for my theory, albeit antedotal. Waiting in a doctor's office, I picked up an issue of *Vogue* magazine. It opened right to a story on a brilliant young pianist, Evgeny Kissin. The reporter writing the story shared an interesting statement by his mother:

> A few days later, at a reception for his twenty-first birthday, I was able to meet his mother and his teacher, Mme Kantor. They were both a good deal more talkative, and as immediately recognizable as characters out of a Broadway show. "I knew Genya was talented at the age of two," his mother tells me. "His older sister was practicing a Bach fugue at the piano. And Genya just started singing it the next day. I asked him to do it again, and he could."[27]

Like Mozart, this young genius was hearing the complex counterpoint of the Baroque Era in his crib. Who but me would have picked up the significance of the song Genya was hearing?

Consider the *60 Minutes* broadcast on December 29, 1996. Lesley Stahl interviewed concert violinist Martha Curtis, who suffered from severe epileptic seizures. Often the seizures would attack in the middle of a symphony performance. Over the years, the medications she had tried were becoming less and less effective in warding off the seizures. In 1991, she decided to undergo risky surgery on her brain to try to remove the origins of the seizures without removing her ability to play music. Surgeons removed part of her right temporal lobe, an area usually associated with interpreting and memorizing music.

As soon as Curtis came out of intensive care, she asked for her violin so she could find out if her life's love could be continued. What did she play? "I played unaccompanied Bach, because that's the hardest stuff (to play) from memory." Again, who but me would pick up that a musician's ultimate test on her own brain would naturally involve the complex music of Bach?

Back when I had called Gordon Shaw to ask why he used the music of Mozart in his Mozart Effect studies, I posed this question: "What about Bach?" He told me that he did not consider himself a musician and that any complex music would probably achieve a similar result. I then called another of the researchers, Frances Rauscher, and asked her the same questions. Having been a concert cellist at one time, Rauscher answered with the same response—hesitation—and then, "Any complex music would probably do."

You can imagine my delight when after years of considering this concept, Shaw included the following suggestion in his own book, *Keeping Mozart in Mind:* "Perhaps the question most asked is what other pieces of music will yield the enhancements in spatial-temporal reasoning generated by the Mozart *Sonata (K. 448)*? (We suggest trying the highly structured music of J. S. Bach.)"[28]

And in fact, serious researchers today are taking this advice. At the Institute for Music Research at the University of Texas at San Antonio, Don Hodges and his team studied the neural networks used for processing music. Their study was designed to determine the brain areas that are activated by melody, harmony, and rhythm by having musicians listen to Bach chorales with intentional errors implanted.

In one experiment, the error was in the melody. In another, it was in the harmony, and in a third, the error was in the rhythm. Dr. Hodges stated, "It is clear that there is no 'music center' (in the brain) and it is also clear that music does not happen only in the right side of the brain."[29] When I asked Hodges why the researchers chose Bach, he answered that it was because of the symmetry and organization. They felt it would most clearly depict the results they were looking for; for example, determining a wrong note. This type of research will eventually help us see why music affects learning the way it does, why math performance is enhanced so by some music, and why spatial-temporal reason is sometimes enhanced by listening to complex music.

GOING FOR BAROQUE

Mozart is considered a Classical composer. But the music that helped with the development of the brain of this young genius was not Classical, it was Baroque. The sounds he heard repeatedly, even before birth, were his older sister practicing counterpoint on the harpsichord and his father's violin students fiddling away at the highly structured, systematic Baroque sounds of the day. And that music was not merely repetitive. It represented the ultimate in melodic design and development in a complex way.

We hear musical sounds the way we do because each note vibrates at a different frequency. Simply put, music can be explained mathematically, and the relationship between tones is in essence a mathematical one. Exposing infants from birth to age three to the highly contrapuntal music of the Baroque Era can stimulate complex neural networking and potentially improve the learning potential, creativity, and resulting intellect of the child later in life. This is especially true if listening to complex music in the crib is followed up with consistent music lessons in the early years. These music experiences enhance neural activity between brain cells. Case study research reveals much evidence to support the theory that Baroque musical exposure may contribute to developing "geniuses" at early ages.

Unfortunately, many neurologists and sociologists have lumped what they refer to as "complex music" into the era of Classical music without recognizing the critical differences between the musical eras that affect child development. Throughout decades of studies of gifted children, when musical factors are considered, these factors are repeatedly labeled and reported in a category referred to as "Classical"; today we have no way of determining if this was specifically music written in the late 1700s and early 1800s.

The Classical music of Mozart is brilliant and should be the standard listening curriculum in the primary grades. However, listening is developmental. Johann Sebastian Bach's contrapuntal compositions are to the music world what Ansel Adams's black-and-white photographs are to the visual art world: extraordinarily complex, but still developmentally appropriate for babies and young children.

Early childhood music clinicians widely use the phrase *developmentally appropriate music making* as though it were defined somewhere and set in stone. It is not. Some aspects of a possible definition are obvious. Clearly children naturally engage in musical activity to help give meaning to experiences or to express themselves. Music can also provide an opportunity for connecting socially to other children and adults.

On a more cognitive level, making music is a fine example of active involvement and has been shown to enhance memory skills and fine motor skills. Many three-year-olds who cannot recite the letter names of the alphabet can easily sing them in the classic ABC song, "Tell me what you think of me." Likewise with numbers: "One, two, buckle my shoe." Many parents use musical tunes to teach their toddlers those critical pieces of information that they may be too young "developmentally" to recall: their full name, phone number, and address.

Early childhood programs do likewise through songs such as the "7 Days of the Week" and other musical chants to cleverly insert important curricular content that needs more ready retention. In this respect, music is used to speed up what may still be considered developmentally inappropriate information for children to process. Yet children can do it and apparently enjoy doing it when music is added.

Music is made up of many types of patterns. When children internalize different kinds of music, they are not only building connections between the rhythmic, melodic, and dynamic patterns of the songs, they are making other connections between neurons within nearby neural networks in their developing brains as well. Music and math skills appear to go hand in hand, and music and memory have some special associations as well. Music may even prepare the brain for all learning since it is a whole-brain activity and does not just involve one or two specific brain areas as previously theorized.

SUPERLEARNING

In 1979, Sheila Ostrander, Lynn Schroeder, and Nancy Ostrander published a book titled *Superlearning*. In it, they claimed that there was a way to learn how to learn more quickly, develop "super memory banks," and speed up learning in general.[30] They cited in particular the work of a Bulgarian researcher, Georgi Lozanov, who had observed outstanding results in helping people achieve a state of relaxed alertness. In this state, the body is relaxed but the mind is alert and especially susceptible to taking in and retaining new information, such as learning a language.

Music was found to be a critical element in achieving this special state of mind. While the authors repeatedly used the terms *Classical* and *Baroque* interchangeably, Lozanov is quoted as emphasizing that the music has to be a special kind of Baroque music, with roughly sixty beats per minute, the approximate number of heartbeats in the body in a minute.

Lozanov also said that string instruments produce better results because of the higher frequencies of the pitches. J. S. Bach wrote most of the music recommended by Lozanov and the authors.

While there were no neurological studies available then to help defend their case, the authors did point out that using a particular style of music to achieve a particular state of mind is certainly not an entirely new concept. They share the well-known story of Bach's composition of the "Goldberg Variations" first found in Johann Forkel's early biography of J. S. Bach.[31]

As the story goes, Russian envoy Count Kayserling had a bad case of insomnia. When he would awaken in the night, he called for the musician Johann Goldberg to be awakened so he could play "that song" for the count yet again. What song? Goldberg played a piece on the harpsichord that had been specifically written for Kayserling by J. S. Bach to help with his sleeplessness. It was "calm, yet bright."[32]

Shortly after Goldberg would begin to play, the count would find himself feeling restful and soon would be able to fall back to sleep, or so the story goes. He even had Goldberg placed in a room near his own bedroom to be ready to play this wonderful healing music immediately upon request. The count was so pleased with the effects of the song that he gave Bach a generous gift of gold. The song was named the "Goldberg Variations" in honor of the obliging harpsichordist.

Lozanov is quoted as claiming that he is quite sure the great composers, philosophers, and poets from ages gone by were well aware of these special musical powers and used them unabashedly. *Superlearning* goes on to promote hypnosis, parapsychology, the development of intuition, and even extrasensory perception, not exactly a scholarly approach to the purported magic of Baroque counterpoint. But as research on "mindfulness" and "healing" and the "energies" associated with these states begin to enter some circles of mainstream scientific research, perhaps the music of Bach will find another avenue of study in these realms.

In 1994, the three *Superlearning* authors published a follow-up book, *Superlearning 2000*. While their work has been criticized by some as being a bit overblown and far-reaching—suggesting we can accomplish a year's worth of learning a new language in only three days—no one has criticized the author's choice of Baroque music for achieving the "superlearning" state. *Superlearning 2000* contains page after page of testimonials of the success of the authors' method. It claims that over two hundred centers have been set up worldwide to use Superlearning methods to learn and heal, and they maintain an updated website.

In *Superlearning 2000*, the music references are more specific. The authors state that the music definitely needs to be a specific type of Baroque music with between sixty and sixty-four beats per minute: "Tests showed music scored for string instruments rich in harmonic overtones produced superior results to music scored for brass, horns or pipe organ."[33] Again, the music of J. S. Bach is cited repeatedly in testimonials, claiming greatly increased learning, the curing of learning disabilities in young children, and the healing of just about any ailment known to man. These stories present a compelling case, however unscientific, for listening to Baroque music to enhance thinking.

In *The Secret Life of the Unborn Child*, Thomas Verny claims that it is easy to tell what kind of music the fetus enjoys listening to: Baroque. "Put Vivaldi on the phonograph and even the most agitated baby relaxes. Put Beethoven on and even the calmest child starts kicking and moving."[34] Unborn babies might not understand words, but somehow they understand tone and tone of voice. They prefer soft, soothing sentences from their mothers, no matter what the words are, and Baroque music with no words at all.[35] Verny suggests that these sounds make babies feel comfortable, loved, and wanted even before they are born.

LISTENING AND LEARNING

If we acknowledge that simply adding some types of music to the environment helps the brain learn better and in some instances faster, then perhaps music should be mandated in standard curriculums in early childhood. If simply listening to a particular style of music helps nurture neural networks and, in turn, helps the brain function better, why would we view exposing infants to wonderfully complex music any differently than providing proper nourishment for a baby? We want our babies to be physically healthy. Why? Is the answer any different than the reason we want our babies to be mentally and emotionally healthy?

The point is, parents who want to provide the best environment for their babies' brains and bodies desire this for the same reasons they do not feed them candy bars, potato chips, or soda pop. They love their children and want them to be healthy, happy, and well developed. They are not trying to create Michael Jordans, Drew Breeses, or Cal Ripkens. They are not trying to create superbabies or tiny Einsteins. They simply want to maximize their children's potential in every domain wherever and whenever possible.

Where is the line to be drawn between providing only for a child's minimal survival needs and child abuse? In the motives of the parents? Is "developmental appropriateness" that which is needed for children's survival? Or is it what we know from research to be best for enhancing their cognitive development? Until scientists can give parents and caregivers a clear definition of what is not only good for enriching a child's development but what is best and what is detrimental, we will continue to have parents and caregivers conducting the vast majority of research in this critical field by trial and error.

What is clear is that we now have enough scientific research to draw the unavoidable conclusion that just "maintenance," or doing just enough to ensure the physical survival of young children, is not nearly enough. Children must be in a developmentally appropriate and stimulating environment. At least in developed countries, this can be accomplished through virtually free resources such as online free visual printables, music sharing sites, and the use of public libraries. We know better, and we must do better!

NAEYC

The National Association for the Education of Young Children (NAEYC) is an organization, founded in 1926, that is dedicated to promoting high-quality, developmentally appropriate programs for all young children and their families. The organization's 2009 website (www.naeyc.org) states:

> Developmentally appropriate practices result from the process of professionals making decisions about the well-being and education of children based on at least three important kinds of information or knowledge:
>
> 1. What is known about child development and learning—referring to knowledge of age-related characteristics that permits general predictions about what experiences are likely to best promote children's learning and development.

2. What is known about each child as an individual—referring to what practitioners learn about each child that has implications for how best to adapt and be responsive to that individual variation.

3. What is known about the social and cultural contexts in which children live—referring to the values, expectations, and behavioral and linguistic conventions that shape children's lives at home and in their communities that practitioners must strive to understand in order to ensure that learning experiences in the program or school are meaningful, relevant, and respectful for each child and family.

In an effort to be somewhat more specific, NAEYC has also outlined the principles of child development and learning that inform developmentally appropriate practice. They are:

1. All the domains of development and learning—physical, social, emotional, and cognitive—are important, and they are closely related. Children's development in one domain influence and are influenced by what takes place in other domains.

2. Many aspects of children's learning and development follow well-documented sequences, with later abilities, skills, and knowledge building on those already acquired.

3. Development and learning proceed at varying rates from child to child as well as at uneven rates within different areas of each child's individual functioning.

4. Development and learning result from a dynamic and continuous interaction of biological maturation and experience.

5. Early experiences have profound effects, both cumulative and delayed, on a child's development and learning; and optimal periods exist for certain types of development and learning to occur.

6. Development proceeds toward greater complexity, self-regulation, and symbolic or representational capacities.

7. Children develop best when they have secure, consistent relationships with responsive adults and opportunities for positive relationships with peers.

8. Development and learning occur in and are influenced by multiple social and cultural contexts.

9. Always mentally active in seeking to understand the world around them, children learn in a variety of ways; a wide range of teaching

strategies and interactions are effective in supporting all these kinds of learning.

10. Play is an important vehicle for developing self-regulation as well as for promoting language, cognition, and social competence.

11. Development and learning advance when children are challenged to achieve at a level just beyond their current mastery, and also when they have many opportunities to practice newly acquired skills.

12. Children's experiences shape their motivation and approaches to learning, such as persistence, initiative, and flexibility; in turn, these dispositions and behaviors affect their learning and development.[36]

If "developmentally appropriate" means appropriate for developing the brain to achieve its inborn capacity, a maximally enriching environment would be important. The principles upon which the accepted definition of "developmental appropriateness" is founded do not conflict with the notion of increasing the complexity of stimuli in the crib and beyond.

Take another look at principle 11. This principle appears to represent Vygotsky's theory of the Zone of Proximal Development. Children who interact with those more capable than they—for example, their parents or more capable siblings—develop knowledge, attitudes, and ideas from these interactions. The learning is dependent, then, upon the quality or complexity that is present in their environment.

For example, the more complex the language present, the more complex the language learned. The more languages present, the more languages learned. The more complex the music present, the more complex the foundation laid for future learning based on nearby or connected neural networking, and in some cases, as with the Bachs and Mozarts, the more musical abilities learned.

Since music is known to translate into improved spatial-temporal reasoning and likely enhanced mathematical and other cognitive abilities, the more complex music present, the more spatially competent and probably the more complex mathematical understanding can be expected later on. Something not yet thoroughly understood or explainable in science through the act of listening to complex music helps set the stage for more complex learning and a variety of other cognitive skills that will be beneficial later on.

So exactly what is developmentally appropriate? It must depend on the expected, defined outcomes. Do we not want all children to develop effective language and communication skills? Do we not want all children to gain understanding and use of logic and mathematics? Do we not want these abilities to be developed as much as we want them to be physically healthy and to know that they are loved?

What about the child's self-esteem? The research in this area seems clear. It says that self-esteem or self-concept is a cognitive structure involving who you believe that you are. This structure is built within a person, not given to him or her. Children develop positive self-concepts through experiences of success throughout their lives. Children who have excellent language and mathematical skills generally perform better in school than children who do not, and they also generally have higher self-esteem.[37]

Martin Gardiner has shown in another of his studies that music training can support powerful thinking in additional areas. He terms this phenomenon "mental stretching." Specifically, it is the cross-fertilization between two different areas in ways that are mutually beneficial. In his study, children receiving music training experienced positive correlations between music and academic achievement, but other important changes were also found. The changes were improvements in class participation, following directions, cooperation with the teacher, cooperation with peers, improvement in self-motivation, self-esteem, responsibility, and initiative. These changes were noted by the students themselves as well as by their teachers.[38]

DEVELOPMENTALLY APPROPRIATE LISTENING

Have you ever dropped something onto the floor near your infant or made an unexpected noise? Something as simple as a sneeze or cough can be so frightening it reduces newborns to tears. The hearing of babies and toddlers is developmental, just like every other aspect of the growth of their little bodies, and should be recognized as such.

What mother in her right mind would offer filet mignon and chocolate-covered almonds for her toothless newborn to eat? Who would read them the tales of Stephen King before the *Tale of Peter Rabbit*? Who would take them to see *Terminator II* before *Winnie the Pooh*? Who would expose them to boiling hot and icy cold before temperatures of warm and chilled? And who would even think of playing the stormy (Classical) symphonies of Beethoven before the counterpoint of Bach?

While newborn babies can see and process works of great detail in black and white, they cannot distinguish between light pastel colors, no matter how simply they are presented. They can understand language of any complexity, and even express that understanding, long before they can actually use the languages themselves. And while their minds can comprehend the rich complexity of contrapuntal music, it is logical to conclude that they are not ready for the volume or emotionally charged frenzy of the more dynamic works of later musical eras.

Today's information explosion, brought about by the technological revolution, has changed our culture. In 2015, it is a necessity for cultural literacy that we strive for our children to become highly effective learners, capable of acquiring, accessing, and using far more knowledge than in prior eras. They need complex language skills and creativity, accompanied by high-level reasoning and critical-thinking capabilities.

With respect to music stimuli, a complex listening base should be built to help all of these skills to blossom, as well as to foster sheer enjoyment of the arts. Music listening and training should be a permanent fixture in the curriculum of our preschools and K–12 schools, alongside reading, writing, working with numbers, and any other content knowledge we as a society believe must be presented (regardless of what can be accessed alone by students). Music programs should include singing and making music, along with continued listening and analysis of complex music. The curriculum should include some songs that are fun, humorous, and designed for enjoyment as well as music designed for a wide range of learning.

My two teenaged children, the impetus for this work, can still recite the presidents and state capitals thanks to Mrs. Frack and her fun and factual songs woven into their elementary educational experience. But this is only one aspect of a developmentally appropriate music program. Learning to read musical notes, rhythm, pitch, tempo, and volume should be incorporated into the program as well. This builds a broader neural foundation of networking for a multitude of knowledge. This important component oftentimes disregarded in many of today's early childhood programs is music that sequentially grows or increases in complexity over time. This should be included to help the brain to develop appropriately, the way it was designed to develop, maximizing capacity for connections.

The Kodaly Method of music training, as used in Gardiner's studies, is basically free, requires no instruments, and should be incorporated into early childhood environments as soon as children can distinguish between a flat hand and a fist moved high or low. In addition, round singing should become a critical part of the beginning program when children are ready. This will be obvious because round singing is too difficult for most young children but can be approached in groups of two parts at first until more parts are developmentally accessible. Round singing allows children to create more complex polyphony themselves as they participate in singing songs. It will surely build more neural networks than singing enjoyable melodies alone.

THE GIFT OF BACH: THE *BACH & BABY* STORY

I spent nearly three decades working in schools. I was a teacher for a decade, then department chair, dean, vice principal, assistant principal, high school principal, director, executive director, and now university professor. I earned a bachelor's, master's, and doctoral degree in education along the way. None of this was done in an attempt to climb career ladders or amass degrees. I was internally driven to find the solution to the huge problem with the education system that I had come to know so well: the problem of the unmotivated student; the student uninterested in learning many of the curricular offerings of schools; the learning problem, the learning gap.

I knew from my studies that the brain, by its very nature, was born to learn. Why, then, were so many teenagers so turned off to learning? Schools were supposed to be a place where teaching and learning was the primary purpose and major focus. Tremendous amounts of time and money had been devoted specifically to creating environments for learning to take place. Yet why did so very many children dislike school, and why were so many failing?

Throughout my career, I tried everything I'd ever heard of, read about, or thought up myself to remotivate the at-risk students and help them to connect or engage with school learning. It wasn't until the birth of my daughter in 1994 that I began to see the light, so to speak. The solution to the K–12 system learning problem might not lie between kindergarten and high school graduation at all but between the maternity ward and the kindergarten door.

This enlightenment was occurring at the same time I was realizing that it was a good idea for babies to be listening to Bach. One morning while my husband was shaving, I said, "Wouldn't it be magnificent if every kindergartner arrived at the schoolhouse door having listened regularly to five years of complex Bach music? Along with lots of complex language and plenty of nurturing love, of course! I am going to put some CDs together of Bach music specifically for young children to hear to help nurture some neural networks. Bach lays neural foundations upon which brains can be better built. This will be my small contribution to the solution of the universal education problem." My analytical husband replied, "You can call them *Bach & Baby*." I still tell him that coming up with such a creative and clever name had to be divine inspiration.

So again, I did what I thought any good mommy would do. I called my piano teacher from twenty years earlier, who had become the dean of the School of Music at the University of Colorado at Boulder. Dr. Daniel Sher, an outstanding Bach pianist in his own right, mobilized his wonderful faculty, and they recorded everything by Bach in their repertoire. (Bach is too difficult even for professional musicians to "work up." Ask them!)

Dan and I sorted the music into the four CDs by theme. The *Bach & Baby* CDs are sorted by titles and tempos: *Bedtime* (slow), *Bathtime* (medium), *Playtime* (fast), and *Traveltime* (everything we had left over). They are presently available through Kindermusik, International, a company devoted to the music education of young children.

BACH & BABY: COMPLEX AND SIMPLE

Adding quality music that is complex yet appropriate to a child's environment has never been simpler. The four *Bach & Baby* titles, *Playtime, Bedtime, Bathtime, Traveltime*, make it especially simple for parents and caregivers to stimulate increased synaptic firing and lay broader neural pathways in their children's brains throughout their normal day with the mere push of a button. This music by J. S. Bach was recorded and placed on different CDs specifically to fit into the various settings of a child's day while maintaining the complexity necessary to help give babies an enriched environment.

These recordings are not like many "Classical" ones that can be found in children's departments everywhere. All four of the *Bach & Baby* titles have won Parent's Choice recognition, and proceeds from the recordings have benefited the Bach Endowment Fund at the University of Colorado at Boulder.

While there has been much ado about Mozart in the last two decades, Bach should be tops for use in building the brains of babies and toddlers. Every newborn should have this wonderful opportunity that only parents or caregivers can bring them. Parents want and need the very best information available to provide their little ones with an enriched learning environment during that most important window of opportunity, the early years before a free education begins. These CDs are one attempt to provide it for them.

There are many outstanding recordings of Bach music available today, and any of them would provide excellent background music for anyone, especially young children and their caregivers. In fact, there are now video recordings of musicians performing Bach music available so that children can watch the music being performed. My personal favorites are *The Essential Bach*, a collection of five DVDs presently available through Amazon.com or Walmart.com.

As a consumer warning, however, be wary of phrases on children's CD packaging like "inspired by the music of Bach" or "especially designed for little ears" or "performed by the toy box symphony." This language can be an indication that the music on the CD is not the actual music of the composer but a rearranged, simplified version of his works. These CDs are analogous in the music world to the black-and-white baby flash cards I discussed in an earlier chapter—unnecessarily simplified.

Children do not want or need "dumbed down" versions of the best our world has to offer. Be aware of this trend, particularly with respect to children's music and children's literature. Leave the *Reader's Digest* versions for another time and give your baby the originals!

SALIENT POINTS

- The music of the Classical Era differs in substantial ways from the music of the Baroque Era. Classical music is typically more homophonic in texture with a wider variety of dynamic variation while Baroque music is typically more polyphonic with less dynamic variation within a song.
- Wolfgang Mozart is a well-known Classical composer who was a child prodigy.
- Johann Sebastian Bach is a well-known Baroque composer and is considered the greatest composer who ever lived by many professional musicians and composers.
- It is conceivable that Mozart was hearing Baroque music rather than Classical music in his crib as his father, mother, and older sister were all musicians and the Baroque style of music was the accepted teaching style of his time.
- It is unknown whether or not Mozart was hearing the music of J. S. Bach in his crib; however, we know through his letters later in life that he viewed Bach's music as great music and was collecting fugues that Bach had written.
- The music of Bach is considered to be of a highly complex nature in texture, particularly his fugues; however, it is developmentally appropriate listening for babies due to the lack of dynamic variation within a piece.
- Listening to complex music in early childhood has been connected to improved cognitive skills. Learning the symbolic representations for reading music as soon as is developmentally possible improves a multitude of cognitive and other school skills later on.
- Early childhood educators should consider the Developmental Listening™ curriculum suggested in this chapter for nurturing neural networks.

NOTES

1. Gordon Shaw, telephone interview by author, December 3, 1997.

2. *The New Grove Dictionary of Music and Musicians*, ed. Stanley Sadie (London: Oxford University Press, 1980), 8:180.

3. Percy A. Scholes, *The Oxford Companion to Music*, 9th ed. (London: Oxford University Press, 1955), 449.

4. Heinz Gartner, *John Christian Bach: Mozart's Friend and Mentor*, trans. Reinhard G. Pauly (Portland, OR: Amadeus Press), 196.

5. Gartner, *John Christian Bach*, 198.

6. Gartner, *John Christian Bach*, 202.

7. T. Wyzewa and G. W. A. Saint-Foix, *W. A. Mozart, sa vie musicale et son oeuvre, de L'enfance, à la pleine maturit é* (Paris: Perrin-Desele'e de Browner, 1912), 122.

8. Louis Biancolli, *The Mozart Handbook* (New York: World Publishing, 1954), 47.

9. Gartner, *John Christian Bach*, 217.

10. Hans T. David and Arthur Mendel, eds., *The New Bach Reader* (New York: W. W. Norton, 1998), 14.

11. David and Mendel, *The New Bach Reader*.

12. Robert Greenberg, *How to Listen to and Understand Great Music*, Learning Company, audiocassette.

13. *The International Encyclopedia of Music and Musicians*, 5th ed., ed. Oscar Thompson (New York: Dodd, Mead, 1949), 817.

14. Stanley Sadie and John Tyrrell, eds., *The New Grove Dictionary of Music and Musicians* (London: Oxford University Press, 1980).

15. Emily Anderson, *The Letters of Mozart and His Family* (London: Macmillan, 1985), 801.

16. David and Mendel, *The New Bach Reader*, 489.

17. Douglas R. Hofstadter, *Godel Escher, Bach: An Eternal Golden Braid* (New York: Basic Books, 1979), 9.

18. Paul Walker, *Theories of Fugue from the Age of Josquin to the Age of Bach* (New York: University Rochester Press, 2003).

19. Hofstadter, *Godel Escher, Bach*, 9.

20. Robert Greenberg, "Bach and the High Baroque," Lecture 9, Course 721, at the San Francisco Conservatory of Music, 1995, Learning Company, audiocassette.

21. Anderson, *The Letters of Mozart and His Family*.

22. *Time*, March 25, 1985.

23. Johann Nikolaus Forkel, "Über Johann Sebastian Bachs Leben, Kunst, und Kunstwerke" ("On Johann Sebastian Bach's Life, Art and Work"). A recent reprint is by Henschel Verlag, Berlin, 2000. An English translation was published by Da Capo Press in 1970.

24. Darold Treffert, *Extraordinary People* (New York: Harper & Row, 1989), 25.

25. Treffert, *Extraordinary People*, 28.

26. John Radford, *Child Prodigies and Exceptional Early Achievers* (New York: Free Press, 1990), 106.

27. David Daniel, "Key Player," *Vogue*, September 1993, 352.

28. Gordon Shaw, *Keeping Mozart in Mind* (San Diego: Academic Press, 2000), 167.

29. Don Hodges, personal communication with author, July 2001.

30. Sheila Ostrander and Lynn Schroeder with Nancy Ostrander, *Superlearning 2000* (New York: Dell, 1994), 86.

31. Ostrander, Schroeder, and Ostrander, *Superlearning 2000*.

32. Forkel, "Über Johann Sebastian Bachs Leben, Kunst, und Kunstwerke."

33. Ostrander, Schroeder, and Ostrander, *Superlearning 2000*.

34. Thomas Verny with John Kelly, *The Secret Life of the Unborn Child* (New York: Dell, 1994), 21.

35. Verny, *Secret Life*, 22.

36. National Association for the Education of Young Children, "Principles of Child Development and Learning That Inform Developmentally Appropriate Practice," position statement adopted July 1996 and updated in 2009, http://www.naeyc.org/positionstatements.

37. Anita Woolfolk, *Educational Psychology* (Boston: Allyn & Bacon, 2000), 71.

38. Martin Gardiner, "Music Learning, and Behavior: A Case for Mental Stretching," *Journal for Learning through Music* 1, no. 1 (Spring 2000): 82.

8

IMPLICATIONS FOR EDUCATION

Of all the civil rights for which the world has struggled and fought for 5,000 years, the right to learn is undoubtedly the most fundamental.
—W. E. B. Du Bois, "The Freedom to Learn"

Based on educational success, or success in schools as measured by grades and test scores as a frame of reference, it would appear that the failure to nurture and develop the potential of the brains of our young children today is widespread. Certainly many schools across the country have been deemed failures, and a variety of reform efforts have come and gone in efforts to improve education in this country and others.

Based on early learning research, the consequences indicate that, deprived of a nurturing environment filled with rich and developmentally appropriate complexity in the earliest years of life, children are left with lower-performing brains later in life. Certainly we have made great strides as a society to improve the environments of our children through passage of a variety of policies, from provisions for food and shelter to the availability of health screenings, safety precautions, and a variety of regulations regarding everything from car seat straps to playground equipment to infant formula ingredients. Still, this is just the aforementioned "maintenance," aimed at keeping children alive and healthy, but it does nothing to stimulate their neural networks.

Securing the minimal physical health and safety of our youngest citizens is not enough; nor is focusing exclusively on their social and emotional development. Cognitive development extends beyond even the intellectual performance of an adult and eventually influences health and welfare as well. A high-functioning mind thinks, questions, reflects, hypothesizes, and tailors behavior accordingly. The problems of the twenty-first century require twenty-first-century brains.

Some aspects of our system today perpetuate a tremendous educational error: the notion that "teaching" babies and very young children is inappropriate. Pure developmentalists may cringe at the initial sound of the phrase, but babies are learning all the time, and we are teaching them whether we recognize it or not. A complete paradigm shift in our thinking about education is needed to address this reality. Perhaps the wild scenario below can help direct our focus outside traditional boundaries.

Put on your most preposterous imaginative thinking cap and consider this analogy: image a country just getting started that is underpopulated. The leaders of this country realize the critical importance of propagating the citizenry and the species, and decide to take action. They set up free reproduction schools for women designed specifically to reach the goal of increasing the population of the country as fast as possible. Their mission? Educate to procreate!

However, since the work of the young women is important to the growing economy and young women are far more productive in the workforce than elderly women, they decide to wait until the women are older to enroll them in this reproduction school. Education becomes compulsory for women at the age of fifty; at that time they are all sent to reproduction school for twelve years. When they graduate at the age of sixty-two, their exit exam is to bear a child. This school system, the nation's leaders believe, will ensure a quick increase in population.

Sure, there is a child or two born to the women in the schools, but overall, the schools fail in their purpose. Reform after reform comes and goes in an effort to fix the reproduction schools. The curriculum is revised, requirements for teachers are increased, class sizes are reduced. Still, very few of the sixty-two-year-olds are able to bear children when they graduate.

Policymakers are baffled. They blame the teachers. Teachers work harder, and more and more money and resources are injected into the system, but there is no noticeable improvement. Teachers blame the students. Students blame their parents. Everyone works harder and harder, but no significant increases in childbearing are seen.

Had the country considered making its schools for fifteen-year-olds instead of fifty-year-olds, no doubt it would have enjoyed considerably more success. It's like a gold prospector who digs and digs in search of the motherload; if he is a foot away from the vein, it doesn't matter how deep he digs. It doesn't matter how technologically advanced his equipment becomes or how much capital he spends on new and improved diggers. He won't find gold unless he considers changing his boundaries.

People do change. The species has evolved. Just ask coffin makers. They will tell you that if they made coffins the size that they made them two hundred years ago, few would fit in them today. Consider the onset of puberty. In my mother's generation, the average age of the onset of menstruation was around fifteen years of age. In my daughter's generation, it is eleven. In his book *Jefferson's Children: Education and the Promise of American Culture*, Leon Botstein notes that high schools were designed for students who were just beginning the journey into adulthood between the ages of fifteen and eighteen. Today, he argues, this is obsolete. Perhaps college should begin after tenth grade instead of after the twelfth.

The faulty assumption that IQ is fixed at birth had significant influence on the education system for generations. This notion led to tracking, profiling, stereotyping, and holding different expectations for different groups of students. Though many schools are trying to break out of this mold of thought, it is simply too well established and deeply ingrained for some systems to break from. The example of the old community merry-go-round comes to mind. The deep trenches dug from decades and decades of racing around the same circle cannot be moved incrementally. Perhaps only by completely dismantling the merry-go-round and moving it to an entirely new location can we escape the depth of the ages-old entrenchment.

As crazy as the hypothetical reproduction schools in our new country sound, the concept is no crazier than a system organized around the assumption that a child should wait until the age of five or six to be taught anything. When the child arrives at the kindergarten door without a proper foundation laid in the brain, teachers become frustrated. Parents and communities blame teachers and schools for their failure to teach their children, year after year after year. Teachers blame parents, legislators blame schools of education, and around and around the blame block we go.

Since the problem appears more pronounced in schools in poor urban areas, more focus on reform is occurring there. Yet despite reform movement after reform movement, the results have continued to disappoint researchers. Billions of extra federal dollars are pumped into these schools in poor socioeconomic communities every year in an effort to help the students learn more and more complex material like their more affluent colleagues in the suburbs. Every effort is aimed at reigniting motivated learning in apparently unmotivated children. When these efforts fail, as they almost always do, schools and teachers find themselves in the headlines being crucified for the lack of learning going on despite so much time and money invested.

We are already facing severe teacher shortages not only in the United States but abroad as well. The blame and humiliation of teachers that presently permeates the media is even more detrimental and further exacerbates the teacher shortages, particularly in low socioeconomic areas. Candidates in college studying to become elementary teachers have brought the lowest standardized testing scores of all the university colleges to the field for decades, and performances spiral downward systemically.

Andrew Gopnik, Alison Meltzoff, and Patricia Kuhl refer to the baby as a scientist in a crib. In education terms, the baby is born a student ready to learn. They come into the world, by nature, as learning machines, and their very existence is focused around learning to adapt to their new environment. Unfortunately, it must be what is happening—or perhaps what is not happening—in the child's environment between the maternity ward and high school that somehow stifles this natural drive to learn. It is stifled when neural circuits that could be formed and want to be formed are not able to be formed because of lack of stimuli, or stimuli not offered in a timely manner.

Recall the grammar studies in which children who were not exposed to proper grammar between the ages of two and four were never able to grasp a natural use of correct grammar. Children should never lose their motivation for learning. No one should assume that babies cannot or should not or do not want to learn. As far as the brain is concerned, learning complex material is the purpose of living, and all children deserve a free and appropriate public education, even babies.

A BRIEF HISTORY OF EDUCATION

The implications of the faulty assumption that babies aren't, or can't be, or shouldn't be taught impel us to reconsider the boundaries of the education system in this and other countries. A look at the history of education in this country reveals even more faulty assumptions. What were schools created for in the first place? One purpose was to rescue children from exploitation by the labor markets of the late nineteenth and early twentieth centuries. The Industrial Revolution was happening in part on the backs of ten-year-olds in sweatshops.

In his provocative work *Separating School and State*, Sheldon Richman makes the case that compulsory education was designed from its inception in Sparta to indoctrinate children and stamp out dissent. Children were taken by the state and educated to obey the state. The modern version of our public schools had its roots in Germany in the 1500s. Again, the primary purpose was to keep the children from hearing the heretics. In 1717, the first national system of schools was set up in Prussia. Children between the ages of seven and fourteen were compelled to go to the schools or parents were subject to having their children removed from their homes.

When American leaders were looking for a model for public school, they visited Prussian schools. There they found order, efficiency, and obedience. They saw large numbers of immigrant children removed from "inappropriate cultural influences" and assimilated successfully. The first public kindergarten in the United States was designed after Friedrich Froebel's kindergarten in Germany. It opened in 1873, and its purpose was to remove children in poverty-stricken areas from their poverty and bad families and subject them to the influence of the school system as early as possible.

COMPELLED TO LEARN

The Massachusetts Bay Colony passed a compulsory literacy law in 1642, just five years before the passage of the country's first compulsory education law. By the beginning of the twentieth century, almost every state had compulsory attendance laws. Another factor that drove widespread compulsory attendance was religious belief. If colonial children were taught to read, it was believed, they would not be deceived by the great deluder, Satan. Schools were set up to teach children how to read the *Bible.*

Learning to read has continued to be viewed as somewhat of a sacred tool. It has continued to be a primary reason for schooling, and children who do not learn to read by the third or fourth grade face considerable hardship throughout their school experience. The schools typically imply that the older children who have not learned to read are failures at schooling. The parents of the children who cannot read consider the schools to be the failures. Regardless of where the fault lies, children who do not learn to read well, regardless of how well they speak, move, or think, make up the vast majority of school dropouts; many then become dependent on the social system. Could schools have convinced these children that they are lazy, disabled, or just can't learn? What went wrong?

The focus on reading has continued for decades, long after the influence of print on our children has been supplanted by other media, specifically television, computer screens, and any other video-showing device. Will we someday hear claims that books are obsolete? Many schools have already gone "paperless," with affluent children purchasing their books on tablets. Some schools now provide schoolwide computers, one for each child.

Early childhood educators, however, are adopting a very different approach. For example, in 2012 the North Carolina Division of Child Development and Early Education passed a state law that limited "screen time" for children in childcare centers to a maximum of thirty minutes per day for children under the age of six. This included not only television but also computers, tablets, Smart Boards, and all other screen-based technology. Which develops more high-level thinking, watching a movie of a book or hearing a book read out loud? The second initiates far more brain activity than the first, so this effort by the state legislature is well founded.

It is interesting to note that in 1925, Thomas Edison predicted that the invention of the motion picture would revolutionize our educational system, supplanting the use of textbooks. Edison said, "In ten years [from 1925], as the principal medium of teaching, [textbooks] will be as obsolete as the horse and carriage are now. Visual education—the imparting of exact information through the motion picture camera—will be a matter of course in our schools."[1] Little did Edison know the power to resist change that is so deeply embedded in the schools.

Political factors also drove compulsory attendance. The fundamental purpose of education was to equip the citizenry to participate fully in (and believe in or trust) our democratic system of government. Large numbers of immigrants were arriving in the United States daily, many speaking different languages and with vastly different cultures. If democracy was to survive, surely some form of assimilation was needed. The burden fell to the public schools to ensure that this took place.

Throughout more recent history, policymakers have continued to add to the school curriculum, in many cases with the aim to help reduce social problems. Courses such as driver's education and health classes are examples. These policymakers erroneously believed that the school influence is the primary influence on a child's life and thus should be used to cure additional social ills.

Research has shown repeatedly that the community and the child's family life have far more influence on the child than the school.[2] However, over time, this myth of the influence of the school has caused society to look more and more to the education system to act as the primary societal change agent. In America, the democratic principle that all children, regardless of the home that they were born into, should have an opportunity to attend school drove our social and educational reform throughout the last century. In one respect, this drive was largely successful. Schools are considered a public good, and almost all children today, regardless of background, attend some form of school.

Attending school, it was believed, was the key to achieving equality and fairness for all in our country, partly by removing them from communities that harbored prejudice and inequity. Attending school at least assured that every child had the opportunity to achieve the American dream. "Children have a fundamental constitutional right to receive an equal opportunity to a free and appropriate education." Every state constitution in this country has laws that have some wording similar to this. So taxes were collected and schools were built. Then when all children did not take advantage of this opportunity, we passed laws to make them attend.

The last quarter of the twentieth century revealed one critical oversight in this plan—or perhaps it was actually another faulty assumption rather than an oversight. It was that children, by simply attending school—showing up for their free and appropriate education—would automatically learn. They did not. At least they did not all learn the standard local or state curricula at the same rate. Compulsory school attendance, while representing an incredible social investment in American human capital, was not the complete answer.

Today, looking again to the school system to help solve society's problems, some reform efforts suggest that the answer will be found in demanding that all students achieve particular standards at particular times in school. This will be ensured, they argue, by setting clear academic standards on a statewide and national level and testing students to be certain that all have achieved. Failure to achieve will be met with failure to move on through the system.

But this may be just another faulty assumption. What evidence is there that we can force all school learning, even with rewards and sanctions attached? Or, as some would argue, especially with rewards and sanctions attached! A decade of leaving no child behind left plenty. In addition, the negative consequences for failing to achieve these lofty goals once again fall squarely upon the schools and, more specifically, the teachers. Following our logical argument of the importance of brain stimulation and development from birth through the age of five, how much can a teacher really accomplish if a child has not had, and continues not to have, a developmentally stimulating environment outside of school hours?

Today, activists such as Alfie Kohn are calling on educators to boycott the recent movement toward widespread standardized testing. His research has shown that rewarding or punishing children can oftentimes discourage learning. Children are naturally curious, he argues, and it is practices such as standardized testing that can cause them to lose interest.[3] Even more so, what if the child's environment outside of school is unsafe and chronically stress-induced? How can a "one size fits all" education system possibly overcome such continuing damage?

This book does not argue against setting high standards and striving to help every child achieve them. In fact, this book is an attempt to help make that happen. However, are we again looking for the silver bullet in the wrong gun? The K–12 school system cannot and will not be able to solve the most recent educational and societal reform problem—the learning problem—within its present (and past) parameters. It can't because of another long-held faulty assumption. This is the assumption that what happens between kindergarten and high school graduation can change the brain enough, change the foundation already laid in the first five years of life, to produce high-powered, motivated learning by children and teens. History (and neuroscience) shows us that it cannot, any more than it can make sixty-two-year-old women bear multiple children, and certainly not by using the kind of instruction that takes place in many schools today.

Asking the present K–12 school system to change the organization of a child's brain wiring once it reaches kindergarten age is like building a skyscraper and then deciding to go back and add plumbing. The endeavor would be much easier and more likely to succeed if the plumbing is included in the original blueprint.

A TALE FROM THE TRENCHES: AN EARLY CHILDHOOD EDUCATOR'S STORY

My friend, Laura Pace, owned and operated two high-quality early childhood education programs for fifteen years. Over the years she began to see patterns in the types of children that were brought to her programs, and she learned to anticipate the challenges that her teachers would face with specific types of children.

One interesting pattern she noticed was that international families who would relocate to our city would bring their children into the program almost universally around the age of three, with the sole goal of enrollment to have their children learn to speak English fluently. They spoke only their native language at home, whether it be Chinese, Tagalog, Gujarati, or other world languages. These children would enroll with little to no spoken English, and, almost without exception, would be understandable within six months and fully fluent in a year. Their acquisition of English was remarkable, and it reinforces the studies that show how quickly children, at the earliest ages, acquire a new language.

The second type of student that she would see involved a much more difficult challenge. Each year a few parents who wanted to enroll their children in the "Transitional Kindergarten," which was a formal, yearlong kindergarten preparation program, would tour the sites. Normally the children would have been at home with a parent, or perhaps with a grandparent, and had been exposed to almost solely media-based learning. These children had literally been allowed to watch television, movies, and play on computers or tablets with no other formal learning structure and very little literacy in the home. Panicked, these families, most of whom were in the high socioeconomic category, would realize that their child needed to be "ready to learn" in one year.

So they would enroll them full time, up to fifty-five hours per week, at their school with the stated expectation that they would have them "kindergarten ready" in nine to twelve months. Her TK teachers were highly skilled practitioners with more than a decade of experience and four-year degrees in education. They were passionate early childhood educators who poured everything they had into these children. In addition, the ratio at the school averaged one teacher to every eleven children, so they had significantly more time with each individual student than a kindergarten teacher in a public school setting would typically have.

At the end of a full year in an intensive learning environment with additional resources sent home to continue the learning past the school day, they were, almost without exception, not able to bring these children up to the level that would be expected for kindergarten readiness. All of their efforts simply were not enough if the preceding four years had not provided the child with a developmentally appropriate stimulating environment. Simply put, their brains could not catch up that quickly.

CONSIDER THIS: A NEW PLAN

All children should have the right to a free and appropriate education. The issue that should be our concern is when that free and appropriate education needs to begin. The failure to acknowledge that this right begins at birth has had tragic consequences, including much discrimination in our society. The failure to maximize brain development in the first three to five years of life can rarely be overcome, and more and more research is confirming this notion.

We cannot go back and correct all of the damage done in the early years. We deny our children the right to life, liberty, and the pursuit of happiness when we do not ensure a maximally enriched, healthy, nurturing, and loving environment for them. In their earliest years of life, children deserve an environment that attends to their cognitive development along with their social, emotional, and physical development.

When children attend school they are typically given free textbooks, materials, tables, heat, air conditioning, and shelter. They even receive free supervision (and instruction) by a teacher with a college degree and, typically, some type of education certification or license. This adult has the legal authority to act in *loco parentis*, in place of the parent, for the better part of each weekday with the children. Some less-advantaged children are even provided with nutritionally balanced free breakfasts and lunches through the public school system. Others receive limited health care at no charge. How do our children become entitled to all this and more? By reaching a magical age of five or six years old, depending on the state in which they live.

Unfortunately, decades of research have shown us that when those five-and-six-year-olds arrive on the schoolhouse steps, they vary widely in background, preparation, and readiness. Some children come to kindergarten reading. Others do not know the names of colors and are nutritionally deprived or emotionally or physically abused. Why are some so advanced and others so underdeveloped cognitively? Is it genetic?

For the most part, educators, with the possible exception of kindergarten teachers, have not questioned seriously enough the reasons for this incredible range of ability, and the learning gap isn't closing. Year after year, from National Assessment of Education Progress scores to SAT scores, this fact is clear. Instead, this consistent disparity has served as a breeding ground for varying types of prejudice.

Lyndon Johnson must have been listening to the kindergarten teachers when he pushed the Elementary and Secondary Education Act of 1965 (ESEA) through Congress, bringing an infusion of cash and federal mandates into a basically state-run system of schools in America. The Head Start program was essentially born here, specifically, through an eight-week summer program administered by the Office of Economic Opportunity in the summers of 1965 and 1966. This was a preschool program specifically designed to improve the learning of children, unlike many day care programs of the time, which were simply designed to ensure health and safety.

Head Start also is one of the few programs using Title I funds that has shown some return on investment in the form of improved learning ability. Almost two decades of Title I research reveal that this is the only area where this federal assistance program (or any compensatory program) has borne significant fruit, and the younger the children, the better the results have been.[4]

So much research was quickly amassed in the 1990s pointing to the problem of the lack of preparation for school, advocates arose and the government had to take notice. In 1994, alongside the reauthorization of ESEA, the federal government began to fund on a limited basis a new program called Early Head Start. This program was designed to serve low-income households, including households with pregnant women, infants, and/or toddlers. In January 2001, an evaluation team summarized some of the outcomes of this program. At the age of two, the Early Head Start children had significantly higher scores in language and cognitive and socioemotional development than a control group. Their parents had much more and more accurate knowledge of infant/toddler development and behavior and used more positive parenting techniques. This knowledge also enabled them to be better prepared to support their child's education throughout their traditional educational experience.

WHERE ARE WE COMING FROM?

There were times throughout our history when childcare was provided for families; sometimes it was even free. But there was little expectation that the care be "educational." The roots of early childcare beyond the extended family can be traced to Boston in the middle 1800s. According to Sandra Scarr and Richard Weinberg, the earliest organized childcare setups "grew out of a welfare movement to care for immigrant and working class children while their impoverished mothers worked."[5] Day care for young children was established as "a social service to alleviate the child care problems of parents who had to work, and to prevent young children from wandering the streets."

Federally sponsored childcare emerged temporarily as a national necessity during the Great Depression and World War II. In the first case, unemployed citizens needed work, and childcare was seen as an employment opportunity. In the second case, with the nation's men off at war, women were seriously needed in the workforce. One way to increase the number of female workers was to provide care for their children, and additional childcare centers were founded. When World War II ended and the men came home, most of these centers closed. Some women, however, chose to remain in the workforce. Others returned home full time but still recognized a value in maintaining some kind of childcare assistance. This probably contributed to the rise seen in partial-day preschool programs after the war.

Preschools, however, were generally different from childcare facilities in several important ways. Preschools typically operated only two to four hours a day. Also, the parents of children in these programs expected that their children would be "taught" something or at least be exposed to something educational. Typically, these preschool programs were used by more affluent parents who didn't need full-day childcare but saw preschools as a type of enrichment.

The definition and use of the terms *preschool* and *day care* are still a bit ambiguous in some areas today, but early childhood education advocates emphasize strongly that it is "school" and not just "care." To some, day care still means full-day childcare, or "babysitting," as some parents call it. Working moms without the support of extended families may have little choice but to put their children in day care. Preschool or prekindergarten is typically a two-to-four-hour-a-day enrichment program for children whose parents can afford it. Today, the vast majority of mothers with young children are currently in some type of day care setting, and it is incumbent upon us to address the quality issues in these settings.

PARENT PERCEPTIONS

More and more affluent parents are opting for high-quality preschool programs, while working moms increasingly need the assurance and convenience of full-time care regardless of the quality of curriculum offered, if any. However, there still seems to be an unfortunate lack of concern or understanding about the ideal environments necessary for fostering the cognitive development of children across the board.

Today, poverty in early childhood is closely tied to low literacy rates and, later, the likelihood of incomplete schooling. On July 27, 2001, the White House sponsored a Summit on Early Childhood Cognitive Development. G. Reid Lyon, then chief of the Child Development and Behavior Branch of the National Institutes of Health, reported estimates that every forty-four seconds, a baby in this country is born into poverty. There is evidence that we have known for almost two centuries that poverty begets poverty and lower school achievement. However, Lyon also pointed out that in 1998, a quarter of our country's children without the noted risk factors (poverty, single-family homes, uneducated parents) also arrived at the kindergarten door not ready to learn.[6] Why is this?

Again, a faulty assumption may be a partial cause. Many people believe that more educated parents have a greater understanding of their children's cognitive development and are consequently better at meeting their children's cognitive needs. A national phone survey conducted in June and July of 2000 by Zero to Three, Civitas Initiative, and Brio Corporation found otherwise. Shockingly, 62 percent of parents surveyed said that children do not take in and react to the world around them until they are two months old or older. Almost a fourth of them said that this doesn't happen until the child is one year old or older. When parents were presented with a scenario that described a twelve-month-old turning TV buttons on the remote control off and on repeatedly, 39 percent said the child was behaving vengefully to get back at his or her parents. Research tells us that a child of this young age couldn't possibly be motivated by revenge and that most likely the child was exploring the cause and effect of the remote control buttons on the television set. After all, the remote control is separated from the television. It does not have to physically touch the set to affect the picture. This is illogical to a young child and is a phenomenon that certainly merits exploration.

Another sad fact was that 62 percent of parents said that educational television was "very effective." Sixty-one percent of these parents said it is appropriate to spank a child as a regular form of punishment. Thirty-seven percent expressed the opinion that this is also appropriate at age two and younger.[7] That a majority of parents would still see corporal punishment as a behavior tool despite widespread research stating that the children who are hit themselves by parents or caregivers are the children who then come to school and hit others is discouraging. The widespread parental misunderstandings of their young children beg for some kind of educational intervention for parents.

One of the popular "educationalese" phrases of recent times has been that we should provide a "seamless" education for children. To achieve this, the implication has been that we need help with transitions for children between school levels—elementary school to middle school to high school, and on to higher education. But this concept has not been systematically applied to the years between the maternity ward and the kindergarten classroom. This important oversight causes the rest of the educational fabric to unravel despite the efforts implemented through the K–12 system.

The five-year-old brain is already an intricately networked organ that any number of highly qualified, effective teachers or any amount of peer pressure cannot easily rewire if at all. Bruce Perry, speaking to the Houston Area Association for the Education of Young Children on September 8, 2001, said, "The five-year-old brain is 90 percent formed. Once it is organized, it is extremely hard to change or reorganize it." Perry used house construction as an analogy. Once a house is built and walls are in place and painted, it is difficult to go back through the building and reconstruct electrical wiring. However, with proper planning, those complex and critical functions can be put into place without difficulty at the outset.

Knowing this, we must ask some serious questions. What educational resources or instructions are new parents given when they leave the maternity ward at the hospital with their new baby? Why are parents sent home with pacifiers and free formula samples yet no developmental guidelines? Why are pediatricians routinely screening for eyesight and hearing and not testing for basic developmental learning milestones? Why is "school" generally denied children until the magic age of five or six? Why are many children given free meals when they arrive at school but are not assured of proper nutrition in the earliest years of their lives, when nutrition is so much more important for brain development? Which is more critical for development: that a high school teenager take physical education classes, or that a newborn's parents have up-to-date knowledge and assistance on how to foster their baby's social, emotional, and cognitive development?

THE RIGHT TO INFORMATION

Most parents have high hopes for their newborn baby, regardless of race, gender, religion, socioeconomic level, or any number of other factors. Parents naturally aspire to success and happiness for all of their children. Many parents even go to great lengths to help provide optimal environments for their young; some even leave their home countries and risk their lives to provide these opportunities for their young children.

As discussed earlier, Hart and Risley documented the language skills of children coming from ten-million-word homes verses thirty-million-word homes. Thirty-million-word moms generally raise thirty-million-word children, and ten-million-word moms generally raise ten-million-word children, as their research shows. What if a parent comes to the realization that she is a ten-million-word caregiver instead of a thirty-million-word caregiver? What can they do or where can they turn to be sure that their child becomes a thirty-million-word child? How do they access what they need to provide the best start in life for the cognitive development of their baby?

Presently in the United States, the availability of these resources is significantly dependent upon the socioeconomic status or the education level of the parents and the availability of services in the area. As has been the case for generation after generation, the wealthy find or buy enrichment for their babies' environments, and these children typically arrive at the kindergarten door considerably more ready to learn—that is, ready to learn what schools teach—than the poor.

If the ten-million-word mom does not have enough wealth or personal knowledge to provide an enriched environment for her baby, her child does not arrive at the kindergarten door ready to learn the curriculum that schools teach in the ways in which they teach. This has been clearly documented by study after study. Research also shows that only in the rarest of cases do the ten-million-word kindergarteners ever become thirty-million-word high schoolers. We are caught in a self-perpetuating spiral that can only be broken by focusing on a child's first years of life.

One problem could be the lack of access to information and goods and services for young children and the parents and caregivers of young children. All new mothers, and certainly the caregivers of infants, need free information on how to create an enriched environment for their babies. In addition, rather than simply attempting to provide for the minimal survival needs of children, society should be offering assistance to maximize the development of these young children.

All children should have a right to a maximally enriched environment, and all parents and caregivers should have a right to obtain information and services that benefit their performance as critically important baby teachers. This is at least as important as teenagers having access to high schools.

Perhaps some state and/or referral secondary school funding should be diverted to the early years. The first high schools were built in the United States in the 1820s. However, a "free and appropriate education" at this time did not include a high school diploma or even an opportunity to earn one. Until the 1890s, secondary school was restricted to the sons of doctors, lawyers, clergy, or anyone else who could afford it.

The curriculum focused on preparation for university training, primarily for the three recognized professions: law, medicine, and theology. Massachusetts passed a law in 1827 that mandated that towns of four thousand or more create a high school, but not all complied. It was not until the 1900s that universal high school education in the United States became a reality and has since become an expectation for all.

Some policymakers today suggest obstetricians become the focal point, claiming that it is their role to "educate" new mothers. Licensed obstetricians have up-to-date training in helping mothers give birth safely. Many also offer information on providing for babies' safety and physical development. However, obstetricians are generally not experts in babies' cognitive development, and they are not equipped to provide the needed training and assistance for this type of education. In fact, some rarely, if ever, see the mothers and children after birth. This important job is far too vast for the present system.

In addition, many new mothers, particularly poor ones, do not even have access to minimal services from any kind of doctor, including a pediatrician. If not through obstetricians, and if we have no guarantee that young children will have caregivers who can provide quality developmental information beyond just the minimal health and safety information, where does a new mother or caregiver turn? How can we morally justify the fact that all children do not have access to quality health care that includes cognitive developmental guidance during the most critical formative years of their lives?

Perhaps every maternity ward should have a parent resource room where information and training is free to all parents or caregivers—a baby library. The adults who affect the cognitive development of children so critically, the baby teachers, could come here regularly to have their questions answered and obtain important resources on an ongoing basis. The federal and local government, sometimes in partnership with businesses, is presently busy trying to provide computers and Internet access to every schoolchild in America. Perhaps a computer and Internet connection should be the birthright of every newborn.

Presently it is generally the more affluent baby teachers who have personal computers and Internet access in their homes. The poor are left without access to this reservoir of potential enrichment for their children in their homes, although this is often readily available at public libraries. The brains of the rich children generally get richer, and the brains of the poor children are often left with poorer-quality environments. This scenario can lead to increased draws on social programs a generation later, as longitudinal studies have shown.

The Family and Medical Leave Act passed in the United States in 1993 was designed to give workers time off to nurture their newborns, to be baby teachers. The act also provided workers time to tend to sick relatives or deal with their own major illnesses. While this law guaranteed that employees would not lose their jobs, it did not provide any financial compensation for the lost time at work. An estimated 2.7 million Americans have wanted to take advantage of this Act but been financially unable to do so.[8] In many states infants cannot be enrolled into a licensed child care program until at least four to six weeks after birth, so what is a mother living at or below the poverty level to do?

Many states in the United States have been investigating ways to remedy this situation. One suggestion has been to tap into states' disability funding. New York, New Jersey, California, Rhode Island, and Hawaii use some of this money for women on maternity leave. Other states are considering expanding the program to include fathers or other caregivers. Still other states are exploring the possibility of using unemployment funds to pay for leaves of absence for infant care. Polls show general support for this type of social assistance.

HATS OFF TO HEAD START

An important step that was taken in the past decade was the passage of the Improving Head Start for School Readiness Act of 2007. This act passed with strong bipartisan support, indicating an increased awareness of the need for more assistance in the early childhood years, and putting in place stronger accountability measures to increase or sustain ongoing high quality in Head Start classrooms or centers.

Administered under the Office of Head Start (OHS), a road map was established setting forth the vision and priorities of the OHS and articulating this through a stronger Child Outcomes Framework and a more accessible Training and Technical Assistance network. In 2010, unannounced visits began in Head Start classrooms and centers to ensure compliance with policies set forth, which resulted in stronger and clearer regulations for the programs.

Then in 2012, a policy that the National Head Start website claims is "arguably the biggest and most impactful reform" even to Head Start, is that Head Start programs that have been in existence but have not proved a high level of service/performance for young children over time are no longer automatically assured that their grants will be renewed. In addition, any provider in the community, even those who have not had prior Head Start grants, can apply for these new five-year Head Start grants.

Much like the infusion of charter school legislation in states to influence the traditional public K–12 system, this latest change in the early childhood landscape brought about by the 2007 Act may provide competition that could in turn increase the quality of existing Head Start programs. Some researchers claim it already has.

Other changes brought about by the 2007 Act included increased education levels for caregivers that work with young children. By the end of 2012, at least 50 percent of Head Start teachers at a center are required to hold a bachelor's or other advanced degree in early childhood or a related area. This was based on research indicating that teachers with BA degrees or higher produced better outcomes for the young children in their care. Also, 100 percent of teachers who do not have a BA were directed to obtain an associate's degree by 2011.

Qualifications were also increased for teacher assistants. All of these increased education requirements were passed with the hope that the quality of the educational environments for young children would be improved. Finally, the Act required Head Start centers to enter into Memorandums of Agreement with their local school districts, probably in an attempt to better bridge the gap toward a more seamless entry into kindergarten. Since so many of the recommendations of this Act have only been fully implemented recently, the jury is still out on whether this will improve learning environments for our youngest citizens.

CHILD'S PLAY

Combining the research results in child development and outcomes of our education system, it would appear that a free and appropriate education should begin at birth. But what would an ideal early childhood curriculum look like? One activity that young children engage in often and quite naturally is play. Play is enjoyable for children, but it is also an important way that cognitive development is advanced and through which young children learn.

Play is generally defined as the casual interaction between very young children and their environment. Children definitely learn through enjoyable, engaging, sometimes challenging and sometimes relaxing interactions. All of these terms are used to describe play. Another important characteristic of play is choice. Children usually play with whatever they choose in their environment that is accessible. It is the adult's responsibility to ensure that the play environment is safe and ideally developmentally stimulating so that the play will result in learning or improved neural circuitry.

Another critical element of play is fantasy. Through fantasy play, young children can act out the inner working of the brain that cannot yet be acted upon in reality. Children can become frogs or firefighters or anything they can imagine through fantasy play. High-quality early childhood education programs encourage this type of play through providing a location in every classroom from twelve months of age and older, often called "Dramatic Play." The shelves are stocked with dress-up clothes from princess to police, athlete to chef, with many and varying props.

There is also typically a play kitchen and, as the children grow older, the environment grows richer with lifelike dolls of multiple ethnicities, strollers, play food, pots and pans, washers and dryers, and other common household items. Children are not formally "taught" in this center, but rather they teach each other as they act out familiar family routines or pretend to be someone else. It is a fascinating location for an adult caregiver to just sit and listen to children's interactions and occasionally interject with questions to stimulate additional verbal interactions.

When the environmental setup is thoughtful and purposefully designed, children are "taught" through play. One important part of the organization of some play environments is to promote the establishment of meaning and understanding in the child's world, using themes where possible and showing connectedness at every opportunity. The environment may also have multiple levels to increase the complexity of design.

For example, a green plastic frog and a green lily pad and a green bucket can propel a storyteller toward a compelling explanation of ecology, colors, full, empty, and everything else an active imagination can generate. Preceding or following up this activity with a trip to a pond will add much more depth and completeness through giving the topic more authentic sense and meaning for the young child. There are many more ideas for increasing complexity in the young child's environment in the final chapters of this book.

Lev Vygotsky's writings reveal some fascinating insights into the function of play in child development. First, while most preschool teachers agree that play is the primary activity of toddlers and is typically abandoned in elementary school, Vygotsky claims that fantasy play remains an important element of the elementary years, and perhaps even longer. He believed that through play, children are capable of achieving more mature behavior than in other settings.

One example is learning the concept of patience through the behavior of waiting. A young child who cannot wait for most activities within the classroom environment may exhibit much more patience in fantasy play (and may need more practice of this!). For example, a little girl pretending that she is a napping baby may be able to wait for her playmate mommy to cook dinner before waking her up. A little boy who is pretending to be an injured puppy may be able to wait far longer for the "veterinarian" to arrive than he can wait to play a ball game. These skills of patience and persistence are moves of higher-level abilities that every skilled early childhood educator looks to develop, and parents should as well.

Vygotsky points out that fantasy play helps children practice self-regulation that they cannot achieve in their real worlds. Thoughtful caregivers can design environments where these difficult-to-manage behaviors become more manageable and increase the strength of the cognitive structures within the brain that regulate them. Remember, neurons that fire together, wire together.

Vygotsky further notes that play provides ways for children to separate their thoughts from actual objects or actions through developing the use of symbolic props. The stick horse is not a real horse, but it serves the imaginary purpose. In fact, even a broom or a simple stick will do. Vygotsky proposes that toys such as generic dishes, pots, and pans provide better fodder for the imagination than plastic food. The children can cognitively explore much wider imaginary boundaries with less-specific props. When children use objects as representations of real life, it is theorized that they are developing the foundation for later use of symbols such as numbers and letters. Any mom or preschool teacher can tell you that children can count objects long before they can recognize *2* as a symbol representing two items.

Some propose that in today's preschool world more adult intervention may be needed to assist with or launch the most basic play. The influence of television and videos on the minds of children can interfere with their own creativity by replacing it with prepackaged programming. If a teacher notices that one group of children is more intent upon acting out superheroes from a television program than stories of their own invention, intervention may be necessary. The teacher can use questions to suggest alternative scenarios that require the children to use their own imaginations instead of the programmed television scenes. "But where is our superhero going? I believe he must be hungry after fighting off all of those villains. What is he going to eat for dinner? What can we fix for our superhero to eat? Perhaps the superhero can head for a different planet tonight after dinner?"

In any event, adult intervention can be critical in helping to scaffold the learning in the brain that child's play can promote. Television watching does not help children build those skills and can, in fact, hinder it. Intervening in a child's play with the direct purpose of developing further knowledge or brain development in that child is teaching. It is also much more effective in most cases than simply administering a "time out" or some other form of punishment. Most disciplinary actions can be transformed into teachable moments through adult intervention and explanation.

Today we know that teaching and learning take place through play and that play is an important method of preschool instruction. But there is a wide range of activity that can fall into this category. Sometimes play with dolls and trucks can lead to scaffolding into more complex cognitive development; sometimes it does not. However, based on Vygotsky's theory, we have an opportunity to guide play toward this higher level of development through planning and careful observation.

"Developmentally appropriate" teaching in the earliest years has generally included a presumption that teachers should wait until a desired skill or behavior is observed in a child before providing activities to encourage that desired skill or behavior. The work of Vygotsky and the additional research presented in this book are intended to show that this is too late. Teachers should be providing children with activities just beyond what they are capable of on their own but still within what they can accomplish with assistance.

Teachers should be helping children to operate at a higher level within their zones of proximal development. This increased complexity will yield more complex learning as it nurtures neural networks and wires the brain for even higher-level learning later on. In addition, we must not underestimate the abilities or possibilities of the infant brain. Who would ever recommend that it is developmentally appropriate to try to teach babies three or four different languages at once? What developmental program recommends that children be trilingual by the age of three? However, we now know that children are capable of accomplishing this. How much more could they accomplish given a complex environment, a different social setting, and a genuinely developmentally appropriate expectation? Most important of all, a child needs a deeply thoughtful, insightful, and curious baby teacher also focused on learning and seeing through the eyes of a young child.

A SOCIAL PLACE IN HISTORY

In his interesting book, *Theories of Development: Concepts and Applications*, William Crain spells out a number of social-historical theories and their implications for cognitive development. We know that Lev Vygotsky's views were influenced by Karl Marx (1818–1883). Marx's writings about human nature were not extensive, but he did emphasize that one must describe human nature in a social-historical context. For example, while he saw that people were distinguished from other animals by their language, use of tools, and capacity for technological production, he pointed out that the conditions under which these activities occur have changed throughout history.

For example, the working conditions of the medieval artisan differed greatly from those of a nineteenth-century factory worker. These different conditions themselves altered the societal changes.[9] Vygotsky took this to the level of the child's developing brain and argued that learning itself changes a child's learning each and every moment. (It also changes the neural activity, which Vygotsky could not have known.)

Marx saw history as a process of continual conflicts and resolutions. New ideas, forces, and methods would arise, causing conflict with the established social system. Crain gives the example of the overthrow of the feudal by the free-enterprise system. A new kind of factory emerged, giving rise to a class of capitalists. These capitalists' desires and new opportunities to make more money for themselves put a strain on the existing social order. The result was genuine systemic change. In summary, changes in behavior begat changes in social structures and systems, which begat more and different changes in behavior, and so on. Social change accelerated behavioral change.

Could the new research pouring out of neuroscience labs today help spur a similarly radical systemic change in our present-day education system? Much as the invention of the printing press changed our social views of literacy from a tool reserved for the elite aristocracy to one accessible and encouraged for the masses, the information revolution necessitates much higher-performing minds managing and using much more information than ever before. The brain can rise to the occasion, given the appropriate early childhood environment.

We know that an enriched early learning environment generally leads to a vastly more successful school life and, in turn, adult life. Most prisoners and welfare recipients were not "A" students throughout school. We also know that the rich enrich. Children from homes in which the mother can afford high-quality care or can afford to stay home with her children, read to them, and take them to see the world and buy them every complex, enriching educational product that comes on the market are often the bluebirds of kindergartens today.

However, these people have become a minority in this country, and the gap between the abilities of rich and poor children at age six is tremendous and growing; not necessarily through any ill will by more affluent upper-class parents hoping for their child to be "better" than another, but through their love of their offspring and hope for them to maximize their potential.

Why should the babies of members of a society with more wealth have more right or access to enrichment than those who are less fortunate to develop their brains and capacities fully? Today, we insist, often through legislation and regulation, that our K–12 schools be equal, focus on equity, and that educators treat students the same. But children today do not enter schools equally equipped. Is equal equitable? Certainly not if we wait until kindergarten to begin teaching our children.

The information revolution is changing society in profound ways. It is also creating a society in which all members need a much higher level of thinking capacity and overall mental functioning than in prior generations. Our culture and consequently our needs are changing, not unlike the changing needs of a capitalistic system evolving from a feudal one. To meet these changing needs, our views about babies and education must change.

On a moral level and on the basis of the priority placed on a free and appropriate education for the citizenry, parents and caregivers should have free access to anything they need to create an ideal environment for their babies' brains. This would include everything from parent and caregiver training to resources at least as plentiful as our high school teachers.

A NEW NAME: FROM DAY CARE TO PRESCHOOL

After World War II as mothers remained in the workforce and an increase in the need for care of young children arose, the terminology generally referred to for taking care of young children in mother's absence was *childcare*. The name alone suggests that it was the minimal health and safety standards of young children that were the target of this service, rather than their cognitive development and learning.

Over the last decade, the term *childcare* is being replaced by the term *preschool*. For those working in early childhood education, preschool is a term far better for indicating that more than just the physical safety of the child is the focus. Interestingly, this new word for taking care of young children is still typically reserved for three- and four-year-olds rather than infants and toddlers. *Preschool* means literally "before school," and younger learners are still often left out of the system thought.

As preschool gained wider acceptance, an additional concern that arose is the lack of quality found in many childcare centers and the lack of education of our important baby teachers. According to Sharon Kagan and Nancy Cohen, the majority of our country's day care settings are presently poor to mediocre in quality and compromise children's long-term development.[10] A democratic society that views its very survival as dependent upon an educated citizenry has a responsibility to provide high-quality learning environments to its young children. Continuing to ignore the fact that parents and early childcare providers are the most important educators in our country is an embarrassing oversight with tragic consequences.

BABY TEACHERS

Babies' brains need teaching. They all need and deserve exceptional baby teachers. We can only meet the cognitive developmental needs of babies through greatly increasing the complexity of curriculum in our cribs and beyond and improving the quality of our day care centers and all early childhood environments wherever they occur and in whatever configurations they happen to exist. This includes increasing and improving the education levels of the baby teachers, or, as some are presently called, caregivers. A basic paradigm shift is needed to change the view of the caregiver to one of a critically important baby teacher.

We also take pride in viewing our society as compassionate. There are well intentioned as well as selfish reasons for providing a free and appropriate education to our children. But we also take care of our elderly. We provide Social Security and Medicare to name a few of the ways we ensure some kind of care in our days of increased vulnerability. Why do we do this for the elderly and not the newborn? (Could it be because the elderly vote?)

Consider this: Perhaps a free and appropriate education should begin upon the discovery that a woman is pregnant. She is granted part-time or full-time leave from her job (with pay and return rights) and enters School for Baby Teachers, or Mother School. She learns with other moms from diverse social and ethnic backgrounds the very best practices for giving birth to and nurturing a healthy baby. She relaxes, reads, and discusses issues with other moms, learning how to become the best possible baby teacher. The bonding of mothers sharing the experience of childbirth and motherhood surpasses any diversity training programs I have ever encountered in any educational system or other organization.

Prejudices will not have the opportunity to take root among these mothers.

After childbirth, the education continues at Baby Teacher School. A network of mothers, fathers, educators, and health care workers is already set up to ensure that every child receives nurturing and enrichment each day. The environment is filled with complex language (moms may even learn new languages in Mother School), complex music, and a multitude of visual, tactile, taste, and other sensory experiences created by developmental experts and implemented by the baby teachers.

After the first year, options may include early preschool if the mothers return to work. However, the environment continues to be rich and nurturing to the cognitive as well as overall physical development of the child. Children are taught to question, hypothesize, predict, discover, and reflect on their environments, interactions, and learning. After all, studies show that high-quality early childhood providers can be as good as moms in most instances, even for social and emotional development. As these diverse parents and their children create new communities among themselves, learning abounds for all. A new social fabric is created by the understanding brought about through the networking of these mothers, fathers, caregivers, and the children.

ONE MODEL: THE NORTH CAROLINA STORY

In the early 1990s, at the onset of a push for standards and accountability in our nation's schools, North Carolina's then governor, Jim Hunt, took notice. The call rang out that too many children were beginning kindergarten unprepared for the kind of learning that was expected of them, and the schools were having difficulty addressing the problem. In 1993, Hunt organized a task force on early childhood issues to explore the problem. The North Carolina Smart Start program grew out of those discussions, and legislation was passed in July 1993 authorizing the program and allocating funds.

Smart Start was designed as a locally driven initiative to ensure the school readiness of all children. Readiness has been defined as all children arriving at kindergarten healthy and ready to succeed. The initiative was to be administered by the North Carolina Department of Health and Human Services. A charge went out to communities to come together and find out how best to meet the needs of their youngest children and their families.

Planning boards were set up and empowered to think broadly. The boards were also given great flexibility to make whatever decisions they deemed necessary concerning the services that could be provided with the over $3 million in funds that had been allocated for this purpose by the state legislature. They were also charged with developing ways to evaluate the long-term benefits of the initiative.

These community-based planning groups found that they couldn't identify just one problem inhibiting school readiness. Rather, they found a broadly interconnected set of issues, such as poverty, work-family strains, lack of parent education, and inadequate access to basic general services such as health care and transportation.[11] By late 1998, all one hundred counties in the state had received some level of funding for their locally established programs.

From these local efforts, incredible partnerships have been formed among a vast array of social services. The types of partnerships include the networking of early childhood education facilities, preschools, public schools, family support services, and health services, including dental, vision, mental health, and immunization services. Programs already up and running, such as Head Start programs, special needs providers, and other nonprofits, were all coordinated with the Smart Start effort. Smart Start funds also provide for salary supplements to early childhood teachers, scholarships to continue teacher and director education, information packages for patients on maternity wards, scholarships for students to attend preschool, and assistance to literally hundreds of supporting organizations.

Some of the county partnerships have even partnered with each other. For example, under the remarkable leadership of Dr. Dean Clifford, former director of the Forsyth Early Childhood Partnership (FECP), other county partnerships contracted with FECP to handle the financial and accounting services for their partnerships. Other counties share resources and technical help. Consequently, both internal and external learning communities became networked.

How is it all working? A Smart Start evaluation team set up at the Frank Porter Graham Child Development Center at the University of North Carolina at Chapel Hill (SmartStart@unc.edu) found that children who have been Smart Start participants have higher school-readiness scores than any other group. Childcare professionals are now significantly better educated, more experienced, and better paid than when the program began. There is also evidence of less early childhood teacher turnover.

Parents from the parent-support programs have increased the time they spend reading to their children and have involved them in more stimulating intellectual development activities; their children now score on average at or above age expectancy. Participating childcare facilities across the state have significantly improved in quality.

The Smart Start program is not without its critics. In the early years of implementation, audits across the state found some counties having difficulties with financial management. As with the charter school movement, another innovative reform initiative in the same state, a pattern of educators possessing weak skills as financial managers emerged. Professional development for leaders on the business functions of educational efforts followed, and more recent audits have shown improvement.

So far the program evaluations of the educational and service components of the North Carolina Smart Start programs show greatly improved outcomes for children and families in Smart Start communities. The program has also influenced other states to design programs, such as South Carolina's First Steps program, and even other countries, as representatives from the British House of Commons, visited Durham County Smart Start as a model for starting a similar program in England.

ANOTHER MODEL: THE NEW JERSEY STORY

More than three decades ago, a class-action suit (*Abbott v. Burke*) against the commissioner of education of New Jersey was initiated by a group of low-income parents concerned that their children were not receiving a thorough and efficient education as compared with their counterparts living in wealthier neighboring communities. In May 1998, the New Jersey Supreme Court finally rendered its decision, mandating the implementation of whole school reform in elementary, middle, and secondary schools; provision of full-day kindergarten for all five-year-olds; and establishment of high-quality half-day preschool programs for all three- and four-year-old residents by the 1999 to 2000 school year in twenty-eight (later thirty) school districts having a large population of low-income families. The commissioner of education was charged with developing regulations to codify the reforms. Included in these regulations was the directive to school districts to use licensed community programs for early care and education in an effort to avoid duplication of services.

In order to ensure educational quality, then Governor Christine Todd Whitman established a special Early Childhood Advisory Council to provide recommendations for program design. In addition, the state Department of Education convened a group of experts to develop program "expectations" for an early childhood program to provide opportunities for growth and development. The expectations were then identified as "standards for programs in early childhood education" following a subsequent court decision. The standards were then aligned with the Core Curriculum Content Standards in order to create a continuum of educational objectives from preschool through high school.

Driven by studies indicating that children who had experienced high-quality preschools were better prepared for academic success, the primary intention of the Abbott early childhood mandate was to ensure that three- and four-year-old children were "education ready" when they entered kindergarten as part of their constitutional right to a thorough and efficient education. In order to meet the definition of a high-quality preschool, Abbott programs had to follow these rules:

- Class size must be limited to fifteen children, with a teacher and an aide.
- Teachers already employed in early childhood programs must earn a specialized P–3 certificate.
- New hires must be certified in early childhood education.
- Districts must provide a master teacher for every twenty classrooms to coordinate the delivery of programs and ensure consistency of delivery throughout the district.
- An appropriate curriculum tied to the kindergarten curriculum must be used.
- A family worker must be provided for every forty families to deliver social services and parenting information.
- Districts must execute a carefully planned outreach program to inform all parents of eligible children of the availability of preschool services.

- Professional development opportunities must be made available to all classroom staff.
- Health and nutritional guidance must be a component of the program.
- Transportation must be available to accommodate all families in need.

What began as half-day, ten-month programs later evolved into full-day, full-year programs upon the completion of an assessment to determine the specialized needs of the children of each district.

The early care and education community united to monitor the execution of the Abbott decision. Known as the Early Care and Education Coalition (ECEC), a group of representatives from advocacy groups, early childhood associations, higher education, resources and referral agencies, funders, and others have the difficult job of providing guidance to policymakers as they steer the implementation of the Abbott mandate.

Funding for the Abbott preschool programs is delivered through a partnership between the departments of education and human services. The department of education funds the "education portion" of the day, or the six-hour-day-180-day year, while the Department of Human Services funds the extended-day-extended-year portion. Funding levels somewhat vary from district to district.

It has been challenging for community providers to meet the standards, especially regarding teacher salaries and benefits, because of a lack of funding overall. In addition, the issue of directors' salaries has been difficult because of varying credentials and nebulous job criteria. The adequacy of facilities remains an ongoing challenge as the state struggles to ensure that community programs have access to public funds to provide Abbott services. In the meantime, districts are eligible for funds to create and renovate early childhood program facilities in an effort to upgrade quality. Although facility standards have been created by the ECEC as well, they have not yet been fully adopted by the state.

More positively, however, the Abbott preschool programs have offered more comprehensive services to children and families within the districts. Staffs have been provided with scholarship opportunities in order to earn the required certifications. Universities have risen to the challenge and have designed a specialized credential to upgrade the qualifications of the teachers in the preschool classrooms. Legislators have become more sensitized to the needs of young children and have become advocates for appropriations to support scholarships and have developed the Commission for Early Care and Education to oversee the implementation of the Abbott decision.

In 2003, the state brought together a diverse group of stakeholders to design preschool teaching and learning standards for the state. This was codified in chapter 13A of the New Jersey Administrative Code, Elements of High Quality Preschool Programs. Then in 2010, they revised their guidelines for school districts, private providers, and Head Start agencies in the state to help plan and implement their standards. The state standards continue to require that preschool classrooms should not exceed fifteen children in a classroom and that classrooms must be sufficiently large (950 square feet) and organized for preschool children. Their standards differ significantly from those for elementary school children.

MORE NEWS FROM NORTH CAROLINA

A longitudinal study called the Abecedarian Project was conducted by the Frank Porter Graham Child Development Center at the University of North Carolina at Chapel Hill. It began over three decades ago with 111 infants from low-income families. Of those, fifty-seven were assigned to a high-quality childcare setting (preschool) and the other fifty-four to a nontreated group. The preschool program was for children in early infancy and continued year-round. Twenty-one years later, 104 of the people from the original group were assessed. Below are highlights of the study:

- More than twice as many children who received intervention attended college than those who did not.
- Young adults in the intervention group were two years older, on average, when their own first children were born.
- Young adults who received early educational intervention had significantly higher mental test scores from toddlerhood through age twenty-one than those who were untreated.
- Enhanced language skills in the children probably increased the effects of early intervention on cognitive skills performance.

- Reading achievement scores were consistently higher for individuals with early intervention. Enhanced cognitive skills appeared to positively affect reading achievement.
- Mathematics achievement showed a pattern similar to reading, with treated individuals earning higher scores, though the differences were moderate in contrast to the major effects on reading scores. Enhanced cognitive functioning appeared to positively affect results. (Upon contacting Joseph Sparling, who helped design the curriculum for this program, I learned that no special music component was present, although there was simple song singing and art.)
- Those with treatment were significantly more likely to still be in school at age twenty-one—40 percent of the intervention group compared to 20 percent of the control group.
- A significant difference was found in the percentage of young adults who ever attended a four-year college. About 35 percent of the young adults in the intervention group had either graduated from or were at the time of the assessment attending a four-year college or university. In contrast, only about 14 percent of the control group was in these categories.
- Employment rates were higher for the treatment group (65 percent) than for the control group (50 percent), although the difference was not statistically significant.

The Abecedarian Project differed from most other childhood projects in that it began in early infancy, whereas other programs generally have begun at age two or older, and treated children had five years of exposure to early education in a high-quality childcare setting, whereas most other programs were of shorter duration. Francis Campbell, the principal investigator, said, "The study clearly emphasizes the importance of providing an enriched learning environment for children from the very beginning of life. Every child deserves a good start in an environment that is safe, healthy, emotionally supportive, and cognitively stimulating."[12]

Over the history of the United States, we have witnessed two tremendous federal investments in human capital that, it could be argued, have had big payoffs for the country. Compulsory education for all children could be viewed as one. The second occurred after World War II through the National Defense Education Act of 1958 and the GI Bill. The expansive effort to rebuild colleges and universities ushered in a trend of greatly increased university attendance nationwide. We ensured that not just the sons of doctors and lawyers but also the daughters of farmers and machinists could attend institutions of higher learning. Both of these efforts cost billions of public dollars, but they have probably brought trillions more to our gross national product. A serious investment in our youngest children today could be the greatest human investment of all.

NOTES

1. Neil Baldwin, *Edison: Inventing the Century* (Chicago: University of Chicago Press, 1995), 371.

2. Margaret C. Wang, Geneva D. Haertel, and Herbert J. Walbert, "Toward a Knowledge Base for School Learning," *Review of Education Research* 63, no. 3 (Fall 1993): 149–94.

3. Alfie Kohn, *Punished by Rewards* (New York: Houghton Mifflin, 1993).

4. David J. Hoff, "Chapter 1 Aid Failed to Close Learning Gap," *Education Week*, April 2, 1997, 1, 29, http://www.edweek.org/ew/articles/1997/04/02/27title.h16.html.

5. Sandra Scarr and Richard Weinberg, "The Early Childhood Enterprise: Care and Education of the Young," *American Psychologist* 41 (1986): 1140–41.

6. G. Reid Lyon, summary of comments presented at the White House Summit on Early Childhood Cognitive Development, July 27, 2001, http://www.ed.gov/PressReleases/07-2001/07272001_lyon.html.

7. J. Ronald Lally, Claire Lerner, and Erica Lurie-Hurvitz, "National Survey Reveals Gaps in the Public's and Parents' Knowledge about Childhood Development," *Young Child* 56, no. 2 (March 2001): 49–53.

8. Debra Rosenberg, "We Have to Sacrifice," *Newsweek*, August 27, 2001, 46.

9. William Crain, *Theories of Development* (Upper Saddle River, NJ: Prentice Hall, 2000), 216.

10. Sharon L. Kagan and Nancy E. Cohen, "Not by Chance," executive summary, The Quality 2000 Initiative (New Haven: Yale University Press, 1997), 2.

11. For an in-depth look at the evolution of Smart Start, see http://www.smartstart.org/.

12. www.fpg.iunc.edu/~abc.

9

CURRICULAR CONSIDERATIONS

Treat children as they are, you make them worse—treat them as they
potentially could be, you make them better.

—Goethe

The following two chapters offer parents and other early childhood educators some practical and effective ways to provide the babies and young
children in their care with increased complex stimulation appropriate to
the development of the child. The activities and suggestions are generally
divided into categories by sense for the first year of life: hearing, sight,
smell, touch, and taste. However, as is so often the case in real-life experiences, many of the activities overlap between categories.

In the first few days of life, your baby will find his mother and father
and others who are regularly present in his environment incredibly stimulating to his senses and, thus, his mind. Everything about this outside
world is new and interesting, and baby is taking it all in. The data arriving
at the newly born brain's doorstep will cause neural firings to form networks by the trillions. Each body has its own special scent, which the
baby will learn to recognize within hours after birth.

The baby will recognize his mother's and possibly others' voices immediately. Talk to him using his name. You can immediately begin reciting the rhythmic rhymes you spoke to him when he could hear but not see
you from the womb. Also, ask him questions as you hold or touch him.
"Bobby, can you see me now? See where Mommy's voice comes from?
This is Mommy's mouth. This is Bobby's mouth."

Gentle, slow, repetitive stroking of your baby's head and back area right from birth can give your baby a sense of calm. Doctors report that this soft, rhythmic stroking helps regulate the infant's breathing and even helps the intestinal functions to begin operating. (Be prepared for that first urination or bowel movement as baby lets you know that he works and shows off his new abilities. Also remember, that first bowel movement will normally be black in color.)

Always be sure to be sensitive to your baby's engagement or lack thereof when interacting with him and stimulating him. Does he appear to be enjoying the activity? If not, discontinue the activity and move to one that promotes comfort and security. The brain is virtually tireless when engaged in something it perceives as meaningful, but we all need downtime, especially babies.

It is not recommended that you strive for constant stimulation during every one of your baby's waking moments. He will need the opportunity to seek out interests for himself in addition to those interesting activities that you provide for him. Most importantly, be responsive to your baby rather than placing expectations for the baby to be responsive to you or your schedule within reason.

EXPECTING

When parents find out that they are going to have a child, they are commonly referred to as "expecting." Expecting what? Expecting a baby to be born. And in the vast majority of cases, it is born. Then parents expect their children to eventually sit, stand up, walk, and talk. And again, in the vast majority of cases, they do. Only children who have specific neurological or physiological problems fail to achieve these expected developmental milestones.

Much research has been conducted over the years on the role of expectations for children, much of it in schools. In the late 1960s, Robert Rosenthal and Lenore Jacobson released results of a study they conducted involving teacher expectations.[1] They told teachers that certain students in their classrooms, selected randomly, should be expected to make above-average intellectual gains over the course of the year. The students did, in fact, make above-average gains, apparently based on nothing more than the teachers' expectations for them to do so. This self-fulfilling prophecy was termed the Pygmalion Effect (after the mythological king, Pygmalion, who created a statue and then "expected" it into real life). The researchers wrote a book with the same title and received tremendous media attention. Expectations matter!

There are many different ways that expectations can be relayed between teacher and student, parent and child. Some are negative, and many are quite subtle. Some involve no more than a facial expression, the raising of a brow. It is critical that parents and caregivers approach their interactions with an attitude of joy and hope as well as realistic expectations. Leave all judgment and criticism and despair outside of the nursery. If you experience a feeling of disappointment concerning the development of your child, check your own motives.

Note that helping children to accomplish what they are already happily attempting is a far cry from pressuring children. Development is not a race, it is a process—the process of living. The parents and caregivers must see themselves in the role of facilitators to be good baby teachers.

MISUNDERSTANDING THE MISUNDERSTANDINGS

Can parents and caregivers push their children too much in attempts to stimulate their brain development? The answer is "yes." This is largely because of misunderstandings of exactly how to stimulate young brains and of the stress factor in forming neural connections. Parents or caregivers who try to force their young children through stages of development by pushing the children to function at inappropriate levels and with capacities that are not ready to be in use are risking developmental dysfunction. Because of the stress connection, parents who pressure babies to undertake activities before they are ready for them can actually inhibit their children's development.

However, most of the time, this becomes obvious, and we do not need a PET scan to tell us to stop a particular activity. For example, few parents try to force their four-month-olds to get up and walk. They do, however, walk around their children. They bring their children to places where they constantly see walking modeled by other humans, including other children. And parents almost intuitively know when to support their child by holding her up by her two little hands to imitate a walking position. If they were to let go, the child would fall.

Few parents repeatedly try to get their children to stand over and over at the expense of bumping and bruising their babies. Most parents today are not solely interested in when their babies walk, just that they do eventually learn to walk. The expectation is there: "I expect that you will eventually walk." The modeling is all around them, and undue pressure is absent. "I don't necessarily care when you walk. I will help you when the time comes. I will know when the time comes by close observation of your development and providing opportunities for you to practice by cruising along a soft couch" and so on. Sensitive parenting and caregiver responsiveness is the key.

Some may poke fun at parents or caregivers who actively attempt to create an enriched learning environment for their children with such materials as flash cards of letters and numbers. A majority of parents believe that these are "very effective" in developing their child's intellect even though symbolic understanding probably cannot be hurried, any more than walking can. However, when the time for that understanding does arrive, which baby will understand better? The one who has seen the letter "A" repeated with the accompanying sound modeled for them, or the one who has never seen a letter "A"?

If used at all, flash cards should be used to supplement real life, not take the place of it. A cardboard picture of an apple is not a replacement for looking at a real apple—feeling the apple, smelling the apple, rolling the apple, and, of course, tasting the apple. However, if after an enriching trip to the supermarket Mommy shows the baby an apple and then shows him the flash card of the apple along with the word *apple*, the child may learn the symbolic representation of the real apple, and it may eventually become meaningful to the child. (Although it may also be confusing to the child.) Only future neurological studies will be able to tell us this on a cellular level.

Pictures of letters mean little to a child who has not developed the neural networking to understand symbolic representation. In addition, apart from their sounds, letters are relatively unimportant in infant phonemic awareness. Parents would do better to teach their toddlers the sounds of letters and not confuse them with the letter names. For example, by repeating that the letter *I* is pronounced "eye" over and over until the child can parrot the sound, parents may create confusion for the child when she attempts to pronounce words such as *pig* or *little*. Which is more important, a child reciting the alphabet letter names, or decoding the sounds of letters to create words?

Think of your toddler navigating your house. Would you force her to memorize a map before exploring the different rooms? Would you wait until she is developmentally ready to understand that a map is symbolic representation of the house? Of course not. The same applies to letters and language. The sounds of letters and quantities represented by numbers are best taught in context. Teach sounds, words, and language by using them. Letter recognition will come along in due time.

Along with environmental considerations, another important key to a baby's cognitive development is in the interactions between the baby and other people or baby teachers. If the baby and caregiver are enjoying an activity that is stress-free and joyful, the baby will gain from it regardless of whether he learns to match the sound of a letter with the letter's symbol. However, if the teacher becomes frustrated with the baby's failure to "understand" what is going on, this will make a negative impression. The disappointment and disapproval will be perceived by the child and will create stress and discomfort. In these cases, the "stimulation" would be best left undone in the first place.

Attentive, observant baby teachers are more likely to detect problems earlier on, thus accelerating their chances of overcoming or correcting these problems with the least amount of damage to the child. For example, in the United States, the technology to detect hearing problems right from birth has been available for years. However, doctors initially would only use this technology if there were an obvious problem. We have learned since this time that hearing problems beget speech and language problems, and the time lost usually cannot be made up.

The sooner a hearing problem is detected, the greater the chance of minimizing damage to speech and language development. Most states now mandate a hearing test before a baby leaves the maternity ward, and all states and territories in the United States have established an Early Hearing Detection and Intervention program. To check on the status or your state or territory, check the National Center for Hearing Assessment and Management website at Utah State University. This Center provides profiles for each state program and coordinator contacts for each.

TOO MUCH TV?

In 1999, the American Academy of Pediatrics published a position state-ment recommending that no children be permitted to watch television or videos before their second birthday.[2] Why would fifty-five thousand pe-diatricians take such a stand? The new technologies in brain research show us why. Some activities are clearly brain builders, while others cause boredom and inactivity. Still others are based on faulty assump-tions, assuming that if a child can parrot back words from a cartoon that this is evidence of learning. (Even a parrot can be taught to repeat words.)

When studies showed the ease with which babies and young children could pick up a second or third language, some parents bought videos in French and Spanish and parked their infants in front of the television or computer to learn the languages. These children did not pick up lan-guages this way. Clearly something was missing. Today, it is believed that the crucial missing element was that of communicative interaction between the speaker and the listener (who is also a watcher).

Hearing talking and being talked with solicit different responses from the brain than just passive observation. Communicative interaction in-volves talking to someone, receiving some kind of feedback, and con-structing a response to that feedback. It is an exchange of language, verbal and nonverbal—a dialogue, if you will. By being spoken to, ques-tioned, and looked at with anticipation and experiencing the wait time needed for a response, babies begin to pick up the rhythm and flow of language in addition to some senses of the purpose of it. They learn that one person generally speaks at a time. And they learn that they are ex-pected to respond afterward. The slightest little response, perhaps a smile or a coo, typically elicits tremendous joy from the adult speaker. From the baby's brain's perspective, this is an activity in which the baby wants to take part. Watching people talk to one another on television does not engage a baby's brain in this way or encourage a verbal response.

Research has shown us that reading a story or hearing a story has a profoundly different impact on our brains than watching that same story played out on a screen. When a child, or even an adult, is hearing or reading a story, the imagination area of the brain—the prefrontal cortex area—is highly active. When reading, the eyes may only be looking at little black symbols on a white page, but the mind's eye is busy creating the image for the brain.

Many studies throughout the 1990s have driven home the importance of visualization and imagination as exercises for the brain. We hear repeatedly that we must visualize our goals and plan for our future to better see those plans actually realized. This is a job for the prefrontal cortex. Studies have shown that gifted children spend significantly more time "hanging out" in their prefrontal cortex—imagining, playing pretend— than average children.[3] This brain area has also been linked to overall intelligence.

Here's an example. If we hear a passage from a story: "The beautiful girl with the long red hair rode the white horse through the field of bluebonnet flowers as the wind blew," our neurons are firing with one another, creating this image in our brains. We see the scene with our mind's eye, and our brain has to "work" and neurons have to fire to create the image. However, if we merely see the scene on a screen, almost no neural work at all is needed. So the difference between telling a story or reading a story is at the far end of the brainwork continuum from watching television.

Investigations of a slice of Albert Einstein's brain showed that his neural networks helped him to imagine himself riding on a light beam. His amazing thinking ability ultimately made his name one commonly associated with brilliant intellectual function (even though he was not entirely able to successfully complete high school) and landed him the title "Man of the Millennium" by *Time* magazine on December 31, 1999. Continually imagining the unimagined supported a brain where increased dendritic branching created exponentially more opportunities for neurons to connect and neural networks to develop. Someone imagined the first wheel before actually seeing one. Someone imagined flying before airplanes could be invented. Closing our eyes and imagining our goals or planned outcomes toward any goals is an important mental step and is good exercise for the brain.

One of the most important brain-stimulation activities one can engage in with their child is to read to him. Probably the most important brain-stimulation activity that you can do for yourself is to read. On a personal note, I began my own personal boycott of television as entertainment three decades ago. At the time, I was responsible for discipline at a large comprehensive high school. I was surprised how often disciplinary issues involved the use of drugs or alcohol, and even more surprised at how common it was to find alcohol problems in the homes of those students' relatives as well. It was obvious to me then that there must be a genetic link.

One night I took particular notice of the advertisements on television, the ones in which beautiful young people drink a six pack of beer and then play flawless volleyball, or drink a six pack and slalom water ski. I saw the deception and brainwashing tactics of advertising in a new light and decided to cleanse my brain as best I could of this propaganda. The result? While I'm rather ignorant of pop culture, it ultimately resulted in a doctoral degree, greatly increased reading speed and comprehension, and gave me some wonderful ideas. I know that I changed my brain over time by changing that single daily activity. Start today. Turn off the TV, turn on some Bach, and pick up a book. And when considering a choice between showing your child a television program or video or reading a story to her, read. Do it for her brain as well as for your own.

THE TOY STORY

We do not need a lot of expensive toys to stimulate our baby or young child, just some thought and time. Nature and your home will probably provide plenty of stimuli. The key to complexity and nurturing neural networks is show-and-tell play and interactions. Complexity is about connections. Explain what everything is, why it is the way it is, and how and why it all fits together the way it does. Then show your child, explain it all again, and how and why it all fits together the way it does. You may find new connections yourself as you try to break down information and processes for your child.

Next, add or subtract a component in the environment. Show your child, explain it all again, and when your child is physically developed enough, include her in the action. You should not assume that your baby or young child automatically understands everything. Showing and telling and interacting and playing with reality teach wonderfully! (As a precaution, never leave your baby alone with toys or other objects in which she may become entangled, that could obstruct breathing, or that could harm the child in any other way.)

One afternoon, while waiting in the carpool lines for his older sister, my two-year-old son, Bobby, pointed out the car window at a truck pouring cement and asked me, "What's that?" I told him that it was a cement truck. He asked what it was for. I told him that's where the cement for sidewalks comes from. He didn't respond. Then I thought about my answer from his point of view. The truck had a big, round, ball-shaped object on the back, out of which was flowing gray, wet cement. Sidewalks are long and flat and hard. How on earth could sidewalks come from there?

I quickly added to my explanation, I reminded him of how Jell-O is liquid when we first stir it up, but then after we put it in the refrigerator for a while, its property changes. I explained to him that cement for sidewalks starts out soft and mushy and then hardens like Jell-O, only even harder. Later we sought out some wet cement and touched it. Since that time, when Bobby sees an imprint of a leaf or a paw or hand in the cement, he always points out to me that the cement must have been wet when that happened.

When a child begins to ask "why" to everything they see or hear, this is evidence of cognitive development and should be celebrated and never stifled. Asking "why" says, "I don't understand this but I want to understand it and I believe you can help me do it." It shows social and emotional health and growth ("I can learn and you can help me") as well as cognitive growth in action. What if we don't know why? Most of us can find the answers to any question a child asks on our phones or some other readily available technological device. By responding with "I don't know but let's find out" we are indicating to our children that we are still learners too. This is the seed of creating a community of learners, hopefully life-long learners.

WORDS OF WARNING

A word of caution concerning adhering to strict time frames in looking for specific developmental achievements in children: the schedule for what is considered "normal" is actually quite loose. Pediatricians' charts show that the average age of walking for most children is closer to fifteen months than twelve. Proud mothers tend to stretch the starting time for the onset of walking, mistaking the first leg motion for the first step and report an earlier age for this big event sooner than it actually occurs. This is evidence of another faulty assumption—the assumption that faster is better with respect to child development. All girls do not begin menstruation at age thirteen. Our hair does not go gray at the same age, or even within the same decade. Life is not a race to the grave. Complexity in the crib is a quality issue, not a competition tactic.

Every child is different and develops differently. In fact, it could be argued that it is unnatural to group children of the same age together year after year for educational purposes. Children generally do not arrive into families in groups of the same age. They typically arrive one at a time and often have an older sibling around to serve as a role model and a younger sibling to take care of it. If you have referred to reliable sources or texts regarding differences in the development of your child and still have a developmental concern, take it up privately with your pediatrician. And always remember, Albert Einstein barely spoke a word before his fourth birthday! Faster doesn't always mean better, and don't let other parents lure you into the comparison game!

Every child has his own developmental timetable, which is usually a mystery to most everyone else. However, being attentive to your child's growing developmental edge can help your timing for enrichment to be just right. For example, there is no harm in holding your seven-month-old up to show her what it feels like to stand with assistance before you would actually expect her to stand alone. With your judgment in check, you are simply offering something for your child to contemplate.

With this in mind, you can play developmentally *appropriate* games with your child but perhaps using developmentally *inappropriate* stimuli. For example, if you have refrigerator magnets in three colors—say, blue, red, and yellow—and you are working with your toddler on identifying colors by sorting them, the fact that the magnets happen to be letters or numbers does no harm.

Your child is developing a visual familiarity with the symbols before she would be developmentally expected to identity or use the symbols. This way, when the child actually does develop the ability to recognize the symbol for what it is, you will know. For example, children can count objects such as two grapes long before they understand that the symbol *2* stands for the word *two*. How will you know that your child has moved on to readiness for symbols or print if she has not had access to the information in an earlier stage?

The point of increasing the level of complexity of the child's environments is not to pressure or force or even speed up the developmental process. It is to keep the process from stagnating or boring the brain or stifling the brain's natural development. Remember, many children who hear three languages in their homes easily learn three languages before they arrive at a schoolhouse door. We have greatly underestimated the learning capacity of children.

As stated previously, if you are considering an enhancement program of any kind for your baby, it is always best to get the approval of your pediatrician first. However, your baby will almost always let you know whether he is enjoying an activity or if it doesn't interest him in the slightest. Watch and listen to your baby. If your baby is tired or hungry or just uncomfortable, it is not likely he will be interested in anything beyond food and cuddling. However, don't give up on an activity after one rejection. There may be other factors involved.

FUTURE TRENDS: DEFINING THE PROFESSION

As shown, the history of education and the history of early childhood education, while having begun as completely separate entities for different purposes, are showing signs of merging. In some respects this can be viewed as positive while in others it may produce insurmountable obstacles. Many preschool classrooms are now found on elementary school campuses, some state-funded and others such as Head Start are federally funded. Consequently, administrators could be faced with multiple layers of expected standards, outcomes, teacher evaluation measures, and other measures of accountability.

In a study by Rebecca Shore, Pamela Shue, and Richard Lambert, elementary principals in North Carolina with preschool classes on their campuses expressed a need for help.[4] While the state had funded much needed preschool classes and hundreds of these wound up on elementary school campuses, few of these school leaders were prepared for the differences between early childhood education and K–12 education. In surveys, over 90 percent expressed a need for help with additional early childhood education information such as health and safety code differences regarding cafeteria furniture, playground equipment, and many other policies and procedures for providing quality environment for the preschoolers that were not present for K–12 students.

How are early childhood educators evaluated? How are outcomes measured? These are important components of a system characterized by variety and fractured through the plethora of different approaches to caring for young children that have evolved over time. Not only are the complex configurations of early childhood education settings very diverse, but trying to follow and administer resources through the complex funding sources can be baffling.

Stacie Goffin, in her book *Early Childhood Education for a New Era*, asks the questions: Exactly what is early childhood education, and who are the professionals within the system? She points out that the field is suffering from a disjointed delivery system and fragmented policies on multiple local, state, and federal levels, making it more and more complex to define and establish early childhood education as a rightful profession. Only through establishing a common denominator can early childhood education be established as a profession, she claims, and leadership is needed to help plot this course.[5]

Within that definition of a purpose for early childhood must be an understanding that babies can and should be taught. This belief must spring from a value that early childhood education is at least as important as elementary or secondary school. Perhaps only then can early childhood education be elevated to its rightful spot within our country's education landscape. Perhaps only then can we make the difficult transition to a free and appropriate public education beginning on the maternity ward.

HIGH-QUALITY EARLY CHILDHOOD EDUCATION: CCRI

In the meantime, parents of young children will likely be faced with choices for the care of their young children before they reach the age when that public education becomes free to all. Those choices will likely involve an economic factor in the decision-making process. Can we afford for mom to stay home with the baby? If not, who will care for him? Grandparents? Neighbors? A private center?

Another important consideration will involve quality indicators. What exactly is a high-quality early childhood education environment? While only individuals can make the financial decision unfortunately associated with choices for childcare, there are some outstanding resources readily available (for free) to help with the quality decision. Perhaps one of the most extensive is the checklist established by Child Care Resources Incorporated (CCRI) in North Carolina.

CCRI was established over three decades ago through a community planning process initiated and commissioned by the Mecklenburg Board of County Commissioners to improve and expand the county's childcare services. CCRI partnered with families, communities, and early care and education and school-age childcare professionals and programs to help families have access to high-quality, affordable early learning experiences. They were Mecklenburg County's first partnership to privatize government services and the first nationally certified Childcare Resource and Referral (CCR&R) agency. They are governed by a twenty-two-member Board of Directors and presently administer $43.4 million of childcare subsidy funds. The extensive work of CCRI is largely credited for 87 percent of the children in their service area (a five-county region in North Carolina) being enrolled in licensed childcare settings with four- and five-star programs. [6]

Beyond its local and regional footprint, CCRI has a long history of successful collaboration at the state level. In 2004, in collaboration and at the request of the North Carolina Division of Child Development, they cofounded the North Carolina Child Care Resource and Referral Council and have served the state on this Council since its inception. In its role with the Council, CCRI ensures quality CCR&R service delivery state-wide; provides competent statewide leadership for one of the Council's special initiatives, Promoting Healthy Social Behaviors in Child Care Centers; and also houses the Council's Consumer Education and Referral and Technical Assistance/Professional Development specialists.

As evidenced by its status as the first CCR&R agency in North Carolina to become International Association for Continuing Education and Training approved for the delivery of Continuing Education Unit (CEU) coursework, CCRI was already developing appropriate curriculum and designing the delivery of effective training to improve the leadership and program management skills of childcare administrators in the region. In 2006, CCRI launched a project in Mecklenburg County known as the Directors Leadership Academy (DLA). The goals of this effort were to 1) strengthen childcare administrators' planning and mentoring for the benefit of their programs; 2) promote and support their leadership roles within the field; and 3) nurture a cadre of lead teachers who would be prepared to succeed current leaders as opportunities arose. To date, DLA has engaged more than two hundred childcare administrators, and its services have penetrated a quarter of the market of Mecklenburg County–licensed childcare programs serving children birth to age five.

CCRI's website houses a thorough and thoughtful checklist of what to look for in a high-quality early childhood educational environment, included below. Other helpful tips can be found at http://www. childcareresourcesinc.org/parents-families/about-quality-child-care/.

For more in-depth study of evaluating the quality of early childhood environments, see Richard Lambert, Martha Abbott-Shim, and Annette Sibley's work, "Evaluating the Quality of Early Childhood Educational Settings" in the *Handbook of Research on the Education of Young Children*.[7] This important work helps clarify the emergence of a culture of accountability within early childhood education, defines quality in early childhood education, and gives important measurements of quality for the early childhood education field.

SALIENT POINTS

- The term *childcare* should be replaced with a term that denotes more attention to cognitive development as well as a focus on health and safety; early childhood education or preschool are more accurate for a paradigm shift toward teaching babies and very young children rather than just caring for them.
- Faster is not necessarily better with regard to child development.
- Attention to developmentally appropriate enrichment activities can be beneficial to developing the cognitive skills of your children. Reading or storytelling is superior to television viewing for young children, particularly those under the age of two.
- Any developmental concerns, problems, or plans for enrichment should be addressed with a licensed pediatrician in addition to referencing scholarly sources through texts or online resources.

NOTES

1. Robert Rosenthal and Lenore Jacobsen, *Pygmalion in the Classroom* (New York: Holt Rinehart and Winston, 1968).

Quality Child Care Checklist

U se the following checklist to keep track of the answers you receive during your search for quality programs. You may need to make additional notes as you ask questions.

The checklist is broken down into several categories covering a wide range of topics, from general program information to the needs of your child.

First, complete the *Program Information Chart* be low for each program you visit. Then, use the checklist as you visit each program. Next to each question on the checklist are three numbered check boxes: ☐1 ☐2 ☐3

The numbers match the program numbers in the Program Information Chart below.

As you ask questions about each program, check the appropriate numbered box when the answer is "Yes." Leave the box unchecked if the answer is "No."

When you have visited all the programs you want to see, compare the answers and determine which program is best for you and your child.

Program Information Chart	
Program: ☐1	
Contact:	Phone:
Hours:	
Fees:	Star Rating:
Referral #1	Phone:
Referral #2	Phone:
Program: ☐2	
Contact:	Phone:
Hours:	
Fees:	Star Rating:
Referral #1	Phone:
Referral #2	Phone:
Program: ☐3	
Contact:	Phone:
Hours:	
Fees:	Star Rating:
Referral #1	Phone:
Referral #2	Phone:

Quality Child Care Checklist

✓ Setting

Do children have a place to store personal belongings?	1	2	3
Are toys on low shelves within reach of infants, toddlers and preschoolers?	1	2	3
Are the furnishings the right size for the ages of the children in care?	1	2	3
Is the children's work displayed at their eye level?	1	2	3
Are there science or sensory activities that encourage the children to experiment and observe?	1	2	3
Does indoor and outdoor equipment (such as low slides, push/pull toys and low climbing equipment) promote physical activity?	1	2	3
Is there sufficient floor space in infant classrooms for cribs, and for infants to crawl and engage in nurturing activities?	1	2	3
Are learning centers and planned activities available outside?	1	2	3
Are there activity areas that allow for different types of play (such as a housekeeping area, cozy book corner, art area, blocks, etc.)?	1	2	3
Is the program accessible to and does it meet the needs of children with disabilities?	1	2	3

✓ Programming

Are learning goals set for each child?	1	2	3
Is there a curriculum that is followed?	1	2	3
Are infant activities (such as play, meals or napping) individualized?	1	2	3
Is a daily record kept on feeding, naps and diaper changes?	1	2	3
Is the children's work creative and individualized as opposed to looking the same?	1	2	3
Is there a variety of clean, developmentally-appropriate materials and equipment for the children, both indoors and outdoors?	1	2	3
Are there strollers or buggies to make outdoor visits easier?	1	2	3
Is there a variety of toys?	1	2	3
Are duplicates of toys available?	1	2	3
Is there a record, CD or tape player?	1	2	3

2. Chana Schoenberger, "Docs Know Best," *Forbes*, September 20, 1999, 190.

3. Barbara Clark, "The Gifted Brain: A Guide to Learning for Parents and Teachers," keynote speech at the California Association for the Gifted Fall Conference, University of California at Irvine, October 30, 1999.

4. Rebecca Shore, Pamela Shue, and Richard Lambert, "Ready or not Here Come the Preschoolers," *Phi Delta Kappan*, (92) 3 (2010), 32–34.

5. Stacie G. Goffin, *Early Childhood Education for a New Era: Leading for Our Profession* (New York: Teachers College Press 2013), 5.

6. Child Care Resources Incorporated, LLC, http://www.childcareresourcesinc.org/parents-families/about-quality-child-care/.

7. Richard Lambert, Martha Abbott-Shim, and Annette Sibley, "Evaluating the Quality of Early Childhood Educational Settings," chapter 26 in the *Hand-*

Quality Child Care Checklist

☑ **Health & Safety**

Are nutritious snacks and meals planned and served? Is there a menu posted for parents?	1 2 3
Does the program encourage vigorous play and plan physical activities that help children maintain healthy weight?	1 2 3
Are foods, bottles and medicines labeled with child's name and date and stored safely and appropriately?	1 2 3
Is there a staff member trained in first aid/CPR at the facility at all times? Is there a first aid kit?	1 2 3
Do staff follow health precautions such as using gloves and washing their hands and children's hands frequently?	1 2 3
Are the toys cleaned daily or as needed?	1 2 3
Can the diaper-changing surface be easily cleaned?	1 2 3
Are there clean and easily accessible bathrooms?	1 2 3
Is the outdoor play area fenced?	1 2 3
Are the children able to move between indoor and outdoor play areas safely and without difficulty?	1 2 3
Are the program's indoor and outdoor areas safe, free from hazards, and large enough for easy movement?	1 2 3
Are there separate outdoor areas for infants that include a variety of safe equipment?	1 2 3
Are safety gates used properly?	1 2 3
Are electrical plugs and radiators covered or protected?	1 2 3
Are there smoke and carbon monoxide detectors?	1 2 3
Are fire drills conducted on a monthly basis?	1 2 3

☑ **The Children**

Are the children allowed to select learning/play activities and toys by themselves?	1 2 3
Can the children choose not to participate in the activities?	1 2 3
Do the children have the opportunity to develop self-help skills as they grow, such as zipping, buttoning and tying shoes?	1 2 3
Are the children encouraged to solve problems constructively?	1 2 3
Do the children appear actively involved and interested?	1 2 3

book of Research on the Education of Young Children, 2nd edition, eds. Bernard Spodek and Olivia N. Saracho (Hillsdale, NY: Lawrence Erlbaum Associates Publishers, 2006).

Quality Child Care Checklist

✓ Staff

Does a staff member greet children warmly when they arrive?	1 2 3
Do staff seem to like and relate well to the children, to families and to each other?	1 2 3
Do staff use a warm and pleasant tone of voice with the children?	1 2 3
Do staff welcome questions and share information with families?	1 2 3
Do staff discipline the children in a caring, consistent and calm manner?	1 2 3
Do staff encourage the children to talk to teachers and one another?	1 2 3
Do staff respond to children's individual needs and do they provide one-on-one attention?	1 2 3
Do staff encourage self-help and independence?	1 2 3
Are staff actively involved with the children (i.e. on the floor with the infants)?	1 2 3
Are staff members required to have special training in early education and child development?	1 2 3
Is there an in-service training program and/or other opportunities for continuous staff training?	1 2 3
Does your child's prospective teacher/provider have a degree from a college or university?	1 2 3
Have the majority of staff members worked at the program for more than two years?	1 2 3
Has your child's prospective teacher/provider been there for more than two years?	1 2 3
Is the staff diverse?	1 2 3
Do staff accept and respect cultural differences?	1 2 3

✓ Activities

Are the planned activities appropriate for the ages and developmental stages of the children?	1 2 3
Are activities planned that help children express ideas and learn about the real world?	1 2 3
Do books, materials and artwork reflect cultural diversity?	1 2 3
Are daily activity plans posted and followed?	1 2 3
Does the program support early literacy by integrating appropriate activities into children's play?	1 2 3
Do activity plans provide for active and quiet play?	1 2 3
Does the activity plan include an opportunity for music, fingerplays, books, art activities and outside play?	1 2 3
Is there an opportunity for large group, small group and individual activities?	1 2 3
Do activities encourage children to solve problems and think creatively?	1 2 3
Are children talked to, read to, and sung to by adults?	1 2 3
Do activities give children opportunities to learn new physical skills?	1 2 3
Are children taken outdoors daily, if weather permits?	1 2 3
Does the program schedule field trips and have written procedures?	1 2 3

Quality Child Care Checklist

✓ Program Policies

Does the program have a written statement that describes its philosophy, and are you comfortable with it?	1 2 3
Does the program have a parent handbook with policies on discipline, illness, medicine and accidents?	1 2 3
Does the program keep records on children and their development?	1 2 3
Does the child/staff ratio meet state standards?	1 2 3
Is the group size small enough so that children do not seem overwhelmed?	1 2 3
Is there a safe sleep policy?	1 2 3
Are there staff benefits (i.e. sick leave)?	1 2 3
Is there a plan for substitutes when staff are sick or on vacation?	1 2 3
Does the program have a policy on toilet learning?	1 2 3
Does the program have a plan for when a child is bitten?	1 2 3
Does the program have policies/procedures in case of accidents, injuries or emergencies?	1 2 3
Does the program have a plan and resources for children with special needs?	1 2 3
Are children's families allowed to visit at any time? Is there an "open door" policy?	1 2 3
Are family members actively involved in the program (i.e. as members of an "advisory committee" or through teacher conferences)?	1 2 3
Does the program offer children's accident insurance?	1 2 3

10

CREATING COMPLEX CURRICULUM FOR THE CRIB AND BEYOND

Learning, I have always felt, is as essential as breathing.
—Linda Darling-Hammond

In the first month of life, a baby's primary needs revolve around food, comfort, and love. They need lots of all three. A crying baby needs attention, even if it is 3 a.m., so be prepared to give it to him. Investigate what could be causing the crying (although you won't always find the culprit). Cognitive stimulation will be occurring naturally all around your baby because, literally, *everything* is new to him. So use this opportunity to make routine chores educational opportunities.

There will be certain health and safety rituals that become established—feeding, bathing, changing diapers, getting the laundry done, and so on. Using a thoughtful, creative approach, these common chores can be wonderful enrichment opportunities for your child. Add lots of explaining (including, of course, how much you are enjoying sharing the experience with your little one), and don't forget to play lots of complex music in the background. Some new parents keep written journals of the early months of parenthood that provide some therapeutic reflection as they are written and provide special memories decades down the road. You may find that how they accomplished feats is much less important than *when* they did after some time has passed.

For the first year, activities suggested in this book are sorted by sense, since a baby's brain is still organizing the separate areas for the senses at birth. While the hearing sense is the first to come to fruition at around twenty to thirty weeks' gestation, babies are born with a more developed network of tactile receptors. Therefore, they will respond well to hugs and loving strokes and lots of cuddling. The more they feel, the more data is sent from the skin to the brain, the more dendrites connect with axons, and the more the neural networks associated with touch develop. This is true, in fact, for all of the senses, so a wide variety of developmentally appropriate experiences leads to a broader foundation of neural networking.

This list is by no means intended to be exhaustive or even close to it. It is meant to provide ideas that may be unique and are for the most part free. There are many recent collections of additional ideas for young children that can provide excellent enrichment online or in books, and many are research based. Those include NuParent for the first year, *Building Brains* by Suzanne Gellens, and especially the Early Head Start National Resource Center.

To stay current on the state of preschool in our country, including important research and quality indicators for curriculum, visit the National Institute for Early Education Research (NIEER) website. Explore other information from reputable companies or institutions sharing research-based ideas to nurture neural networks, and use your own neural networks to translate that research into ideas for you and the young children in your care.

HEARING: THE EARS HAVE IT

Birth to Six Months

- You cannot explain too much to your baby or use too big a vocabulary. Studies have shown repeatedly that parents and caregivers who speak many words to their children hear more words back sooner than parents and caregivers who do not. This positive language skill effect lasts a lifetime. Learn new vocabulary as a family, and build your own neural networking as you go.
- No activity is too simple to be explained to your baby. Examples: "And now Mommy is pulling your red shirt over your head. Where's baby? Where's baby? There she is! And now we put one arm through this

sleeve. And now we put one arm through the other sleeve. Where's that arm? Where is it? There it is!" this process can go on and on.

- Be especially responsive to your baby. When she attempts a sound, repeat it to her, encouraging her to attempt more sounds. Look at her closely when talking and listening to her and elongate these time periods as much as possible.

- Include many questions with your explanations, and follow questions with some wait time. Recent research suggests that looking at your baby while talking to them and then using wait time for their possible responses after questions builds the attention infrastructure in the brain, potentially leading to better self-regulation later in life. The baby's brain is working hard to try to figure out language, and it is masterful at detecting patterns and every nuance of dialect. The more this interaction takes place in early childhood, the better delayed gratification skills develop later on according to some researchers. All it takes is time and talking.

- For a primary focus of conversation for you and your baby, point out difference and similarities in everything in the environment. This, it can be argued, is the basis of all learning. "This red apple is bigger than this yellow lemon." "This dresser is taller than this bed, and I'm taller than you." And more.

- There are multiple wonderful board books such as *Big and Little* or *Opposites* that are appropriate for the youngest children.

- Make animal and insect sounds and show your baby the animal or insect that makes that sound through pictures, stuffed toys, or best of all, real life. Realistic pictures are always better than pink elephants and blue giraffes, which may be confusing to a baby's developing sense of the world.

- Play Bach music at regular times throughout the day for your baby. This is simple if you are prepared, so:

- Set up iPods or CD players throughout your house. (*In the bathroom or kitchen or any other potentially hazardous area, be sure that electrical appliances never come near water.*)

- Keep the volume medium to soft.

- Stick to Bach and other Baroque composers in the first few months, adding Mozart and other Classical composers later.

- Pandora Radio is a free app with a wonderful Baroque station that is appropriate and convenient.

- Don't play music constantly for your baby. Do not play it all night long or during every waking hour. The sound of quiet and the sounds of nature are important for your child's development as well.

Six Months to Twelve Months

- As with the first six months, lots and lots of complex language spoken to your child is critical. Keep the dialogue going whenever and wherever possible!
- The different sounds made with kitchen utensils can be wonderful teaching tools. Let your baby discover the different sounds of silverware on a paper plate, on a plastic plate, and on a glass plate (with your supervision, of course).
- Wooden spoons on pots and pans and rubber containers make interesting musical instruments.
- Start with math concepts early. "I have two ears and you have two ears. Mommy has one nose and you have one nose. But look! How many fingers do you have? How many do I have? How many toes?"
- If you have access to a city orchestra, string quartet, or even a high school chamber music group of some kind, ask if it would be possible for you to sit in on rehearsals occasionally with your little one. Exposure to string instruments and keyboards will delight your baby while it builds neural networks. (Hold off on the symphonic band concert until baby's hearing is better developed. However, watching a marching band at your local high school football game would fascinate your young child as they watch patterns created as music patterns are played, so long as it is not too loud.)
- The sounds of birds signing in the morning, raindrops in the afternoon, crickets and frogs in the evenings, and all of the sounds in the natural environment are essential for a full spectrum of auditory stimulation. Try to find places where the sounds of nature are audible over the sounds of moving vehicles, and frequent those most in the first year. Ask a baby, "What's that sound?" and you will see him or her slowly learn to identify the source of sounds.

SIGHT: SEEING IS BELIEVING

Birth to Six Months

- Show your baby everything and explain everything. Describe shapes, colors, and why you are doing what you are doing. Show how items are alike and how they differ.
- Keep observation objects within seven to nine inches of the baby's face in the early months to keep visual stimulation developmentally appropriate.
- Prop your baby up. Try to envision the world through your baby's eyes, and match as closely as possible the appropriate angle of vision at which adults see the world as well. Frequent staring at the ceiling is probably not the most visually stimulating scene for your little one. In time, the ceiling will better come into focus and become more interesting. Meanwhile, there are a variety of soft pillows—Boppys—that will gently prop your child up to vary the view.
- Use a variety of crib mobiles or other objects for the baby to see when she is lying down. Change them regularly and, if possible, use them thematically—stars and moons for nighttime, sunshine and flowers before walks, and so forth.
- Be sure to include objects with dark contrasts such as black and white. Ansel Adams photographs or other complex black-and-white photos or prints, preferably of nature, are ideal. Also, be sure to include prints with discernible patterns in sharp, contrasting colors. The more patterns and the more complex the patterns, the better. The drawings of M. C. Escher are ideal.
- Show your baby objects with movable parts, both parts that you move yourself and later, parts that move by battery operation. Explain the difference to your baby. Examples include manual can openers, nutcrackers, salad servers connected at the center, and scissors. There are also classic baby toys with "popup." (Always be careful with sharp edges or any other qualities that could be harmful to your child, and never leave them unattended near items that could hurt them in some way.)
- As your baby grows older, share colors, contours, shapes, designs, animals, plants, insects, and everything else that you can find or create in his environment. Describe them all and point to parts where appro-

priate. You are not just your baby's language teacher, you are his biology teacher, arts teacher, and so on.

- Include objects that make interesting sounds when crinkled, such as aluminum foil and paper. After you have shown your baby crinkling paper and foil, then crinkle it behind your back and name it based on the sound it makes. (Any time you can turn an activity into a guessing game, the brain usually responds positively to the novelty and challenge.) Choose a variety of similar-looking objects with different consequential effects when altered. Show your baby an apple, then take a big bite out of it and show your baby the result. Show them the difference between peeling a banana and peeling an orange.

- Show your baby the insides of drawers and cabinets. "These drawers appear the same, but look! There are spoons inside this one and spatulas inside this one." Show her all the different sizes of spoons (measuring spoons, baby spoons, soup spoons, etc.) and explain their uses.

- Prepositions are your friends! Help your baby develop spatial recognition through the use of words such as *more, less, over, under, beside, in front of.*

- Put your baby's favorite toy on a blanket on the floor. Show your baby how you can pull the toy toward you by pulling the blanket. Let her try it.

- Don't forget tummy time! Putting your baby on their tummy helps to develop their neck and core muscles and gives them a new visual perspective.

Six Months to Twelve Months

- Take your baby everywhere, show her everything, and explain everything you show her in as much detail as you possibly can. If you do not know how something operates, look it up online or in a book and learn something new alongside your baby. Motherhood needs to be stimulating for mom as well as baby.

- At intersections whether driving or walking, explain what we do at green lights and red lights and what yellow lights are for. Spare no details.

- Make stops at anything and everything interesting or engaging to your child, especially fountains, interesting flowers or plants, different animals, children of different ages, and other people.

- Point out similarities between objects such as cats, kittens, leopards, panthers, and lions, or the color of frogs and the color of the places they prefer to live. Talk to your baby about natural selection and explain that it's easier to hide when living things are the same color as their environment: they blend in. (Yes, use words like *environment*.)

- When back at home, use a felt or flannel board (or poster board if you prefer to draw) to review interesting things that you saw and did that day. Take every opportunity to make connections between your day and what you are showing and talking to your baby about at home.

- Talk about the differences between living and nonliving things (those that breathe and grow and those that don't).

- As you go through the morning chores of putting dishes and laundry into cabinets and drawers and closets, let your baby watch you; explain what you are doing and why.

- Let your baby watch you sort the colors of clothes as they go into the washer and match the socks as the laundry comes out of the dryer. Let him watch you fold those great big T-shirts into little squares and rectangles. Later, he can help you with these chores. They will be meaning-making learning experiences for him and more tolerable for you if you know that you are contributing to his cognitive growth.

- Begin playing peek-a-boo with your baby. This will help develop memory skills, and babies clearly love finding out that your face is still there behind your hands or hat!

- Bubbles here, bubbles there, bubbles in the bathtub, bubbles in the air. Your baby will love to observe objects that don't fall back to Earth when dropped and that form somehow in the tub when he splashes in the water.

TOUCH: IF IT FEELS GOOD, DO IT!

Birth to Six Months

- There is plenty of research today indicating that baby massage is a tremendously positive experience for your baby. Premature and low-birth-weight babies have shown remarkable weight gain and overall improvement of condition simply through the power of touch. Get in the habit of routinely massaging your baby gently after diaper changes, after changing clothes, after floor play, or after riding in the car. Knowing that this pleasurable experience is waiting can help your baby look forward to all of the activities that precede it. And of course, talk to your baby constantly while massaging her, describing body parts and function.

- Some doctors believe that there is nothing more soothing than a warm bath for a baby, even right after birth. A bath can help simulate baby's prior life in the amniotic fluid. The bath experience can continue to be one of the most stimulating activities for your child for many years to come. The bath helps your baby learn much about his own body. Sensory receptors rushing back and forth from the skin cells to the brain let your baby know where his body ends and the water begins. He learns about temperature through the feel of the cool or warm water touching his body. Add to this the sensation of soap, a soft cloth, and even water poured gently over his hands or back. Bath water is also a wonderful visual tool for learning about the properties of liquids and solids. "If the cup has a hole in it, it can't keep the water in. If it doesn't, the water stays in! Just like it stays in the tub and doesn't go out on the floor. But look at this drain. The water goes down these little holes and doesn't stay in the tub unless we plug it up." Tell your baby to "watch where the water comes from" when you turn it on. (Never, ever leave young children alone in the bathtub or the bathroom.) Expect bathtime to be messy, and do not be perplexed by being splashed or having to wipe up water that winds up outside of the tub. Also, try not to rush this experience. Babies will usually want to participate in a warm bath (once they are in the tub) longer than you will. Prepare ahead of time and mentally work to make baths an enjoyable learning experience as well as a health and safety effort.

- Rain, rain, don't go away. Another good teaching tool is rain. You can imitate rain in the shower, but be sure to explain the difference in where the water comes from. Your baby will be fascinated watching and then feeling rain and coming into understanding the difference between wet and dry.

- Weather is a wonderful teacher of touch. Where possible and appropriate, let your baby feel the cold of snow, the heat of the sun on a sidewalk, the fragility of a flower's petals, and the tree's rough bark. (The refrigerator and freezer can help teach cold from a different perspective.)

- Don't be afraid to bring nature inside! Grow nonpoisonous plants, have large seashells, rocks, and even pinecones available for supervised play.
- Mealtime is an especially easy way to expose your baby to a variety of textures, not only through her mouth but also through her fingers. Make gelatin in different colors, and let your baby manipulate it on her highchair tray as you speak descriptive words to her. Let your baby push an ice cube around on her tray (with supervision to keep it out of her mouth). And of course, play some wonderful Bach music in the background. As your baby gets older, you will be able to add more and more variety to this activity.
- Make a game of touching different body parts and naming them. Add songs and rhymes to the activity. "Eye-winker, tom-tinker, nose-rooter, chin-chopper," "This little piggy." Don't forget the perennial favorite, "Head, Shoulders, Knees, and Toes."
- Take your baby into your closet and let her see and touch all of the different textures of your clothes, your shoes, your scarves. Explain when you wear what and why. If your closet doesn't offer enough variety, take them to a clothing store or a fabric store to see similar textures.
- When appropriate (safe and warm), consider shedding restrictive clothing or blankets that could inhibit your baby's interest in exploring how her body works on the floor or in her crib. This is particularly important after around three months, when your baby becomes uncurled.
- When she can, let your baby turn the pages of cardboard books.
- Pain—recent research indicates that your baby does in fact feel it. If a medical procedure would hurt you, it would probably be painful to your baby as well. While most pediatricians today know this, few act upon it. Be advised.

Six Months to Twelve Months

- Your baby may be sitting up now. This developmental milestone adds a whole new dimension to the sense of touch. She will begin to reach for what she sees and wants to explore further. Where safe and reasonable, accommodate her.
- Put on a hat. Put different hats on yourself and then on your baby to help connect the visual image with the feeling of the hat on the head.

(For added visual stimulation, have a mirror handy to show him how delightful he looks!)

- The feet are important sensory receptors. Whenever possible, leave the feet bare for exploration and tactile enrichment.
- Baby bouncers are especially enjoyable for most babies during this period. They also help the baby with conceptualizing his body as a whole as well as cause and effect. Pushing the ground harder with the feet causes a higher bounce. However, as with car seats and carriers and other baby corralling devices, don't overdo, as free-range movement is best.
- Put on some wonderful complex music and dance with your baby. Include music with different time signatures such as waltzes and minuets as well as marches and symphonies. (Aaron Copland's *Rodeo* is a popular favorite. My daughter especially loved the music of Bobby McFerrin—along with that of J. S. Bach.)
- Lift your baby up and use words like *up, tall, higher*. Then lower her to phrases like *Now we are short, small, lower, down*. Use words like *tall*, then *very tall*, then *extremely tall*, or *very, very tall*. When moving down, say, "Now we are moving lower, going down to the ground until we touch the floor." Use as many adjectives or other descriptive phrases to explain the motions as you can think of. Your baby will want to learn them all!
- If possible, expose your baby to other languages and, if at all possible, use living people speaking those languages rather than videos. Remember that fifty-five thousand American pediatricians united to proclaim that no child should be staring at a screen before her second birthday! It is recommended that any video be watched *with* your child and only for brief periods once every few days at most.
- Count fingers and toes by touching them one at a time. Include songs and rhymes in this activity.
- Steer clear of technology. Babies have no need to be entertained by smartphones, tablets, or computers. And certainly don't use these devices as a babysitter.

BUDDING TASTE BUDS

Birth to Six Months

- It's no secret that breast milk is tops for your newborn for as long as Mom can manage. And in the first few months, taste is not a sense that should be widely explored because of health and safety precautions, and breast milk offers the nutrition that baby needs. Since sucking is critical for survival, just about anything that finds its way to your baby's mouth will be explored, so utmost care should be taken to monitor exactly what gets close to it. Fortunately, babies have a more sensitive sense of taste and smell than adults do, so there is some built-in protection. Your baby will turn away from unpleasant smells and typically turn toward anything that smells like Mom.

Six Months to Twelve Months

- You'll soon have no doubt about how important the sense of taste is to your young child because he will show you. How? By putting every-thing he can reach into his mouth, including that roly-poly crawling out on the front porch. The mouth serves as the little scientist's own per-sonal Petri dish or test tube, and anything that will fit into it could become an experiment. Beware! But try not to stifle his curiosity un-less his health or safety is at risk.
- Do not give your child your keys or phone at this age. Both of these items are likely to be covered in potentially harmful germs and bacte-ria, and a curious child won't be able to resist tasting them.
- As your baby develops his own taste—that is, what he likes and doesn't like—help guide his budding taste buds toward foods that are healthy and away from sugary or less nutritious foods. Be creative. A large, unmanageable banana can easily become "banana buttons" sliced in a clever formation on a plate. Apples, sliced and arranged in a bowl of peanut butter, can become a sunflower. With a bit of creativity and forethought, healthy meals can also build additional neural net-working while it provides the needed nutrition. If you're having trou-ble thinking of additional similes, metaphors, or analogies, just ask a young child for their help. ("What does this look like to you?" "What

can we make it look like?") Let them touch and work with their food and see what interesting creations emerge.

A SENSE OF SCENT

Birth to Six Months

- Newborn babies probably have a more sophisticated sense of smell, or "olfaction," than adults do. Some studies have shown that at two weeks old, a baby can tell the difference between the smell of his own mother's breast milk over a different mother's milk. It may be that the sense of vision is so underdeveloped at birth that the sense of smell is so strong. Skin-to-skin contact immediately after birth for about an hour has been shown to increase babies' recognition of Mom's smell and the smell of her milk.
- It will be obvious when a particular scent is not appreciated by your little one. Spare nothing within the bounds of reason and safety. The puppy in the backyard, the fresh preaches at the grocery store, the newly cut grass—expose your baby to them all and point out the smell of each as you smell the object yourself. Just watch for that curious mouth! (See the section on taste.)
- During this period it is unlikely that any scent will take preference over Mom's scent. Also, familiar scents have been shown to be comforting to babies, so taking that blanket that she loves along for the first vaccine visits can be helpful. Also, discouraging strong perfumes or aftershaves for family members or other caregivers can help in maintaining a natural, calm environment for baby.

Six Months to Twelve Months

- Begin to help your baby connect words to describe scents as well as the objects from which they emanate. Line up a banana, an apple, and an orange. Take a bite and let your baby smell the different scents from the new spot you created. You can identify the fruits individually as members of the fruit category. Also do this with vegetables or any other interesting-smelling food. It's a good idea to save smelling smaller items that are not edible for a later time when your child can better distinguish which objects go into the mouth and which are best explored only with the eyes and fingers.

FOLLOWING THE FIRST YEAR

Twelve to Twenty-Four Months

- During these months, your child will be excited about their newly developing motor abilities. Tasks such as putting in and taking out will become especially delightful. Have special drawers in the kitchen set aside at just the right level for your young child to access. Filling them with different shapes and sizes of your plastic bowls or other containers with lids will set the stage for some wonderful challenging opportunities. "Stack the bowls from biggest to smallest. See how they fit into each other? Which tops match which bowls?" When play is over, make a game of fitting all of the dishes back into the drawer. And of course, *Bach & Baby Playtime* is the perfect background music for this brain-building activity.
- Continuing with the theme of in and out, take a smaller container and help your child find their own objects to try to put in and out. What happens if they are too big? Closer to the second year, have them put coins in and take them out again. This activity must be closely supervised to keep the coins in the cup and not in the mouth! You can start to identify coins by their names. Your child will probably not be able to identify the different denominations yet, but when she does reach this stage, the visual foundation will be laid. Broaden their color spectrum by including colors such as silver and copper.
- Line up an apple, an orange, and any other round fruit that you have on hand. Then line up a banana, a cucumber, and a zucchini. Now is the time to begin to point out "alike" and "different" and identity the qualities that distinguish items. How is a dog like a kitten? How is it unlike a kitten? If your child finds sorting fruits and vegetables easy, mix up different shapes of pasta or different kinds of beans and help him sort them out. Games to differentiate differences can get more and more complex as your child develops. (Empty egg cartons make great sorting containers.)

- Your child may begin the birthday party circuit during these months. She will love watching you wrap gifts. Fold the bright paper slowly so that she can see the object of the activity. "What's inside? How will Jenny know what we got her for her present?" While your baby will probably not be ready for actually attaching objects with tape, she will enjoy the sticky sensation of trying to help with the wrapping. Tear off a piece of masking tape and show her how fabric sticks to it. What about cellophane tape? Describe the differences in color and in use. If you do not own a variety of these types of objects, local home supply stores have a wide range of them, usually all lined up ready to be compared and contrasted. This outing can be a wonderful and educational field trip for you and your child, so don't be in a hurry.

- Exploring with food coloring or paints can help show your child how different colors are created. Get several clear containers so that your child can see clearly that yellow added to red becomes orange, yellow added to blue becomes green, and red added to blue becomes purple. "What color do we get when we mix them all up?" The same activity will be enjoyable to your child if you use nontoxic water-soluble paints. While most refrigerators today come with automatic icemakers, many households have old ice trays around. Find a white or clear ice tray and start on one end with the primary colors of blue, red, and yellow. Let your child be the artist, and create different colors in the remaining compartments of the tray.

- Play-Doh becomes a great item to introduce at this age. Let them mix the colors and experiment with shapes and colors, and they will strengthen their fingers and hands as they work the dough.

- The produce section of the grocery store could be one of the most enriching "schools" that your child ever attends in early childhood. Make the most of it on each visit. Show your child all of the different colored apples and bell peppers to help reinforce understanding of colors and categories. Explain what you are doing as you count out five oranges and put them into one bag. Then count out six carrots, and so on. When your child begins to say the numbers, have him do the counting with you. When he can pick up the produce himself, delegate as much of the sorting and counting as you can to him. Green beans make a good starting vegetable, since they are light and easy for small hands to manage. And if you have access to a garden or farm, take regular tours to find out where all of those fruits and vegetables come from. If possible, plant your own and watch your garden grow together.

Twenty-Four to Thirty-Six Months

- Grocery store trips become a treasure hunt during this stage. Tell your child that you need three of something long and yellow and that it is something that monkeys like to eat. Describe what you are thinking of and let your toddler find it for you. "Now I need something small, oval-shaped and yellow that tastes very sour. That's right, I need a lemon." Conjuring up these clues will be great for your own mental stimulation. For an added challenge, try to weave them all into a grocery store story through the experience. These same activities can be used when putting the groceries away at home.
- While it is possible that your child may be able to handle a pencil, it is unlikely that her fine motor skills will be anywhere near the required ability level to write letters and words during these months. She will, however, love to scribble, and should be allowed to—on paper, of course. And chalk on the sidewalk is even better! Post your child's artwork somewhere in the home. Refer to it as the "nice picture you drew yesterday." Have them describe it the following day to build memory.
- Toddlers develop wonderful abilities to tell stories. This should be encouraged, as it helps the development of many brain parts—including the prefrontal cortex, the imagination area. Sometimes a little creative assistance can provide the little storyteller with structure. Try adding a visual component. Three-year-olds typically can handle stickers. Take your toddler to a teacher supply store or arts and craft store and help him pick out his favorite stickers—ones that he would like to make a story or "write a book" with. (You might encourage him to get stickers of animals or houses or people and not just pretty designs.) Listen to Bach on the drive home to help prime his brain to be ready for creative activity. When you get home, get out some blank paper, the stickers, and let the story begin. Sit back, relax, and be a spellbound audience for your child. He will probably want to tell the story many times, possibly for several days. The story may take new and interesting turns over time. You can enhance this activity by connecting it to the day's activities. For example, follow a trip to the zoo with an

animal-sticker story, a trip to the grocery store with fruit and vegetable stickers, and so on. The possibilities are limited only by your child's imagination and your willingness and ability to spend time listening and being responsive.

• After the story is set, help your toddler select background music for the storytelling activity. See how changing the music affects the story line. Change rooms. See how this changes your child's perception of the story. Have your child tell the story while looking in the mirror.

• Over time, you can compile the sticker stories into a book. You can teach the concept of chapters this way. You will see the sophistication of your toddler's storytelling abilities progress before your eyes as he develops the imagination area of his brain, the seedbed of intelligence, and develops a sense of structure with language and narrative.

• The refrigerator can be a wonderful teaching tool in the kitchen, as a child this age will love maneuvering magnets all over it. Again, this can be used as a storyboard with just the right magnets. Sort magnets into categories and let your toddler select the type of story he wants to create. Is today's story about fruit? Is it about fish? Be sure to keep an eye out for interesting magnets in discount stores to keep some variety in this activity.

• Have your child help you sort objects into groups. Different kinds of beans or pasta or birthday candles or rocks or shells or buttons work wonderfully. Sort them by size, shape, color—any categories you can think of. Talk about what you have the most, the least, some, a little, a lot of. These concepts will all lay a foundation for later math and reasoning skills.

• Empty popsicle-making containers, muffin pans, or ice cube trays can help with sorting as well as counting to twelve. Ask your child to drop one bean into each cup, then one rock into each cup, and so on. Talk about the concept of a dozen. On your next grocery trip, look for other food items that come in packages of a dozen: rolls, juice boxes, raisins, and so on.

• While we are experimenting with quantities and pouring, in and out, and full and empty, use actual measurements such as cup, pint, quart, and gallon. "How many cups does it take to fill up a pint? How many are in a quart? A gallon?" Your child will be expected to know these terms and quantities later in school. Why not give him the proper labels right from the start?

- When traveling, point out the red car, the blue car. "Can you find another red car? Where?" This can be done in parking lots as well. Include words like *first*. "This is the first red car in this row. Where is the second? The third?" "What is the difference between a car and a truck? A really big truck?"
- At around thirty months, you may be able to line up toys or fruit or a mixture of items, then have your toddler cover her eyes. Take away one item and ask your toddler to identify what is missing. This is fun for the child and builds memory skills.
- There may be opportunities in your community to involve your toddler in more structured exposure to music. Kindermusic or Musikgarten programs are excellent, but some may lack a cognitive development component such as Kodaly teaching, so look for programs that actually teach music reading skills, even if only rudimentary ones. Your child is not likely to have the fine motor skills to manipulate keys on a piano yet; however, they could hold mallets to bang on a xylophone or glockenspiel. In addition, children usually love mixing the enjoyment of socializing with other children through music.

Thirty-Six to Forty-Eight Months

- Some children are ready to work with printed words during these months rather than just look at them in a book that is being read to them. Get yourself some poster board and cut it into rectangles. With a wide-tip permanent marker (which you keep hidden!), label the objects in your child's room: bed, lamp, window, and so on. Occasionally ask your child to point to the word that says *bed.*" He will quickly begin to attach the symbols to the words. You may want to follow this activity up at some point in the day with flash cards with pictures and words on them. However, the flash cards alone are no substitute for the real thing. Once he has the words in his room down, add other rooms—the bathroom, or playroom, or even the kitchen. Let him place the words by the objects. (Later, you can move them to incorrect positions and see if he can fix them.)
- Have your child help with setting the table. "How many people are going to be eating at our table tonight? How many plates do we need? Forks? Napkins?" Plan this event out verbally before actually beginning the task of setting the table. "Where do the plates go?" Between

these items, to the left or right of these items, and so on. If your place settings are no more than a fork and a napkin, this activity helps with one-to-one correspondence, area, and location and lays a foundation for math and reasoning and other spatial skills.

- Post a large monthly calendar somewhere accessible to your child. (We keep ours inside the pantry door.) Have her help you cross off each day and count the number of days until a trip to the park, a birthday party, the weekend. Point out the days of the week. Later, use a yearlong calendar to point out the months of the year. There are plenty of songs to help reinforce these concepts, or you can make up your own.

- Each morning, discuss with your child what you plan to do that morning and on through the day. Ask your child what must be done before an activity is begun. Help her with visualizing the plan. "Do we need to brush our teeth? Get dressed? What should we put on first, our socks or our shoes? Why?" Discuss the concepts of "before" and "after."

- Empower your children! Allow them to dress themselves. Avoid shirts that snap between the legs or overalls. Buy elastic waistband pants and shorts that are easily managed by small fingers.

- Come on baby, and do the twist! If you are like many moms, you have a drawer in the kitchen full of "stuff." Some of that stuff can make for great brain-building activities for your child. Keep a baggie on hand for collecting those little twist ties—for example, the ones that come with some brands of trash bags or loaves of bread—and see what your child can make. Start out small: "How about making the sun and the moon? A flower? How about a statue of Mommy? Daddy? Baby sister?" Use the statues to create a story or play. Have your child help select music for the production.

- To add some variety to the twist-tie activity, use pipe cleaners. Encourage your child to form shapes such as triangles, circles, squares, and spirals around his fingers. He can make chains, headdresses, animals—whatever his imagination and fine motor skills can create. Pipe cleaners make great travel-activity materials and can keep children fascinated for quite a while. (Note: Sometimes pipe cleaners have sharp ends, so close supervision may be necessary with younger children.) This type of activity is superior to putting a video into a device and ignoring the child for the duration of the trip.

- During these months, tape becomes more than just fascinating, it becomes something your child may be able to connect things with. Let your imagination flow along with your child's, considering what can be attached to what with tape. Always discuss why. "Why are you connecting all the pages of the newspaper? So Daddy can't read it?"

- There are plenty of good books recorded on CD for children. Some come with the printed book. Snuggle up with your child and point to the words as the audio plays. If possible, have your child follow along with her fingers. She will learn that print reads from left to right and up to down in the English language.

- For more active times, get (or make!) some puppets. Play audio books and have the puppets act out the book. Your child will need to know the story somewhat to do this. As much as possible, sometimes let it be your child's production, not yours. At other times, you can ask to be the director. Be sure to let them go "off story" and change the plot!

- When you believe the creative artists are ready, write your own story or play with your child, have your child help select music, and create an entirely original production. You may want to help direct the story toward a particular lesson you are working on with your child, such as picking up toys.

- Your child probably indicated measurements earlier with outstretched arms for "this big" or scrunched-together hands for "tiny." Now rulers can be a fun and more accurate means of measuring your front door, your refrigerator, or any other accessible object or area in your home or office. Make a chart and graph the widths of familiar household objects and areas. Especially enjoyable is measuring the different heights of family members in inches and then feet and inches. Keep track of growth through light pencil marks on an inside doorframe. If you move frequently, just use a tape measure and mark growth on the measure itself. Older children love going back and looking at how far they've come.

- Routinely incorporate play using board games in which the child must count out the forward progression of the play pieces one by one. Board games have been shown to help build both spatial skills and self-regulation. Make this a regular event during the week, and involve as many family members as possible.

Forty-Eight to Sixty Months

- Start collections of things you and your child find on your daily outing: feathers, interesting insects—any treasures will do. Match like objects, and have boxes or baggies ready to keep things organized. Label everything clearly to help with print and word identification. Go to the library and try to identify where your leaf or feather came from. If you have Internet access, you can do this from home.

- To add some variety to the nature walks, occasionally have your child glue all of his newfound treasures onto a piece of poster board and label it with the date of the walk. One collage a month or one per season can make a wonderful "museum" of your yard or walking area for future years. They will make great artifacts for learning about seasons. Having physical evidence of your outings helps to build memory and provides a springboard for planning the next outing. "We went there last month, I wonder if the colors of the leaves have changed this month?"

- Since you have been reading to your child every day of her life, she will probably begin to be comfortable with print this year, so maximize her exposure to it. Point out the name of your street on your street sign or on letters in your mailbox for as long as is relevant. Children this age still enjoy a concrete piece of evidence over electronic forms of communication. Keep books by her bed and encourage her to "read" if she wakes up early.

- Discuss the locations of neighbor's houses with words like *closer* and *farther*, and count how many houses away different neighbors live.

- Take the poster board signs you made last year labeling the items in your child's room such as the window, lamp, and bed. Now take the cards into another bedroom and see if your child can match the right words with the item. Compose a story using the cards and words. Talk about a moral to a story, a theme of a story. You might want to record the stories in a journal for your child to look back at in later years.

- Comfort with numbers is probably catching up with your child's understanding of quantity, so looking up your own address and phone number in the phone book or on the computer will be fun for him. Continue with height and age charts and measuring anything that needs to be measured, liquid or solid.

- Use pennies to identify different ages, days of the month—anything numerical that you can think of. If it takes five pennies to make your age, how many nickels does it take?
- Discuss time. What time is it? What is an hour? A minute? Talk about how numbers are used to tell time. Get a clock with hands to help teach this concept before going completely digital. You may want to plot out the time of the day's activities on a poster or tablet.
- Animals are fascinating to children. Trips to the city zoo or a smaller petting zoo or a farm or even a neighbor's backyard can create wonderful opportunities for discussions with your child. See if she can categorize animals into mammals, amphibians, and so on. Which animals have fur? Which lay eggs? Do the same type of sorting activity with insects. Of course, having her own pets teaches the added enrichment of responsibility and care for animals or insects over time. Her future science teachers will love you for it!
- Outings to concerts, plays, or other cultural events are wonderful for children this age and may even have been appropriate for some time, depending on your child. There are usually plenty of free concerts or plays around if there is a high school nearby. If not, check out your local museum. If you are fortunate enough to have a children's museum in your town, think about getting involved in sponsoring some partnership programs to bring greater enrichment to your own community.
- Above all, keep reading and speaking to your child. Ask him lots of questions that require more than a yes-or-no answer. Always speak in a vocabulary that you believe is just a bit above the head of your child and see if he asks what the words mean (you are striving to stay in what Vygotsky termed their Zone of Proximal Development). Learn new information and skills yourself. This will help instill in your child a love of learning that will lead to a lifetime of ever increasing neural networks.

DR. SHORE'S ALL-TIME FAVORITES

Birth to One Year

Picture Book: *Ansel Adams at 100*, by John Szarkowski (New York: Little, Brown, 2001).

Storybook: *Brown Bear, Brown Bear, What Do You See?* by Bill Martin, illustrated by Eric Carle (New York: Henry Holt, 1996). This board book includes large, brightly colored pictures of common animals. The text is simple and repetitive, and it rhymes. The unique feature of this book is that it engages the imagination area of the brain. The text on one page says, "I see a red bird looking at me." The red bird does not appear until the following page. The child hears the words and then envisions the red bird before actually turning the page and seeing it, so when the child sees what he has just heard of and imagined, there is reinforcement of the mental imaging. Then, while the child is seeing the red bird, the text reads, "Red bird, red bird, what do you see?" "I see a blue horse looking at me." The reader must again turn the page before the blue horse is visible. This is a wonderful book for the brain!

Music: *Bach & Baby Bedtime, Bathtime, Playtime, and Traveltime.* This series of CDs features the music of Johann Sebastian Bach. The CDs are thematically arranged to match the different moods or activities of the child's day and provide complex audio stimulation in a developmentally appropriate format. It is also performed by actual musicians on actual instruments and is not simplified or altered computer versions from the notes that Bach wrote. Also, recordings of Kit Armstrong performing Bach would be tops!

Video: Home videos of your child and family engaging in enjoyable activities can help build up your child's memory. These should be watched together and narrated by you. (Make this an annual event at birthday time or New Year's in future years.)

Two Years to Three Years

Books: *The Rainbow Fish*, by Mark Pfister (New York: North South Books, 1992); and *The Snow Child: A Russian Folktale*, by Freya Littledale (New York: Scholastic, 1989).

Music: *Teacher's Pet*, by Beth Frack (http://bethfrack.com/); and the *Brandenburg Concertos* by J. S. Bach.

Video: *Silly Willy Workout*, by Brenda Colgate (Freeport, NY: Educational Activities Inc., 1998); phone 800-645-3739; *The Many Adventures of Winnie the Pooh*, Walt Disney Masterpiece Collection. (Most of the Barney and Richard Scarry videos are educational and have excellent character-building stories as well.)

Four Years to Five Years

Books: *James Herriot's Treasury for Children* (New York: St. Martin's Press, 1992).

Music: Bach & Kids, *Schooltime* and *Studytime*, by Rebecca Shore; *A.E.I.O. & U.*, by Beth Frack (http://bethfrack.com/).

Video: *Between the Lions* series by PBS; and Dr. Seuss's Orchestra.

For an excellent resource and activity guide for children ages one through twelve, see Marian Diamond and Janet Hopson's *Magic Trees of the Mind* (New York: Plume, 1999).

CONCLUSION

If you care for your own children, you must take an interest in all, for your children must go on living in the world made by all children.
—Eleanor Roosevelt, 1933

This book is optimistic. Many ideas are presented here in an effort to help turn the tide of unintended infant neglect into a paradigm shift for parents, caregivers, and the entire educational and social system. The present system has assumed that Earth is flat for too long. With respect to recent revelations on brain development and the consequences of brain development on building lives, the effects of a child's environment between the kindergarten years and high school graduation on their neural networks pale in comparison to the effects of the environment between birth and kindergarten.

We have been focusing on the K–12 education system in this and other countries to "fix" the child who does not love learning. We have blamed teachers, programs, parents, and even other children for our schools' failures. But the solution to the K–12 system's learning problems lies between the maternity ward and the kindergarten door, and we need visionary educational leadership to make this paradigm shift happen.

I had the good fortune of taking an English class while attending the University of California at Berkeley that was as devoted to lifting our social consciousness as well as teaching us English. I recall the professor leading us along (through questioning) to addressing the dirty problem of litter in the city. With all of the homeless people in Berkeley in the 1970s, litter was literally everywhere you looked. After much discussion, one student finally remarked, "Well, who is responsible, then? Surely you don't expect *us* to pick up all of the litter in this city!" To this she replied, "Only if you see it."

Society doesn't fully "see" the neglect of the infant brain yet. If it did, there would be high-quality, free, universal preschool or home-assistance programs from conception to kindergarten. Preschool teachers would not be the least-educated, least-paid, and least-recognized educators in the system. (Actually, they aren't even considered part of "the system" yet in most states.) No child would go unfed—not their stomachs, not their brains. No mother or father or other caregiver would be left helpless until the child reaches age five. And we would see the need for welfare and prisons greatly reduced.

We can do it. This vision of a moral, just, and enlightened society can become reality. But only if we all help the fire spread. The infant brain needs more attention, more nurturing, more complexity, and we are all responsible for developing young minds.. Pass it on.

SDG!

BIBLIOGRAPHY

Abercrombie, Karen. "Wisconsin District Requires Piano Lessons for K–5 Students." *Education Week*, October 14, 1998.

Acredolo, Linda, and Susan Goodwyn. *Baby Minds*. New York: Bantam, 2000.

Agid, O., B. Shapira, J. Zislin, M. Ritsner, B. Hanin, H. Murad, T. Troudart, M. Block, U. Heresco-Levy, and B. Lerer. "Environment and Vulnerability to Major Psychiatric Illness: A Case Control Study of Early Parental Loss in Major Depression, Bipolar Disorder, and Schizophrenia." *Molecular Psychiatry* 4, no. 2 (1999): 163–72.

Americans for the Arts. "New Harris Poll Reveals That 93% of Americans Believe That the Arts Are Vital to Providing a Well-Rounded Education," 2005. http://www.artsusa.org.

Anderson, Emily, ed. *The Letters of Mozart and His Family*. London: Macmillan, 1985.

Baldwin, Neil. *Edison: Inventing the Century*. Chicago: University of Chicago Press, 1995.

Beachy, Jodi M. "Premature Infant Massage in the NICU." *Neonatal Network: The Journal of Neonatal Nursing* 22, no. 3 (May–June 2003), 39–45.

Berk, Laura E. *Development through the Lifespan*. Needham Heights, MA: Allyn & Bacon, 2001.

Biancolli, Louis. *The Mozart Handbook*. New York: World Publishing, 1954.

Botstein, Leo. *Jefferson's Children*. New York: Doubleday, 1997.

Brown, Richard E., and Peter M. Milner. "The Legacy of Donald O. Hebb: More Than the Hebb Synapse." *Nature Reviews Neuroscience* 4 (December 2003): 1013–19. doi:10.1038/nrn1257

Bruner, Jerome. "The Course of Cognitive Growth." *American Psychologist* 19 (1964): 1–15.

Buell, S., and P. Coleman. "Quantitative Evidence for Selective Dendritic Growth in Normal Human Aging but Not in Senile Dementia." *Brain Research* 214, no. 1 (1981): 23–41.

Butzlaff, R. "Can Music Be Used to Teach Reading?" *Journal of Aesthetic Education* 34, no. 3/4 (2000): 167–79.

Caine, Geoffrey, Renate Caine, and Sam Crowell. *Mindshifts*. New York: Avon Books, 1997.

Campbell, Don. *The Mozart Effect*. New York: Avon Books, 1997.

Caplan, Frank. *The First Twelve Months of Life*. New York: Bantam, 1973.

Child Care Resources, Incorporated (CCRI). Charlotte, North Carolina. http://www.childcareresourcesinc.org/.

Childs, C. P., and P. M. Greenfield. "Informal Modes of Learning and Teaching: The Case of Zinacanteco Weaving." In *Advances in Cross-Cultural Psychology*, vol. 2, edited by N. Warren, 269–316. London: Academic Press, 1982.

Chomsky, Noam. *Language and Problems of Knowledge*. Cambridge: MIT Press, 1988.

Clark, Barbara. *Growing Up Gifted*, 6th ed. Columbus, OH: Merrill/Prentice Hall, 2002.

Colangelo, Nicholas, and Gary A. Davis. *Handbook of Gifted Education*. Boston: Allyn & Bacon, 1997.

Collins, James. "The Day-Care Dilemma." *Time*, February 3, 1997, 58.

Crain, William. *Theories of Development*. Upper Saddle River, NJ: Prentice Hall, 2000.

Cuddy, Lola L., ed. *Music Perception: An Interdisciplinary Journal* 29, no. 3 (December 2011). University of California Press.

Daniels, Michael, Bernie Devlin, and Kathryn Roeder. "Of Genes and IQ," chapter 3 of *Intelligence, Genes, and Success*, edited by B. Devlin et al. New York: Springer-Verlag, 1997.

Darwin, Charles. *The Origin of Species: 150th Anniversary Edition*. New York: Signet Classics, 2003.

David, Hans T., and Arthur Mendel, eds. *The New Bach Reader: A Life of Johann Sebastian Bach in Letters and Documents*, revised and expanded, Christopher Wolff. New York: W. W. Norton, 1998.

DeCasper, Anthony, and Melanie J. Spence. "Prenatal Maternal Speech Influences Newborn's Perception of Speech Sounds." *Infant Behavior and Development* 9 (1986): 133–50.

Dege, Franziska, Claudia Kubicek, and Gudrun Schwarzer. "Music Lessons and Intelligence: A Relation Mediated by Executive Functions." *Music Perception: An Interdisciplinary Journal* 29, no. 2 (December 2011). University of California Press.

Dennis, Wayne, and Pergrouhi Najarian. "Infant Development under Environmental Handicap." *Psychological Monographs* 71, no. 7 (1957): 1–13.

Diamond, Marian. "Brain Research and Its Implications for Education," paper presented at the Twenty-Fifth Annual Conference of the California Association for the Gifted, Los Angeles, February 1986.

Diamond, Marian, and Janet L. Hopson. *Magic Trees of the Mind: How to Nurture Your Child's Intelligence, Creativity, and Healthy Emotions from Birth through Adolescence*. New York: Plume, 1999.

Elashoff, Janet, and Richard Snow. *Pygmalion Reconsidered*. Worthington, OH: C. A. Jones, 1971.

Forkel, Johann Nikolaus. *Über Johann Sebastian Bachs Leben, Kunst, und Kunstwerke* ("On Johann Sebastian Bach's Life, Art and Work"). A recent reprint is by Henschel Verlag, Berlin, 2000; ISBN 3-89487-352-3. An English translation was published by Da Capo Press in 1970.

Freeman, W. J. *Societies of Brains: A Study in the Neuroscience of Love and Hate*. Hillsdale, NY: Lawrence Erlbaum Associates, 1995.

Galton, Francis. *Hereditary Genius*. London: Macmillan and Company, 1869.

Gardiner, Martin. "Effects of Arts on Learning." *Nature* 384 (May 26, 1996): 192.

———. "Music, Learning, and Behavior: A Case for Mental Stretching." *Journal for Learning through Music* 1, no. 1 (Spring 2000).

Gardner, Howard. *Frames of Mind: The Theory of Multiple Intelligences*. New York: Basic Books, 1983.

Gartner, Heinz. *John Christian Bach: Mozart's Friend and Mentor*. Translated by Reinhard G. Pauly. Portland, OR: Amadeus Press, 1989.

Gass, Robert, and Kathleen Brehony. *Chanting: Discovering Spirit in Sound*. New York: Broadway Books, 1999.

Gellens, Suzanne R. *Building Brains*. St. Paul: Red Leaf Press, 2012.

Goffin, Stacie. *Early Childhood Education for a New Era*. New York: Teachers College Press, 2013.

Goldstein, Avram. "Thrills in Response to Music and Other Stimuli." *Physiological Psychology* 8, no. 1 (1980): 126–29.

Gopnik, Alison, Andrew N. Meltzoff, and Patricia K. Kuhn. *The Scientist in the Crib*. New York: Morrow, 1999.

Graziano, Amy B., Gordon L. Shaw, and Eric L. Wright. "Music Training Enhances Spatial-Temporal Reasoning in Young Children: Towards Educational Experiments." *Early Childhood Connections* (Summer 1997): 30–36.

Green Gilbert, Anne. *Brain-Compatible Dance Education*. Reston, VA: NDA/AAHPERD, 2006.

Greenberg, Robert. *How to Listen to and Understand Great Music*. Learning Company, audio-cassette.

Greenfield, Susan. *Brain Story*. London: BBC Worldwide, 2000, 32.

Hallowell, Edward M., and John J. Ratey. *Delivered from Distraction*. New York: , Ballantine Books, 2005.

Hannaford, Carla. *Smart Moves: Why Learning Is Not All in Your Head*, 2nd ed. Salt Lake City: Great River Books, 2005.

Hart, Betty, and Todd R. Risley. *Meaningful Differences in the Everyday Experience of Young American Children*. Baltimore: Paul H. Brooks, 1995.

Hart, Leslie A. *Human Brain and Human Learning*. New York: Longman, 1983.

Harvard Dictionary of Music. Edited by Willi Apel. Cambridge: Harvard University Press, 1951.

Healy, Jane M. *Your Child's Growing Mind*. New York: Doubleday, 1994.

Hoff, David J. "Chapter 1 Aid Failed to Close Learning Gap." *Education Week*, April 2, 1997.

Hofstadter, Douglas R. *Godel, Escher, Bach: An Eternal Golden Braid*. New York: Basic Books, 1979.

Horvath, A. Tom, Kaushik Misra, Amy K. Epner, and Galen Morgan Cooper. "Stress Regulation and Withdrawal: Addictions' Effect on the Hypothalamus," edited by C. E. Zupanick. *Sevencounties.org* .

Huron, David. "Music and Mind: Foundations of Cognitive Musicology." Six lectures presented in the 1999 Ernest Bloch Lecture Series at the University of California at Berkeley, September–December 1999. http://www.musiccog.ohio-state.edu/Music220/Bloch.lectures/Bloch.lectures.html.

———. *Sweet Anticipation: Music and the Psychology of Expectation*." Cambridge: MIT Press, 2006.

International Cyclopedia of Music and Musicians. Edited by Oscar Thompson. New York: Dodd, Mead, 1949.

Jacobs, Bob, Matthew Schall, and Arnold B. Scheibel. "A Quantitative Dendritic Analysis of Wernick's Area in Humans. 2. Gender, Hemispheric, and Environmental Factor." *Journal of Comparative Neurology* 327 (1993): 97–111.

Kagan, Sharon L., and Nancy E. Cohen. "Not by Chance," executive summary, *The Quality 2000 Initiative*. New Haven: Yale University Press, 1997, 2.

Kemper, Kathi J. *Addressing ADD Naturally: Improving Attention, Focus, and Self-Discipline with Healthy Habits in a Healthy Habitat*. New York: Xlibris Corporation, 2010.

———. *The Holistic Pediatrician (Second Edition): A Pediatrician's Comprehensive Guide to Safe and Effective Therapies for the 25 Most Common Ailments of Infants, Children, and Adolescents*. New York: Harper Perennial, 2002.

———. *Mental Health, Naturally: The Family Guide to Holistic Care for a Healthy Mind and Body*. New York: American Academy of Pediatrics, 2010.

Kohn, Alfie. *Punished by Rewards*. New York: Houghton Mifflin, 1993.

Kotulak, Ronald. "Q&A." *Chicago Tribune*, "Perspective," March 24, 1998, 3.

Kuhl, Patricia K. "Cracking the Speech Code: How Infants Learn Language." *Acoustical Science and Technology* 28, no. 2 (2007): 71–83.

———. *The Linguistic Genius of Babies*. TED Talks, 2010. www.ted.com/talks/patricia_kuhl_the_linguistic_genius_of_babies?language=en.

Kuzawa, Christopher W., Harry T. Chugani, Lawrence I. Grossman, Leonard Lipovich, Otto Muzik, Patrick R. Hof, Derek E. Wildman, Chet C. Sherwood, William R. Leonard, and Nicholas Lange. "Metabolic Costs and Evolutionary Implications of Human Brain Development." PNAS, August 2014.

Lacerda, Francisco, Claes von Hofsten, and Mikael Heimann, eds. *Emerging Cognitive Abilities in Early Infancy*. Mahwah, NJ: Lawrence Erlbaum Associates, 2001.

Lally, J. Ronald, Claire Lerner, and Erica Lurie-Hurvitz. "National Survey Reveals Gaps in the Public's and Parents' Knowledge about Childhood Development." *Young Child* 56, no. 2 (March 2001).

Lambert, Richard, Martha Abbott-Shim, and Annette Sibley. "Evaluating the Quality of Early Childhood Educational Settings," chapter 26 from the *Handbook of Research on the Educa-*

tion of Young Children, 2nd ed., edited by Bernard Spodek and Olivia N. Saracho. Mahwah, NJ: Lawrence Erlbaum Associates, Publishers, 2006.

Lamont, Bette. "Learning and Movement." *Pathways: Creative Dance Center Newsletter*, Seattle, WA (Spring 1996): 4–5.

Leach, Penelope. *Children First*. New York: Vintage, 1995.

———. *Your Baby and Child: From Birth to Age Five*, revised edition. New York: Alfred A. Knopf, 2000.

Lees, Caitlin, and Jessica Hopkins. "Effect of Aerobic Exercise on Cognition, Academic Achievement, and Psychosocial Function in Children: A Systematic Review of Randomized Control Trials." *Preventing Chronic Disease* (2013). 10:130010. doi: http://dx.doi.org/10.5888/pcd10.13010.

Levi-Montalcini, Rita. *In Praise of Imperfection*. New York: Basic Books, 1988.

Lorenz, Ralph. "Health Benefits of Singing: A Perspective from Traditional Chinese Medicine and Chi Kung." *The Phenomenon of Singing* 9 (January 2014): 154–66.

Lozanov, Georgi. "A General Theory of Suggestion in the Communications Process and the Activation of the Total Reserves of the Learner's Personalities." *Suggestopaedia-Canada* 1 (1997): 1–4.

Ludington-Hoe, Susan, with Susan K. Golant. *How to Have a Smarter Baby*. New York: Bantam, 1985.

Lyon, G. Reid. Summary of Comments before the White House Summit on Early Childhood Cognitive Development, July 27, 2001. www.ed.gov/PressReleases/07-2001/07272001_lyon.html.

MacLean, Paul. "A Mind of Three Minds: Educating the Triune Brain." In *Education and the Brain: The Seventy-Seventh Yearbook of the National Society for the Study of Education*, part 1, edited by J. Chall and A. Mirsky. Chicago: University of Chicago Press, 1978.

Manrique, B., M. Contasti, M. A. Alvarado, M. Zypman, N. Palma, M. T. Ierrobino, I. Ramirez, and D. Carini. "A Controlled Experiment in Prenatal Enrichment with 684 Families in Caracas, Venezuela: Results to Age Six." *Journal of Prenatal and Perinatal Psychology and Health* 12, nos. 3 and 4 (Spring and Summer 1998): 209–34.

Medina, John. *Brain Rules: 12 Principles for Surviving and Thriving at Work, Home, and School*. Seattle: Pear Press, 2008, 10.

Merriam-Webster's Collegiate Dictionary, 11th ed. Springfield, MA: Merriam-Webster, 2005.

Meyer, Marianne S. "What We Have Learned from Reading Research: Implications for Teaching Struggling Readers," paper presented at Mineral Springs Elementary School, Winston-Salem, NC, October 5, 2000, 1.

Moreno, Sylvain, Deanna Friesen, and Ellen Bialystok. "Effect of Music Training on Promoting Preliteracy Skills: Preliminary Causal Evidence." *Music Perception: An Interdisciplinary Journal* 29, no. 3 (December 2011). University of California Press.

Mozart, Leopold. *A Treatise on the Fundamental Principles of Violin Playing*. New York: Oxford University Press, 1959.

Myers, David. *Psychology*. New York: Worth Publishers, 1998.

National Assembly of State Arts Agencies. "Critical Evidence: How the Arts Benefit Student Achievement," 2006.

National Association for the Education of Young Children. "Developmentally Appropriate Practice in Early Childhood Programs Serving Children from Birth through Age 8." Position statement of NAEYC, 2009.

———. "Principles of Child Development and Learning That Inform Developmentally Appropriate Practice." Position statement adopted July 1996, updated 2009. https://oldweb.naeyc.org/about/positions/dap3.asp.

National Institute for Early Education Research (NIEER). Rutgers University, New Jersey. http://www.nieer.org/.

New Grove Dictionary of Music and Musicians. Edited by Stanley Sadie. London: Macmillan, 1980.

Ogawa, Seiji, T. M. Lee, A. R. Kay, and D. W. Tank. "Brain Magnetic Resonance Imaging with Contrast Dependent on Blood Oxygenation." *Proceedings of the National Academy of Sciences of the United States of America* 84, no. 24 (December 1990): 9868–72.

Ostrander, Sheila, and Lynn Schroeder, with Nancy Ostrander. *Superlearning*. New York: Delacorte, 1979.

―――. *Superlearning 2000*. New York: Dell, 1994.

Oxford Dictionary of Music. Edited by Michael Kennedy. Oxford: Oxford University Press, 1985.

Perrett, Peter. *A Well-Tempered Mind: Using Music to Help Children Listen and Learn*. New York: Dana Press, 2006.

Perris, Eve, Nancy Myers, and Rachel Clifton. "Long-Term Memory for a Single Infancy Experience." *Child Development* 61 (1990): 1796–1807.

Pinker, S., D. S. Lebeaux, and L. A. Frost. "Productivity and Constraints in the Acquisition of the Passive." *Cognition* 26 (1987): 195–267.

Poduslo, S. E., and Y. Jang. "Myelin Development in Infant Brain." *Neurochem Research* 11 (November 9, 1984): 1615–26.

Ponter, James R. "Academic Achievement and the Need for a Comprehensive Developmental Music Curriculum." *NASSP Bulletin* (February 1999): 108–13.

Purves, D., W. T. Wojtach, and R. B. Lotto. *Understanding Vision in Wholly Empirical Terms*. *Proceedings of the National Academy of Science* 108, no. 3 (2011): 15588–95.

Qin, Shaozheng, Christina B. Young, Xujun Duan, Tianwen Chen, Kaustubh Supekar, and Vinod Menon. "Amygdala Subregional Structure and Intrinsic Functional Connectivity Predicts Individual Differences in Anxiety During Early Childhood." Biological Psychiatry 75, no. 11 (2014): 892. doi: 10.1016/j.biopsych.2013.10.006.

Radford, John. *Child Prodigies and Exceptional Early Achievers*. New York: Free Press, 1990.

Rauscher, Frances, Gordon Shaw, and K. Ky. "Listening to Mozart Enhances Spatial-Temporal Reasoning: Towards a Neurophysiological Basis." *Neuroscience Letters* 185 (1995): 44.

―――. "Music and Spatial Task Performance." *Nature* 365 (1993): 611.

Rauscher, Frances, Gordon Shaw, L. Levine, E. Wright, W. Dennis, and R. Newcomb. "Music Training Causes Long-Term Enhancement of Preschool Children's Reasoning." *Neurological Research* 19 (1997): 2.

Ravitch, Diane. *Left Back*. New York: Simon & Schuster, 2000.

Raymond, Joan. "The World of the Senses." *Newsweek* (special issue) (Fall/Winter 2000), 18.

Restak, Richard M. *The Infant Mind*. Garden City, NY: Doubleday, 1986.

Richman, Sheldon. *Separating School and State*. Fairfax, VA: Future of Freedom Foundation, 1994.

Ridley, Matt. "Is IQ in the Genes? Twins Give Us Two Answers." *Wall Street Journal*, June 22, 2012.

Rivera, Enrique J., Alison Goldin, Noah Fulmer, Rose Taveres, Jack R. Wands, Suzanne M. de la Monte. "Insulin and Insulin-Like Growth Factor Expression and Function Deteriorate with Progression of Alzheimer's Disease: Link to Brain Reductions in Acetylcholine." *Journal of Alzheimer's Disease* 8, no. 3 (2005): 247–68.

Rose, Dale, and Michaela Parks. "The Arts and Academic Achievement: What the Evidence Does (and Doesn't) Show." *Grants in the Arts Reader* 13, no. 3 (2002).

Rosenberg, Debra. "We Have to Sacrifice." *Newsweek*, August 27, 2001, 46.

Scarr, Sandra, and Richard Weinberg. "The Early Childhood Enterprise: Care and Education of the Young." *American Psychologist* 41, no. 10 (1986).

Schellenberg, E. Glenn. "Cognitive Performance After Listening to Music: A Review of the Mozart Effect." *Music, Health, and Wellbeing* (2012).

Schoenberger, Chana. "Docs Know Best?" *Forbes*, September 20, 1999.

Scholes, Percy. *The Oxford Companion to Music*, 9th ed. London: Oxford University Press, 1955.

Shaw, Gordon. *Keeping Mozart in Mind*. San Diego: Academic Press, 2000.

Shetler, Donald. "The Inquiry into Prenatal Music Experience: A Report of the Eastern Project, 1980–1987." In *Music and Child Development: The Biology of Music Making, Proceeding of the 1987 Denver Conference*, edited by Frank R. Wilson and Franz L. Roehmann. St. Louis, MO: MMB Music, 1990.

Shore, Rebecca A. "Music and Cognitive Development: From Notes to Neural Networks." *National Head Start Association: Dialog* 13, no. 1 (2010): 53–65.

Shore, Rebecca A., Pamela L. Shue, and Richard G. Lambert. "Ready or Not, Here Come the Preschoolers." *Phi Delta Kappan*, (92), 3 (2010), 32–34.

Shore, Rebecca, Jenna Ray, and Paula Goulkasian. "Applying Cognitive Science Principles to Improve Retention of Science Vocabulary." *Learning Environments Research*, 18, 2 (2015), 313–28.

Shue, Pamela L., Rebecca A. Shore, and Richard G. Lambert. "Prekindergarten in Public Schools: An Examination of Elementary School Principals' Perceptions, Needs, and Confidence Levels in North Carolina." *Leadership and Policy in Schools* 11, no. 2 (2012): 216–33.

Skeels, Harold, and H. B. Dye. "A Study of the Effects of Difference Stimulation on Mentally Retarded Children." *Proceedings of the American Association on Mental Deficiency* 44 (1939): 114–36.

Sousa, David. *How the Brain Learns*. Thousand Oaks, CA: Corwin Press, 2011.

Sparks, Sarah D. "Scientists Trace Adversity's Toll." *Education Week* 32, no. 11 (November 7, 2012).

Terry, Charles Sanford. *John Christian Bach*. New York: Oxford University Press, 1967.

Teyler, T. "An Introduction to the Neurosciences." In *The Human Brain*, edited by M. Wittrock. Englewood Cliffs, NJ: Prentice Hall, 1977.

Thompson, Oscar. *The International Cyclopedia of Music and Musicians*, 5th ed. New York: Dodd, Mead, 1949, 817.

Toth, Heidi. "Hearing Loss Most Common Birth Defect in U.S." *Daily Herald*, October 11, 2009. http://www.heraldextra.com/news/local/hearing-loss-most-common-birth-defect-in-u-s/article_dc41c731-2ff5-5320-aad4-9b332ab17223.html.

Treffert, Darold A. *Extraordinary People*. New York: Harper & Row, 1989.

Van de Carr, Rene, and Marc Lehrer. "Enhancing Early Speech, Parental Bonding, and Infant Physical Development Using Prenatal Intervention in Standard Obstetric Practice." *Pre-and Peri-Natal Psychology* 1, no. 1 (1986): 20–30.

———. *While You Are Expecting: Creating Your Own Prenatal Classroom*. Atlanta: Green Dragon Publishing Group, 1996.

Verny, Thomas, with John Kelly. *The Secret Life of the Unborn Child*. New York: Dell, 1981.

Viadero, Debra. "Music on the Mind." *Education Week*, April 8, 1998.

Vygotsky, Lev S. *Mind in Society: The Development of Higher Mental Processes*. Cambridge: Harvard University Press, 1978.

———. *Thinking and Speech*. In *Problems of General Psychology*, vol. 1 of *The Collected Works of L. S. Vygotsky*, edited by R. W. Rieber and A. S. Carton, translated by N. Minick. New York: Plenum, 1987.

Walker, Elaine, Carmine Tabone, and Gustave Weltsek. "When Achievement Data Meet Drama and Arts Integration." *Language Arts* 88, no 5 (2001): 365–72.

Wang, Margaret C., Geneva D. Haertel, and Herbert J. Walberg. "Toward a Knowledge Base for School Learning." *Review of Education Research* 63, no 3 (Fall 1993): 149–94.

Wertsch, J. V., and P. Tulviste. "L. S. Vygotsky and Contemporary Developmental Psychology." *Developmental Psychology* 28, no. 4 (1992): 548–57.

Westman, Jack. *Licensing Parents*. New York: Plenum Press, 1994.

Winner, Ellen, and Lois Hetland, eds. "The Arts and Academic Achievement: What the Evidence Shows." *Journal of Aesthetic Education* 34, nos. 3–4 (Fall/Winter 2000).

Wittrock, M. C. *The Human Brain*. New York: Prentice Hall, 1977.

Woolfolk, Anita. *Educational Psychology*. Boston: Allyn & Bacon, 2001.

Wyzewa, T., and G. W. A. Saint-Foix. *Mozart, sa vie musicale et son oeuvre, de l'enfance à la pleine maturité*. Paris: Perrin-Desele'e de Browner, 1912.

INDEX

Abbott preschool programs, 179–182
Abbott-Shim, Martha, 198
Abbott v. Burke, 179
Abecedarian Project, 182–183
ACE. *See* Adverse Childhood Experiences study
acetylcholine, 22
Acredolo, Linda, 46
Adams, Ansel, xix, xx, xxi, 97
Addressing ADD Naturally (Kemper), 70
adrenaline, 22, 23
Adverse Childhood Experiences study (ACE), 70
Alzheimer's disease, 22
Amadeus, 117
amnesia, 33, 45
amygdala: anxiety and, 30; emotional development and, 30, 90; fear and, 23, 29. *See also* brain
animals, learning and, 225
Ansel Adams at 100 (Szarkowski), 226
anxiety, amygdala and, 30
apoptosis, 59–60, 63
Armstrong, Kit, 130–131, 132–133
Armstrong, May, 130–131, 132–133
arts: benefits of, 78; dance and, 82–84; dramatic play and, 84–85; educational benefits of, 78; infants and visual, 78–81; learning enriched by, 78; paper activities and, 81; standardized testing impacting, 85; tools and toys for, 80–81

axons, 19–21

Babe, Divje, 95
Baby Minds (Acredolo and Goodwyn), 46
baby teachers, cognitive development and, 189
Bach, J. C., 122–123, 123
Bach, J. S., 123; Armstrong, Kit, on, 131; *Brandenburg Concertos* of, 227; complexity of Mozart's work compared to, 132, 135; complexity of work of, 118–135, 123, 136; counterpoint of, 126; fugues of, 127–130; *Goldberg Variations* and, 138; legacy and brilliance of, 124–125, 132; Mozart collecting fugues of, 127; Mozart influenced by, 125; *Musical Offering* of, 129, 130; personal life of, 125, 130, 132; religion and, 130; Schumann on importance of, 123–124
Bach, P. E., 123, 132
Bach & Baby CDs, 146–147, 217, 226, 227
balance, cerebellum and, 27–28
Baroque Era of music, 96, 97, 100; characteristics of, 120; Classical Era compared to, 121; complexity and, 120–121, 136; counterpoint and, 100–101, 120; harpsichord and, 121; Mozart influenced by, 119, 135–136; piano and, 121–122; pianoforte and, 121; prenatal environment and, 139;

ABOUT THE AUTHOR

Rebecca Shore is an associate professor in the Department of Educational Leadership in the College of Education at the University of North Carolina at Charlotte. Prior to joining the academy, she worked in schools for twenty-eight years in three states—thirteen years as a teacher and fifteen years as an administrator. She started her career as a music teacher and also taught multiple core subjects in two different private schools. She was principal of Los Alamitos High School, a multiyear National Blue Ribbon School in Southern California. Prior to this she served in varied administrative roles in the Huntington Beach Union High School District while teaching as a lecturer at the University of California at Irvine. Her bachelor's degree in Music Education is from Louisiana State University, where her father, Bruce, graduated in chemical engineering in 1955. Her master's degree in School Leadership is from California State University at Northridge, and her doctorate in Educational Administration and Policy is from the University of Southern California. Her dissertation investigated new professional opportunities for teachers in the California charter schools. She is the author of three books, over fifty journal articles, and speaks widely on a variety of educational topics. She can be reached at rshore6@uncc.edu.